# Celebrate with *Country Woman Christmas 2002!*

Bright bedecked wreaths adorning frosted windows… twinkling lights wrapped around fragrant pines…plates of warm cookies cooling on the kitchen counter. These familiar sights and scents are telltale signs that the Yuletide season is on its way!

No other holiday quite compares to Christmas, with its message of hope and goodwill. To help you make the most of this enchanting time of year, we've packaged the season's best in our seventh edition of *Country Woman Christmas*.

What makes this annual edition such a treat is its country flavor. That's because most of the yummy recipes, cheery photos, heartwarming stories, clever crafts and fun gift ideas come from readers of *Country Woman* magazine.

Here's a peek at what you'll find inside…

**Goodies Galore.** You'll discover over 100 holiday recipes, from appetizers and entrees to breads and sweets, that are bound to become favorites at your Christmas festivities. Many make appetizing gifts, too!

Our Test Kitchen home economists prepare each and every recipe to ensure that it's both tasty *and* timely. And you don't have to worry about searching for unusual ingredients. These dishes can be made with ingredients you likely have on hand.

**Clever Crafts.** What's Christmas without crafts? You're likely to find more than one project that catches your eye among the dozens we've selected this year.

Each homespun craft features charts, patterns and easy-to-follow instructions, so you can complete the project in plenty of time for decking your halls or giving as gifts.

You'll also enjoy reading about country ladies who spread the spirit of the season with their own individual style, whether they're fashioning wreaths, painting ornaments or decorating the house. And take a few minutes to relish a poem, a handy holiday hint or nostalgic memories of Christmases past.

**More in Store.** With a bright new edition added to this series each year, you can look forward to many more country-flavored holiday celebrations. But, for now, simply settle back with *Country Woman Christmas 2002*. We hope you enjoy it as much as we've enjoyed bringing it to you.

3

**Executive Editor**
Kathy Pohl

**Editor**
Kathleen Anderson

**Food Editor**
Janaan Cunningham

**Associate Food Editor**
Coleen Martin

**Senior Recipe Editor**
Sue A. Jurack

**Recipe Editor**
Janet Briggs

**Test Kitchen Assistant**
Suzanne Hampton

**Craft Editor**
Jane Craig

**Associate Editors**
Barbara Schuetz
Jean Steiner
Susan Uphill

**Editorial Assistant**
Joanne Wied

**Art Director**
Emma Acevedo

**Art Associate**
Tom Hunt

**Photographers**
Rob Hagen
Dan Roberts

**Food Photography Artists**
Stephanie Marchese
Vicky Marie Moseley

**Photo Studio Manager**
Anne Schimmel

**Production Assistants**
Ellen Lloyd
Catherine Fletcher

© 2002 Reiman Media Group, Inc.
5400 S. 60th Street
Greendale WI 53129

International Standard
Book Number:
0-89821-341-X
International Standard
Serial Number:
1093-6750

## INSIDE...

## *AND MUCH MORE!*

**PICTURED ON OUR COVER.** Clockwise from top right: Soft-Sculpture Reindeer (p. 64), Drummer Boy Cake (p. 41), Quilted Wall Hanging (p. 72), Eggnog Cutout Cookies (p. 31), Angel Basket (p. 88), Sugared Twists (p. 14) and Plastic Canvas Gift Bags (p. 82).

# WELCOME TO MY COUNTRY KITCHEN

*By Patricia Ingold-Wright of Asheboro, North Carolina*

IT'S easy to warm up to Christmas in my cozy kitchen. The red brick fireplace and rich oak cabinets and flooring create such a homey atmosphere…one that becomes even more inviting when I wrap the room in red and green.

My husband, Jim, and I joke that we built our house around the fireplace, but it's a popular gathering place and so much fun to decorate for any holiday.

The neutral-toned countertop and walls let me change colors with the seasons. But Christmas is my favorite time of year. (Even the cattle I raise with my brothers have a Christmas connection—they're registered Santa Gertrudis breed!)

So once Thanksgiving dinner is done, I haul out my holiday trims and fill the kitchen with seasonal spirit. I start by ringing the room in holly, placing it over the patio doors, across the mantel and desk, around the sink and stovetop and twining through my pottery collection above the cupboards.

Holly garland adorns the window treatments, too. The curtains are actually a piece of red fabric I wire to the curtain rod and drape across the double window over the sink. For a finishing touch, I loop the fabric through gold grapevine wreaths and add berries and braid.

Sprigs of holly give a festive flair to vases, pots and napkin rings, too. I even tie red bows to holly candle rings and hang them like wreaths on the patio door.

The kitchen really comes alive when my animated dolls move in for the season. I'm sure the carolers on top of the refrigerator look forward to the Yuletide tunes my Christmas clock plays every hour. Nearby, Santa builds toys while Mrs. Santa bakes cookies.

### All Dolled Up

The jolly pair also light up my handy desk, where I often sit and browse through cookbooks stored in the cupboard overhead. At Christmas, the books are replaced by a band of merry mice, some playing the piano or blowing bubbles.

The mice are just a few of the crafty characters that peek out from every nook and cranny of my kitchen. I've been doing ceramics since 1978, so I have amassed quite a number of Noel figurines…and I find a spot for every one of them!

Whimsical elves and bears get tucked among the antique dishes in the corner cupboard. Reindeer, Santa and snowman cookie jars hold tasty holiday treats on the countertop. And gingerbread boys and girls, painted with a different expression ♂

**DECKED IN BOUGHS** of holly, the North Carolina kitchen of Patricia Ingold-Wright (shown at far left) is seasoned to please. The cheery room shows off Patricia's collection of animated dolls and playful seasonal ceramics, including the cute Claus couple (above) warming up on the brick hearth. A plaid tablecloth and "Country Christmas" dishes (far left) lend a festive flair to holiday meals, and Noel-themed cookie jars and plates hold homemade goodies for guests to enjoy.

on each side, dance atop the cupboards and peer out the window.

### Seasoned with Santas

Folks always get a chuckle from the ceramic Claus couple warming up on the hearth. I pose a variety of other St. Nicks, including a farmer Claus and a Spanish Santa, on a German crocheted scarf that graces the mantelpiece. But it's the white porcelain Nativity that I make the center of attention.

Since family, friends and neighbors stop by throughout the holiday season, my "Country Christmas" dinnerware gets a lot of use. I love its playful pattern featuring festive farm animals and a cow pulling Santa's sleigh.

The oak dining table, covered with a red and green plaid tablecloth, is always ready for guests. Two hurricane candle holders flank an arrangement of red roses and holly in a sugar bowl. There are even a few mice peeking out!

Our breakfast bar provides extra seating, so I keep it set with matching plaid place mats. Jim and I prefer to eat here when it's just the two of us. We can gaze at a crackling fire in the fireplace or watch the cattle graze in the pasture beyond our patio.

We find such peace and joy in our country kitchen...at Christmas and all year-round. It's truly the heart of our home, and I'm glad I could share it with you. Happy holidays! ♥

**AN OLD-FASHIONED ATMOSPHERE** fills the kitchen when the red brick fireplace is all aglow. Patricia displays some of her nifty St. Nicks on the mantel. Whimsical ceramic mice take over the cookbook cupboard above the built-in desk and peek around antique dishes in the corner cupboard.

8

# 'Gingerbread Lady' Helps Build Homes for Holidays

SUGAR AND SPICE and everything nice are built into every house Eleanor Twardy constructs. But sturdy as they are, her structures are bound to crumble.

That's because the rural Shaftsbury, Vermont woman designs dwellings that are edible from the ground up. And Eleanor encourages folks to follow in Hansel and Gretel's footsteps and sample the enticing edifices.

"The smoke in the chimney is the only thing that can't be eaten, because it's a cotton ball," she says. "Everything else is sweet to eat, from the steps to the windows to the frosted roof.

"The treetops are candy kisses, and the bushes are gumdrops. The fence posts, latticework and lights are made from frosting. I also use candy canes and M&M's as accents."

Eleanor, who is known as the "Gingerbread Lady of Shaftsbury", erected her first house 30 years ago. Her primary tool was a basic cookie recipe, a formula she revised over the years to create the "perfect dough".

"Each year I made renovations to my little gingerbread house," she recalls. "Eventually, I started giving them as Christmas gifts, then people began asking me to make houses for *them* to give as gifts."

Soon the entire family was in the construction business. Her husband, Mike, worked with her on lighting the houses, while their five children helped in the kitchen and at craft fairs.

And shoppers ate them up. "Before long, I found myself making over 100 in one season," remembers Eleanor, who was honestly overwhelmed by the building boom.

"I knew I couldn't keep up the pace, plus people were always asking me how I made them, so I decided demonstration was the best route."

About 4 years ago, Eleanor produced "Gingerbread Creations", a 1-hour videotape and instruction booklet, with help from college-age daughters Jenny and Jessica.

The kit also includes a cassette of carols to cook by and full-size blueprints for two lighted houses, including one that's just right for kids.

"From start to finish, you can make a complete house in about 3 hours," Eleanor assures.

She hasn't turned in her own tool belt, though. Eleanor still builds gingerbread structures for friends, family and charities from designs she creates.

"I make country stores, covered bridges, carousels, barns, mills, birdhouses, Victorian villages, gazebos and trains," she says. "If it can be made of gingerbread, I can build it!"

**Editor's Note:** *For more information or to order Eleanor's gingerbread house kit, call 1-802/447-3618, visit her Web site at www.gingerbreadcreations. com or send her an E-mail at gingerb@ sover. net.* ♥

**HOME SWEET HOME.** Eleanor Twardy's candy-covered gingerbread houses can be made in just a few hours and gobbled up just as quickly. She doesn't limit herself to designing homes, however. She has constructed carousels (left), birdhouses and even entire Victorian villages.

**BEAUTIFUL BRUNCH.** Shown clockwise from top: Creamy Strawberry Breeze (p. 11), Farmhouse Omelets (p. 11) and Homemade Sage Sausage Patties (p. 11).

# Holiday Brunch

## FARMHOUSE OMELETS
**Roberta Williams, Poplar Bluff, Missouri**
(Pictured on page 10)

*We really enjoy eating brunch after church on Sundays, so I make an effort to serve something special. This pretty omelet provides a pleasant blend of tastes and textures.*

 4 bacon strips, diced
 1/4 cup chopped onion
 6 eggs
 1 tablespoon water
 1/4 teaspoon salt, optional
 1/8 teaspoon pepper
Dash hot pepper sauce
 3 teaspoons butter *or* margarine, *divided*
 1/2 cup cubed fully cooked ham, *divided*
 1/4 cup thinly sliced fresh mushrooms, *divided*
 1/4 cup chopped green pepper, *divided*
 1 cup (4 ounces) shredded cheddar cheese, *divided*

In a skillet, cook bacon over medium heat until crisp. Remove with a slotted spoon to paper towels. Drain, reserving 2 teaspoons drippings. In the drippings, saute onion until tender; set aside.

In a bowl, beat eggs, water, salt if desired, pepper and hot pepper sauce. Melt 1-1/2 teaspoons butter in a 10-in. nonstick skillet over medium heat; add half of the egg mixture. As the eggs set, lift edges, letting uncooked portion flow underneath.

When eggs are set, sprinkle half of the bacon, onion, ham, mushrooms, green pepper and cheese over one side; fold over. Cover and let stand 1-2 minutes or until cheese is melted. Repeat with remaining ingredients for second omelet. **Yield:** 2 omelets.

## HOMEMADE SAGE SAUSAGE PATTIES
**Diane Hixon, Niceville, Florida**
(Pictured on page 10)

*Oregano, garlic and sage add zippy flavor to these quick-to-fix ground pork patties. I've had this Pennsylvania Dutch recipe for years, and it always brings compliments.*

3/4 cup shredded cheddar cheese
1/4 cup buttermilk
 1 tablespoon finely chopped onion
 2 teaspoons rubbed sage
3/4 teaspoon salt
3/4 teaspoon pepper
1/8 teaspoon garlic powder
1/8 teaspoon dried oregano
 1 pound ground pork

In a bowl, combine the first eight ingredients. Crumble pork over mixture and mix well. Shape into eight 1/2-in. patties. Refrigerate for 1 hour. In a nonstick skillet over medium heat, fry patties for 6-8 minutes on each side or until meat is no longer pink. **Yield:** 8 servings.

## CREAMY STRAWBERRY BREEZE
**Amy Cruson, Dodge City, Kansas**
(Pictured on page 10)

*Get Christmas Day off to a refreshing start with this frothy fruit drink. For a festive touch, garnish with a strawberry and a dollop of whipped topping. The pretty pink smoothie makes an attractive addition to a Yuletide brunch.*

 2 cups whole strawberries
 2 cups apple juice
 3 cups whipped topping

Place half of the strawberries and apple juice in a blender; cover and process until smooth. Add half of the whipped topping; cover and process until blended. Pour into glasses. Repeat. **Yield:** 4 servings.

## CHRISTMAS COFFEE CAKE
**Sue Meckstroth, New Carlisle, Ohio**

*Christmas morning wouldn't be complete at our house without this yummy moist coffee cake. A streusel filling and topping sweetens the delightful cake, and red and green cherries add a festive touch. It's a perfect addition to any holiday breakfast buffet.*

 1 cup pecans, chopped
 1/3 cup packed brown sugar
 1/4 cup sugar
 1/4 cup butter *or* margarine, melted
 1 teaspoon ground cinnamon
CAKE:
 7 green maraschino cherries, finely chopped
 7 red maraschino cherries, finely chopped
 1/2 cup shortening
 1 cup sugar
 2 eggs
 1 teaspoon vanilla extract
2-1/4 cups all-purpose flour
 1 teaspoon baking powder
 1 teaspoon baking soda
 1/2 teaspoon salt
 1 cup (8 ounces) sour cream

In a small bowl, combine the first five ingredients; mix well. Set aside. Drain cherries on paper towels. In a mixing bowl, cream shortening and sugar. Add eggs, one at a time, beating well after each addition. Add vanilla; mix well. Combine the flour, baking powder, baking soda and salt; add to creamed mixture alternately with sour cream. Fold in cherries.

Pour half of the batter into a greased 9-in. springform pan; sprinkle with half of the pecan mixture. Top with remaining batter and pecan mixture. Bake at 350° for 45-50 minutes or until a toothpick inserted near the center comes out clean. Cool on a wire rack for 10 minutes. Carefully run a knife around edge of pan to loosen. Remove sides of pan just before serving. **Yield:** 12 servings.

# BUTTERNUT SQUASH DOUGHNUTS
### Elizabeth Leighton, Lincoln, Maine

*My mother and I used to make several batches of these cake doughnuts at a time. They're not only different, they're delicious, too!*

        2 eggs
1-1/4 cups sugar
      1 cup mashed cooked butternut *or* winter squash
          of your choice
  1/2 cup buttermilk
      2 tablespoons butter *or* margarine, softened
      2 teaspoons vanilla extract
3-1/2 cups all-purpose flour
1-1/2 teaspoons baking soda
1-1/4 teaspoons ground nutmeg
      1 teaspoon baking powder
      1 teaspoon cream of tartar
  1/2 teaspoon salt
  1/4 teaspoon ground cinnamon
  1/4 teaspoon ground ginger
Confectioners' sugar *or* additional sugar, optional

In a mixing bowl, combine the eggs, sugar, squash, buttermilk, butter and vanilla. Combine the dry ingredients; add to squash mixture and mix well. Cover and refrigerate for 2 hours (dough will be very soft).

Turn onto a heavily floured surface; roll to 1/2-in. thickness. Cut with a 2-1/2-in. doughnut cutter. In an electric skillet or deep-fat fryer, heat 1 in. of oil to 375°. Fry doughnuts, a few at a time, until golden brown on both sides. Drain on paper towels. Dust with sugar if desired. **Yield:** about 2 dozen.

# PETITE SAUSAGE QUICHES
### Dawn Stitt, Hesperia, Michigan

*You won't be able to eat just one of these cute mini quiches. Filled with savory sausage, Swiss cheese and a dash of cayenne, the mouth-watering morsels will disappear fast from the breakfast or buffet table.*

      1 cup butter *or* margarine, softened
      2 packages (3 ounces *each*) cream cheese, softened
      2 cups all-purpose flour
FILLING:
      6 ounces bulk Italian sausage
      1 cup (4 ounces) shredded Swiss cheese
      1 tablespoon minced chives
      2 eggs
      1 cup half-and-half cream
  1/4 teaspoon salt
Dash cayenne pepper

In a mixing bowl, beat butter, cream cheese and flour until smooth. Shape tablespoonfuls of dough into balls; press onto the bottom and up the sides of greased miniature muffin cups.

In a skillet, cook sausage over medium heat until no longer pink; drain. Sprinkle sausage, Swiss cheese and chives into muffin cups. In a bowl, beat eggs, cream, salt and pepper. Pour into shells. Bake at 375° for 28-30 minutes or until browned. Serve warm. **Yield:** 3 dozen.

# RAISED YEAST WAFFLES
### Helen Knapp, Fairbanks, Alaska

*These waffles bake up crispy on the outside and light and tender on the inside. Since they aren't too filling, they leave room for sampling the rest of a brunch buffet—or for munching on more waffles!*

      1 package (1/4 ounce) active dry yeast
      1 teaspoon sugar
  1/2 cup warm water (110° to 115°)
      2 cups warm milk (110° to 115°)
      2 eggs
  1/2 cup butter *or* margarine, melted
      2 cups all-purpose flour
      1 teaspoon salt
  1/8 teaspoon baking soda

In a mixing bowl, dissolve yeast and sugar in warm water; let stand for 5 minutes. Beat in the milk, eggs and butter. Combine the flour, salt and baking soda; stir into yeast mixture just until combined. Cover and let rise in a warm place until doubled, about 45 minutes.

Bake in a preheated waffle iron according to manufacturer's directions until golden brown. **Yield:** 10 waffles.

# BUFFET SCRAMBLED EGGS
### Elsie Beachy, Plain City, Ohio

*These are my favorite scrambled eggs. The white sauce, flavored with chicken bouillon, keeps the eggs creamy and moist. It's a tasty twist on a morning mainstay.*

      4 tablespoons butter *or* margarine, *divided*
      2 tablespoons all-purpose flour
      1 cup milk
      2 teaspoons chicken bouillon granules
      8 eggs, beaten
Minced fresh parsley, optional

In a saucepan, melt 2 tablespoons butter. Stir in flour until smooth. Add milk and bouillon. Bring to a boil; cook and stir for 2 minutes or until thickened. Set aside.

In a large skillet, melt remaining butter. Add eggs; cook over medium heat until eggs begin to set, stirring occasionally. Add white sauce; mix well. Cook until the eggs are completely set. Garnish with parsley if desired. **Yield:** 4 servings.

# PRALINE FRENCH TOAST
### Jean Kruse, Bowling Green, Missouri

*There's quite a crowd when our family gathers for Christmas, and I'm always asked to fix this French toast. The praline syrup is a nice change of pace from traditional maple.*

      9 eggs
      3 cups half-and-half cream
  1/3 cup sugar
1-1/2 teaspoons vanilla extract
  1/2 teaspoon ground cinnamon *or* nutmeg
      24 to 30 slices French bread (3/4 inch thick)

**PRALINE SYRUP:**
1-1/2 cups packed brown sugar
  1/2 cup corn syrup
  1/2 cup water
  1/2 cup chopped pecans, toasted
    2 tablespoons butter *or* margarine

In a large bowl, lightly beat eggs. Stir in the cream, sugar, vanilla and cinnamon. Arrange bread in a single layer in two greased 15-in. x 10-in. x 1-in. baking pans. Pour egg mixture over bread. Cover and refrigerate overnight.

    Remove from the refrigerator 30 minutes before baking. Bake, uncovered, at 400° for 20-25 minutes or until golden brown. Meanwhile, for syrup, combine brown sugar, corn syrup and water in a saucepan. Bring to a boil over medium heat. Reduce heat; simmer, uncovered, for 3 minutes. Stir in pecans and butter; simmer 2 minutes longer. Serve with the French toast. **Yield:** 10-12 servings.

# CINNAMON CREAM ROLL-UPS
### Helen Clem, Creston, Iowa

*These fancy breakfast roll-ups are a cinch to make with everyday sandwich bread. Each slice wraps around a rich cream cheese filling, and the cinnamon-sugar coating not only looks pretty, it tastes terrific!*

    1 package (8 ounces) cream cheese, softened
    1 egg yolk
1-1/4 cups sugar, *divided*
    1 loaf (1 pound) sandwich bread, crusts removed
    1 tablespoon ground cinnamon
  1/4 cup butter *or* margarine, melted

In a small mixing bowl, combine the cream cheese, egg yolk and 1/4 cup sugar; mix well. Flatten bread slices with a rolling pin. Spread cream cheese mixture over each slice to within 1/2 in. of edges. Roll up diagonally from point to point.

    In a shallow bowl, combine the cinnamon and remaining sugar. Dip roll-ups in melted butter, then in cinnamon-sugar mixture. Place in an ungreased 15-in. x 10-in. x 1-in. baking pan. Bake at 350° for 16-19 minutes or until lightly browned. Remove to wire racks to cool. **Yield:** 8-10 servings.

# SPICED FRUIT BOWL
### Linda Cary, Albany, New York

*Juicy grapes and handy canned peaches and pears are spiced just right in this delicious dish. Allspice, cinnamon and cloves give the fruit a punch of holiday flavor. It's an easy and wonderful way to add fruit to your morning meal.*

    2 cans (29 ounces *each*) sliced peaches
    1 can (29 ounces) pear halves
  1/4 cup cider vinegar
  1/4 teaspoon salt
    4 cinnamon sticks (3 inches), broken
  3/4 teaspoon whole allspice
  1/2 teaspoon whole cloves
    1 pound seedless red grapes, halved

Drain juice from peaches and pears into a saucepan; set fruit aside. Add vinegar and salt to juices. Place cinnamon, allspice and cloves on a double thickness of cheesecloth; bring up corners of cloth and tie with string to form a bag. Place in the saucepan. Bring to a boil. Reduce heat; cover and simmer for 10 minutes. Remove from the heat; cool for 15 minutes.

    In a large bowl, combine the peaches, pears and grapes. Add juices and spice bag. Cover and refrigerate for 12 hours or up to 3 days, stirring occasionally. Discard spice bag before serving. **Yield:** 10-12 servings.

# BACON 'N' EGG PIZZA
### Georgiann Franklin, Canfield, Ohio

*Pizza for breakfast? Kids especially will enjoy eating the bacon, cheese, hash browns and eggs layered on an easy-to-cut pizza-like crust. This attractive entree is sure to be a hit with grown-ups, too.*

    1 tube (8 ounces) refrigerated crescent rolls
  12 bacon strips, cooked and crumbled
    1 cup frozen shredded hash brown potatoes
  3/4 cup shredded cheddar cheese
    4 eggs
    2 tablespoons milk
  1/2 cup grated Parmesan *or* Romano cheese

Unroll crescent roll dough into one long rectangle. Press onto the bottom and 1/2 in. up the sides of a greased 13-in. x 9-in. x 2-in. baking pan. Seal seams and perforations. Sprinkle with bacon, potatoes and cheddar cheese.

    In a bowl, beat eggs and milk. Pour over cheddar cheese. Sprinkle with Parmesan cheese. Bake, uncovered, at 375° for 25-30 minutes or until eggs are completely set. **Yield:** 8 servings.

# SUGAR 'N' SPICE MUFFINS
### Monica Penner, Elma, Manitoba

*These sugar-and-spice treats are so tasty! The moist streusel-topped muffins are perfect for parties or nibbling with a hot cup of coffee, tea or hot chocolate.*

    2 cups all-purpose flour
    1 cup sugar
  3/4 cup cold butter *or* margarine
    1 teaspoon baking soda
    1 teaspoon ground cinnamon
    1 teaspoon ground cloves
    1 cup buttermilk
    1 egg, lightly beaten

In a bowl, combine flour and sugar; cut in butter until crumbly. Set aside 1/2 cup for topping. Add baking soda, cinnamon and cloves to the remaining crumb mixture. Stir in buttermilk and egg just until moistened.

    Fill greased or paper-lined muffin cups two-thirds full. Sprinkle with reserved topping. Bake at 375° for 18-20 minutes or until a toothpick comes out clean. Cool for 5 minutes before removing from pan to a wire rack to cool. Serve warm. **Yield:** 1 dozen.

# Christmas Breads

## SUGARED TWISTS
**Shelley Blythe, Indianapolis, Indiana**
(Pictured on page 16)

*Folks like these tender twists because they aren't rich or overly sweet. I usually double the recipe to feed our five eager eaters and fill holiday gift plates for friends.*

```
        1 package (1/4 ounce) active dry yeast
    1/4 cup warm water (110° to 115°)
3-1/2 cups all-purpose flour
1-1/2 teaspoons salt
    1/2 cup cold butter or margarine
    1/2 cup shortening
        2 eggs, lightly beaten
    1/2 cup sour cream
2-1/2 teaspoons vanilla extract, divided
        1 cup sugar
Red and green or multicolored nonpareils
```

In a small bowl, dissolve yeast in warm water; set aside. In a large bowl, combine flour and salt. Cut in butter and shortening until mixture resembles coarse crumbs. Add eggs, sour cream and 1 teaspoon vanilla; mix well. Add yeast mixture. Cover and refrigerate for 2 hours or overnight.

Punch dough down; divide in half. Combine sugar and remaining vanilla; sprinkle some over work surface. Roll each portion of dough into a 15-in. x 5-in. rectangle. Fold in thirds; sprinkle with additional sugar mixture. Repeat rolling and folding twice.

Cut into 5-in. x 1-in. strips. Twist and place on greased baking sheets. Sprinkle with nonpareils; press down lightly. Bake at 350° for 18-20 minutes or until golden brown. Remove from pans to wire racks to cool. **Yield:** 2-1/2 dozen.

## PUMPKIN COFFEE RING
**Carol McCartney, Danville, Ohio**
(Pictured on page 16)

*I make this delicious coffee cake, with its creamy pumpkin filling, for almost every holiday gathering, and everyone loves it.*

```
2-1/4 cups all-purpose flour
    3/4 cup sugar, divided
        1 package (1/4 ounce) active dry yeast
    1/2 teaspoon salt
    1/4 cup water
    1/4 cup milk
        3 tablespoons butter or margarine
        1 egg
        1 package (3 ounces) cream cheese, softened
    1/2 cup cooked or canned pumpkin
        1 teaspoon ground cinnamon
    1/2 teaspoon salt
    1/2 teaspoon ground ginger
    1/2 teaspoon ground nutmeg
    1/2 cup chopped walnuts
    1/2 cup raisins
        1 egg yolk, beaten
```

**GLAZE:**
```
    1/2 cup confectioners' sugar
    1/8 teaspoon vanilla extract
        1 to 2 tablespoons milk
    1/4 cup finely chopped walnuts
```

In a mixing bowl, combine 1-1/2 cups flour, 1/4 cup sugar, yeast and salt. In a saucepan, heat water, milk and butter to 120°-130°. Add to dry ingredients; beat just until moistened. Beat in egg. Stir in enough remaining flour to form a soft dough. Turn onto a floured surface; knead until smooth and elastic, about 6-8 minutes. Place in a greased bowl, turning once to grease top. Cover and let rise in a warm place until doubled, about 1 hour.

In a small mixing bowl, beat cream cheese and remaining sugar until smooth. Add the pumpkin, cinnamon, salt, ginger and nutmeg. Punch dough down; turn onto a floured surface. Roll into a 20-in. x 10-in. rectangle; spread pumpkin mixture to within 1/2 in. of edges. Sprinkle with nuts and raisins. Roll up jelly-roll style, starting with a long side; pinch ends together to form a ring. Place on a greased baking sheet. Cover and let rise until doubled, about 1 hour.

Brush dough with egg yolk. Bake at 350° for 20-25 minutes or until golden brown. Remove from pan to a wire rack. For glaze, combine the confectioners' sugar, vanilla and enough milk to achieve drizzling consistency. Drizzle over warm ring. Sprinkle with nuts. **Yield:** 1 ring.

## CHERRY CRESCENTS
**Leona Luecking, West Burlington, Iowa**
(Pictured on page 17)

*These light flaky pastries are so easy to make, and they always get raves at our house. The festive cherry filling suits the season, but you can substitute other flavors.*

```
        2 cups all-purpose flour
    1/2 teaspoon salt
        1 cup cold butter or margarine
        1 egg yolk, lightly beaten
        1 cup (8 ounces) sour cream
        1 can (21 ounces) cherry pie filling
    1/2 teaspoon almond extract
Confectioners' sugar
```

In a bowl, combine flour and salt. Cut in butter until mixture resembles coarse crumbs. Combine egg yolk and sour cream; add to crumb mixture and mix well. Refrigerate for several hours or overnight. Coarsely chop cherries in the pie filling; place in a small bowl. Stir in extract; set aside.

Divide dough into quarters. On a lightly floured surface, roll each portion into a 12-in. circle. Cut each circle into 12 wedges. Place 1 teaspoon filling at the wide end. Roll up from wide end and place point side down 1 in. apart on ungreased baking sheets. Curve ends to form crescent shape.

Bake at 375° for 20-24 minutes or until golden brown. Immediately remove from pans to wire racks to cool. Dust with confectioners' sugar. **Yield:** 4 dozen.

## RAISIN ORANGE BREAD

**Eva Sue Jones, Shell Knob, Missouri**
(Pictured on page 17)

*I've won many blue ribbons over the years with this recipe. No doubt my daughters will pass on the tradition and bake this bread for their own families.*

    5 to 5-1/2 cups all-purpose flour
    1/2 cup sugar
    5 teaspoons grated orange peel
    2 packages (1/4 ounce *each*) active dry yeast
    1-1/2 teaspoons salt
    1 teaspoon ground ginger
    1 cup milk
    1/2 cup butter *or* margarine, softened
    1/4 cup water
    2 eggs
    1-1/2 cups raisins
**WALNUT GLAZE:**
    1 cup confectioners' sugar
    2 tablespoons orange juice
    2 teaspoons butter *or* margarine, softened
    1/2 cup finely chopped walnuts

In a mixing bowl, combine 2 cups flour, sugar, orange peel, yeast, salt and ginger. In a saucepan, heat milk, butter and water to 120°-130°. Add to dry ingredients; beat just until moistened. Add eggs; beat on low speed for 30 seconds. Beat on high for 3 minutes. Stir in raisins. Stir in enough remaining flour to form a soft dough. Turn onto a floured surface; knead until smooth and elastic, about 6-8 minutes. Place dough in a greased bowl, turning once to grease the top. Cover and let rise in a warm place until doubled, about 1-1/4 hours.

Punch dough down. Turn onto a floured surface; knead for 1 minute. Cover and let rest 15 minutes. Divide in half. Roll each portion into a 9-in. x 7-in. oval; fold in half lengthwise. Pinch edges to seal. Place in two greased 8-in. x 4-in. x 2-in. loaf pans. With a sharp knife, make three 1/4-in.-deep diagonal slashes across top of each loaf. Cover and let rise until doubled, about 45 minutes.

Bake at 375° for 45-50 minutes or until golden brown. Cover loosely with foil after 20 minutes to prevent overbrowning. Remove from pans to wire racks to cool. For glaze, combine the sugar, orange juice and butter until smooth. Stir in walnuts. Spread over loaves. **Yield:** 2 loaves.

## CRANBERRY STICKY BUNS

**Anne Frederick, New Hartford, New York**
(Pictured at right)

*The aroma of fresh bread baking reminds me of my childhood and the wonderful cinnamon rolls Mom used to make. This recipe is a variation of those treats with the seasonal addition of cranberries.*

    4 cups all-purpose flour
    1 package (1/4 ounce) active dry yeast
    1/4 cup sugar
    1/4 cup butter *or* margarine
    1 teaspoon salt
    1 cup milk
    2 eggs

**TOPPING:**
    3/4 cup chopped fresh *or* frozen cranberries
    2/3 cup packed brown sugar
    1/2 cup butter *or* margarine
    1/2 teaspoon ground cinnamon
    3/4 cup chopped walnuts
    2 tablespoons butter *or* margarine, melted
**FILLING:**
    1/2 cup packed brown sugar
    1/2 cup chopped walnuts
    1/2 cup chopped fresh *or* frozen cranberries
    1/2 teaspoon ground cinnamon

In a mixing bowl, combine 2 cups flour and yeast. In a saucepan, heat sugar, butter, salt and milk to 120°-130°. Add to dry ingredients; beat on low speed for 30 seconds. Add eggs; beat on high for 3 minutes. Beat in remaining flour. Turn onto a floured surface; knead until smooth and elastic, about 6-8 minutes. Place in a greased bowl, turning once to grease top. Cover and let rise in a warm place until doubled, about 1 hour.

In a saucepan, combine the first four topping ingredients; cook and stir over low heat until brown sugar is dissolved and butter is melted. Stir in walnuts. Spread into two greased 9-in. square baking pans; set aside.

Punch dough down; divide in half. Roll each portion into an 18-in. x 6-in. rectangle; brush with butter. Combine filling ingredients; sprinkle over dough to within 1/2 in. of edges. Roll up jelly-roll style, starting with a long side; pinch seam to seal. Cut each roll into nine slices; place cut side down over topping and flatten slightly. Cover and let rise until doubled, about 1 hour.

Bake at 375° for 10 minutes. Reduce heat to 350°; bake 15 minutes longer or until golden brown. Immediately invert onto serving plates. **Yield:** 1-1/2 dozen.

**BOUNTIFUL BREADS.** Shown clockwise from top left: Sugared Twists (p. 14), Honey Whole Wheat Pan Rolls (p. 18), Cherry Crescents (p. 14), Raisin Orange Bread (p. 15) and Pumpkin Coffee Ring (p. 14).

# HONEY WHOLE WHEAT PAN ROLLS
### Nancye Thompson, Paducah, Kentucky
(Pictured on page 16)

*With their pleasant wheat flavor and a honey of a glaze, these rolls impress my guests. Every time I take them to potluck dinners, I come home with an empty pan.*

        4 to 5 cups bread flour
    1/4 cup sugar
        2 packages (1/4 ounce *each*) active dry yeast
        1 teaspoon salt
        1 cup milk
        1 cup butter (no substitutes)
    1/2 cup water
        2 eggs
        2 cups whole wheat flour
HONEY BUTTER:
        1 cup butter, softened
        7 tablespoons honey
HONEY GLAZE:
        2 tablespoons honey
        1 tablespoon butter, melted

In a mixing bowl, combine 2 cups bread flour, sugar, yeast and salt. In a saucepan, heat milk, butter and water to 120°-130°. Add to dry ingredients; beat just until moistened. Add eggs; beat until smooth. Stir in whole wheat flour and enough remaining bread flour to form a soft dough. Turn onto a floured surface; knead until smooth and elastic, about 10 minutes. Cover and let rest 15 minutes.

Divide dough into thirds. Roll each portion into a 20-in. rope. Cut each into 20 pieces; shape each into a ball. Grease three 9-in. round baking pans; arrange 20 balls in each pan. Cover and refrigerate overnight.

Let rise in a warm place until doubled, about 1-1/4 hours. Bake at 350° for 18-22 minutes or until golden brown. Meanwhile, in a small mixing bowl, cream butter. Add honey; beat until light and fluffy. Remove rolls from pans to wire racks. Combine glaze ingredients; brush over warm rolls. Serve with honey butter. **Yield:** 5 dozen (1-1/4 cups honey butter).

# PECAN-FILLED COFFEE RINGS
### Charlotte Schoening, Waterford, Wisconsin

*This old recipe was handed down to me by my great-grandmother. The easy-to-handle sweet dough produces two tempting rings that look lovely drizzled with a powdered sugar glaze.*

        1 package (1/4 ounce) active dry yeast
        2 teaspoons plus 1/2 cup sugar, *divided*
        1 cup warm milk (110° to 115°)
        1 cup butter *or* margarine, softened
        3 egg yolks, beaten
        1 teaspoon vanilla extract
    1/2 teaspoon salt
        4 to 4-1/2 cups all-purpose flour
FILLING:
1-1/2 cups ground pecans
    1/2 cup sugar
        1 egg
        3 tablespoons butter *or* margarine, softened
        1 teaspoon vanilla extract

GLAZE:
        1 cup confectioners' sugar
        1 tablespoon lemon juice
        1 tablespoon milk

In a bowl, dissolve yeast and 2 teaspoons sugar in warm milk; let stand for 5 minutes. In a mixing bowl, cream butter and remaining sugar. Beat in the egg yolks, vanilla and salt. Add yeast mixture and 1 cup flour; beat until smooth. Stir in enough remaining flour to form a soft dough. Turn onto a floured surface; knead until smooth and elastic, about 6-8 minutes. Place in a greased bowl, turning once to grease top. Cover and let rise in a warm place until doubled, about 1-1/4 hours.

Punch dough down. Turn onto a lightly floured surface; divide in half. Roll each portion into a 16-in. x 9-in. rectangle. Combine filling ingredients; spread over dough to within 1 in. of edges. Roll up jelly-roll style, starting with a long side; pinch seam to seal.

Place seam side down on greased baking sheets; pinch ends together to form a ring. With kitchen scissors, cut from the outside edge two-thirds of the way toward center of ring at 1-in. intervals. Separate strips slightly and twist to allow filling to show. Cover and let rise until doubled, about 45 minutes.

Bake at 350° for 30-35 minutes or until golden brown. Remove from pans to wire racks; cool for 20 minutes. Combine glaze ingredients; drizzle over warm rings. **Yield:** 2 rings.

# CREAM CHEESE COFFEE CAKES
### LaDonna Andeel, Yukon, Oklahoma

*Since these coffee cakes freeze well, they make a welcome "instant" breakfast during all the Christmas morning craziness. Friends and family love receiving them, too, wrapped up with a holiday bow.*

    1/2 cup butter *or* margarine
        1 cup (8 ounces) sour cream
    1/2 cup sugar
        1 teaspoon salt
        2 packages (1/4 ounce *each*) active dry yeast
    1/2 cup warm water (110° to 115°)
        2 eggs, lightly beaten
        5 to 5-1/2 cups all-purpose flour
CREAM CHEESE FILLING:
        2 packages (one 8 ounces, one 3 ounces) cream cheese, softened
    1/2 cup sugar
        1 egg
1-1/2 teaspoons vanilla extract
    1/4 teaspoon salt
GLAZE:
        2 cups confectioners' sugar
    1/4 cup milk
        2 teaspoons vanilla extract

In a saucepan, melt butter over low heat. Remove from the heat. Stir in sour cream, sugar and salt; cool to 110°-115°. In a mixing bowl, dissolve yeast in warm water. Add the eggs, sour cream mixture and 2 cups flour; beat until smooth. Stir in enough remaining flour to form a stiff dough. Turn onto a floured surface; knead until smooth and elastic, about 6-8 minutes. Place in a greased bowl, turning once to grease top. Cover and let rise in a warm place until doubled, about 1 hour.

In a mixing bowl, beat filling ingredients until smooth; set aside. Punch dough down. Turn onto a lightly floured surface; divide into four portions. Roll each into a 12-in. x 10-in. rectangle; spread with filling. Roll up jelly-roll style, starting with a long side; pinch seam to seal and tuck ends under. Place seam side down on greased baking sheets. With a scissors, cut two-thirds of the way through dough at 1-in. intervals. Cover and let rise until doubled, about 45 minutes.

Bake at 350° for 15-20 minutes or until golden brown. Remove from pans to wire racks to cool. Combine glaze ingredients; drizzle over coffee cakes. **Yield:** 4 coffee cakes.

# CARAMEL CINNAMON ROLLS
### Marjorie Miller, Haven, Kansas

*My husband and our four sons are delighted when I bake these sweetly satisfying cinnamon rolls with a terrific caramel glaze. They make any meal special.*

2 packages (1/4 ounce *each*) active dry yeast
1/4 cup warm water (110° to 115°)
2 cups warm milk (110° to 115°)
1 cup butter *or* margarine, softened
1 cup sugar
1 cup mashed potatoes (prepared without milk or butter)
2 eggs, beaten
1 teaspoon salt
1-1/2 cups whole wheat flour
7-1/4 cups all-purpose flour
FILLING:
1/4 cup butter *or* margarine, melted
1 cup packed brown sugar
3 tablespoons ground cinnamon
CARAMEL GLAZE:
1/2 cup whipping cream
1/3 cup sugar
1/3 cup packed brown sugar
3 tablespoons butter *or* margarine
1 cup miniature marshmallows
2 cups confectioners' sugar
1 teaspoon vanilla extract

In a mixing bowl, dissolve yeast in warm water. Add the milk, butter, sugar, potatoes, eggs, salt and whole wheat flour; beat until smooth. Stir in enough all-purpose flour to form a soft dough. Turn onto a floured surface; knead until smooth and elastic, about 6-8 minutes. Place in a greased bowl, turning once to grease top. Cover and let rise in a warm place until doubled, about 45 minutes.

Punch dough down. Turn onto a floured surface; divide into thirds. Roll each portion into a 12-in. x 8-in. rectangle; spread with melted butter. Combine brown sugar and cinnamon; sprinkle over dough to within 1/2 in. of edges. Roll up jelly-roll style, starting with a long side; pinch seams to seal. Cut each into 12 slices; place cut side down in three greased 13-in. x 9-in. x 2-in. baking pans. Cover and let rise until doubled, about 45 minutes.

Bake at 350° for 27-30 minutes or until golden brown. Cool on wire racks. For glaze, combine the cream, sugars

and butter in a saucepan. Bring to a boil; cook and stir for 2 minutes. Remove from the heat; stir in marshmallows until melted. Beat in confectioners' sugar and vanilla. Drizzle over rolls. **Yield:** 3 dozen.

# APPLE NUT COFFEE CAKE
### Bonnie DeMeyer, New Carlisle, Indiana

*My family really enjoys this sweet, moist coffee cake with its crunchy cinnamon topping. On chilly winter days, a warm slice hits the spot, but it tastes just as good served cold.*

1/2 cup butter *or* margarine, softened
1/2 cup shortening
1-1/2 cups sugar
2 eggs
3 cups all-purpose flour
2 teaspoons baking powder
1 teaspoon baking soda
1/4 teaspoon salt
1-3/4 cups buttermilk
2 medium tart apples, peeled and thinly sliced
TOPPING:
1/2 cup all-purpose flour
1/2 cup sugar
1-1/2 teaspoons ground cinnamon
1/4 cup cold butter *or* margarine
1/2 cup chopped pecans

In a mixing bowl, cream butter, shortening and sugar. Add eggs, one at a time, beating well after each. Combine the dry ingredients; add to creamed mixture alternately with buttermilk and mix well. Spread half into a greased 13-in. x 9-in. x 2-in. baking dish. Top with apples. Carefully spread remaining batter over apples.

For topping, combine flour, sugar and cinnamon. Cut in butter until crumbly; stir in pecans. Sprinkle over batter. Bake at 350° for 40-45 minutes or until a toothpick inserted near the center comes out clean. Cool on a wire rack. **Yield:** 12-16 servings.

# SAVORY BISCUITS
### Rose McClure, McClure, Ohio

*Shredded cheese and a sprinkling of herbs give refrigerated biscuits great flavor. This is one of my favorite bread recipes.*

2 tubes (12 ounces *each*) refrigerated buttermilk biscuits
1/2 cup shredded Monterey Jack cheese
1/2 cup shredded cheddar cheese
3 tablespoons butter *or* margarine, melted
3/4 teaspoon dried basil
1/4 teaspoon dried oregano
1/8 teaspoon dill weed
1/8 teaspoon garlic powder

Separate each tube of biscuits into 10 biscuits; place in a single layer in a greased 11-in. x 7-in. x 2-in. baking pan. Sprinkle with cheeses. Drizzle with butter; sprinkle with seasonings. Bake at 350° for 25-30 minutes or until golden brown. Serve warm. **Yield:** 20 biscuits.

**APPEALING APPETIZERS.** Shown clockwise from top right: Cranberry Orange Punch (p. 21), Orange-Ginger Fruit Dip (p. 21), Everything Nice Nuts (p. 21) and Ranch Jalapeno Dip (p. 21).

# *Appetizers*

## RANCH JALAPENO DIP
**Charolette Westfall, Houston, Texas**
(Pictured on page 20)

*My family often asks me to make this zippy ranch-style dip. The recipe, from a local Mexican restaurant, stirs up a creamy blend that tastes great with crunchy tortilla chips or raw vegetables.*

　　1 envelope original ranch salad dressing mix
　　2 pickled jalapeno peppers, seeded
　　1 jalapeno pepper, seeded
　　2 tablespoons minced fresh cilantro *or* parsley
Tortilla chips

In a blender or food processor, prepare the ranch salad dressing according to package directions. Add peppers and cilantro; cover and process for 2-3 minutes or until combined. Cover and refrigerate for at least 1 hour. Serve with tortilla chips. **Yield:** 2-1/2 cups.

　　**Editor's Note**: When cutting or seeding hot peppers, use rubber or plastic gloves to protect your hands. Avoid touching your face.

## ORANGE-GINGER FRUIT DIP
**Trisha Faulk, Athens, Michigan**
(Pictured on page 20)

*A platter of colorful cut-up fruit surrounding a bowl of this fluffy no-fuss dip will sweeten any holiday buffet table. It's a great way to get kids to eat fruit, too!*

　　1 package (8 ounces) cream cheese, softened
　　1 jar (7 ounces) marshmallow creme
　　1 tablespoon grated orange peel
　　1/8 teaspoon ground ginger
Assorted fresh fruit

In a mixing bowl, beat cream cheese until smooth. Beat in the marshmallow creme, orange peel and ginger. Cover and refrigerate until serving. Serve with fruit. **Yield:** 2-1/2 cups.

## EVERYTHING NICE NUTS
**Janet Forden, Okotoks, Alberta**
(Pictured on page 20)

*I wasn't satisfied with any spiced nut recipes I tried, so I created my own crunchy concoction. They're great to take to a party or to give as a tasty holiday gift.*

　　1/2 cup packed brown sugar
　　1/2 teaspoon ground cinnamon
　　1/4 teaspoon ground allspice
　　1/8 teaspoon ground cardamom
　　1/8 teaspoon ground cloves
4-1/2 teaspoons water
　　2 cups mixed nuts

In a microwave-safe bowl, combine the first six ingredients. Microwave, uncovered, on high for 1 minute. Stir; heat 30-60 seconds longer or until syrupy. Add nuts; stir to coat. Spread into a microwave-safe 9-in. pie plate. Microwave, uncovered, on high for 4 to 4-1/2 minutes or until syrup is bubbly. Immediately spread onto a greased baking sheet. When cool, break apart. **Yield:** 2 cups.

　　**Editor's Note**: This recipe was tested in an 850-watt microwave.

## CRANBERRY ORANGE PUNCH
**Sandy McKenzie, Braham, Minnesota**
(Pictured on page 20)

*This tangy punch is festive, refreshing and easy to prepare. I float orange wedges studded with cloves in the pitcher or bowl as a garnish. And instead of plain ice cubes, I add frozen orange juice cubes.*

　　2 bottles (32 ounces *each*) cranberry juice, chilled
　　1 cup lemon juice
　2/3 cup sugar
　　2 cans (12 ounces *each*) orange soda, chilled
Ice cubes
Whole cloves and orange wedges, optional

In a large punch bowl or several pitchers, combine the cranberry juice, lemon juice and sugar; stir until sugar is dissolved. Just before serving, add orange soda and ice. If desired, insert cloves into orange wedges for garnish. **Yield:** about 3-1/2 quarts.

## BACON CHEESE WREATH
**Lisa Carter, Warren, Indiana**

*My grandmother makes this smoky bacon and Parmesan spread for parties and holiday get-togethers. For a pretty Yuletide presentation, accent the cream cheese wreath with parsley and pimientos.*

　　2 packages (8 ounces *each*) cream cheese, softened
　1/2 cup mayonnaise *or* salad dressing
　1/3 cup grated Parmesan cheese
　1/4 cup sliced green onions, optional
　　10 bacon strips, cooked and crumbled
Parsley sprigs and diced pimientos, optional
Assorted crackers

In a small mixing bowl, beat the cream cheese, mayonnaise, Parmesan cheese and onions if desired; mix well. Stir in bacon. Cover and refrigerate for 1-2 hours.

　　Invert a small bowl in the center of a serving platter. Drop cream cheese mixture by rounded tablespoonfuls around edge of bowl. Remove bowl. Smooth cream cheese mixture, forming a wreath. Garnish with parsley and pimientos if desired. Serve with crackers. **Yield:** about 3 cups.

## PIZZA SWIRLS
### Linda Gerrald, Nacogdoches, Texas

*My children helped me dream up this snappy bread that tastes like pizza. The from-scratch flavor makes it a family favorite, but it's great for parties, too.*

     1 package (1/4 ounce) active dry yeast
1-1/3 cups warm water (110° to 115°)
     1/4 cup vegetable oil
     1/2 teaspoon sugar
     1/2 teaspoon salt
3-3/4 to 4-1/4 cups all-purpose flour
SAUCE:
     1/4 cup chopped onion
     2 garlic cloves, minced
     1 can (8 ounces) tomato sauce
     1/4 teaspoon dried basil
TOPPINGS:
     4 cups (16 ounces) shredded mozzarella cheese,
      *divided*
     2 packages (3 ounces *each*) sliced pepperoni
     1 can (2-1/4 ounces) chopped ripe olives, drained

In a mixing bowl, dissolve yeast in warm water. Add oil, sugar, salt and 2 cups flour; beat until smooth. Stir in enough remaining flour to form a soft dough. Turn onto a floured surface; knead until smooth and elastic, about 6-8 minutes. Place in a greased bowl, turning once to grease top. Cover and let rise in a warm place until doubled, about 1 hour. Punch dough down. Turn onto a floured surface; divide in half. Roll each portion into a 12-in. x 8-in. rectangle; set aside.

   For sauce, combine the onion and garlic in a microwave-safe dish. Cover and microwave on high for 1 minute. Add tomato sauce and basil; cover and cook at 50% power for 3 minutes or until bubbly. Spoon over crust to within 1/2 in. of edges. Sprinkle with 3 cups mozzarella cheese, pepperoni and olives.

   Roll up jelly-roll style, starting with a long side; pinch seam to seal. Cut each roll into 12 slices. Place cut side down on a greased baking sheet. Sprinkle with remaining cheese. Bake at 400° for 15 minutes or until crust is golden and cheese is melted. Serve warm. **Yield:** 2 dozen.

## CREAMY GUACAMOLE SPREAD
### Lynn Thomas, Lakewood, New York

*All my brothers and sisters like to bring appetizers to our Christmas gatherings. This delectable dip came from my brother. It can be attractively displayed on lettuce with tomato wedges.*

     2 large ripe avocados, peeled and cubed
     1/2 cup mayonnaise
     1/4 cup chopped onion
     2 teaspoons lemon juice
     2 teaspoons Worcestershire sauce
     1 teaspoon salt
     1 teaspoon hot pepper sauce
Crackers *or* raw vegetables

In a blender or food processor, combine the first seven ingredients. Cover and process until smooth. Serve with crackers or vegetables. **Yield:** 2 cups.

## BROCCOLI VEGGIE DIP
### Wanda Ward, Louisville, Mississippi

*This yummy variation on spinach dip gets a bit of crunch from chopped broccoli. Everyone enjoys this delicious blend, which you can serve with crackers or in a bread bowl.*

     2 cups (16 ounces) sour cream
     1 package (10 ounces) frozen chopped broccoli,
      thawed and well drained
     1/2 cup mayonnaise
     1 envelope vegetable soup mix
Crackers *or* raw vegetables

In a bowl, combine the sour cream, broccoli, mayonnaise and soup mix; mix well. Cover and refrigerate for 3 hours or overnight. Serve with crackers or vegetables. **Yield:** 3-1/2 cups.

## MOCHA EGGNOG
### Beth Ann Hill, Dayton, Ohio

*This chocolaty twist on traditional eggnog will spread good cheer at your Christmas or New Year's celebration. My family makes a batch each year to sip while opening presents.*

     5 cups chocolate milk
     4 cups eggnog*
     1 cup whipping cream, *divided*
     2 tablespoons instant coffee granules
2-1/2 teaspoons vanilla extract
     1 teaspoon rum extract

In a large saucepan, combine the milk, eggnog, 1/2 cup cream and coffee granules; heat through. Remove from the heat; stir in extracts. In a small mixing bowl, beat remaining cream until stiff peaks form. Dollop over eggnog. **Yield:** 2-1/2 quarts.

   **\*Editor's Note:** This recipe was tested with commercially prepared eggnog.

## HOT BEAN DIP
### Donna Trout, Las Vegas, Nevada

*My hearty dip is extra smooth, thanks to the cream cheese and sour cream I add. It's easy to assemble ahead and then bake before serving. People keep dipping until the dish is empty.*

     1 can (16 ounces) refried beans
     1 package (8 ounces) cream cheese, softened
     1 cup (8 ounces) sour cream
     1 can (4 ounces) chopped green chilies
     3/4 cup salsa
     3 tablespoons taco seasoning mix
     6 green onions, chopped
Tortilla chips

In a mixing bowl, combine the first six ingredients; mix well. Transfer to a greased shallow 2-qt. baking dish. Sprinkle with onions. Bake, uncovered, at 350° for 25-30 minutes or until heated through. Serve with tortilla chips. **Yield:** 5 cups.

## HOT BACON CHEESE SPREAD
### Bonnie Hawkins, Burlington, Wisconsin

*This creamy spread, made with Monterey Jack and Parmesan cheeses, is sure to warm up your next holiday party. Guests never wander too far from the table when I put out this fragrant dip.*

- 1 unsliced round loaf (1 pound) Italian bread
- 2 cups (8 ounces) shredded Monterey Jack cheese
- 1 cup (4 ounces) shredded Parmesan cheese
- 1 cup mayonnaise*
- 1/4 cup chopped onion
- 5 bacon strips, cooked and crumbled
- 1 garlic clove, minced

Cut top fourth off loaf of bread; carefully hollow out bottom, leaving a 1-in. shell. Cube removed bread and set aside. Combine the remaining ingredients; spoon into bread bowl. Replace top. Place on an ungreased baking sheet. Bake at 350° for 1 hour or until heated through. Serve with reserved bread cubes. **Yield:** 2 cups.

**\*Editor's Note:** Reduced-fat or fat-free mayonnaise may not be substituted for regular mayonnaise.

## LOUISIANA CRAB DIP
### Ruby Williams, Bogalusa, Louisiana

*When friends visit from other parts of the country, I treat them to a Cajun-style Christmas. This flavor-packed seafood dip gives them a delicious taste of the Bayou State.*

- 2 packages (8 ounces *each*) cream cheese, softened
- 2 tablespoons prepared horseradish, drained
- 2 teaspoons Worcestershire sauce
- 1/4 teaspoon hot pepper sauce
- 2 cans (6 ounces *each*) crabmeat, drained, flaked and cartilage removed
- 1 medium onion, chopped
- 1 tablespoon dry bread crumbs
- 1/8 teaspoon paprika
Assorted crackers

In a mixing bowl, combine the cream cheese, horseradish, Worcestershire and hot pepper sauce; mix well. Stir in crab and onion. Spoon into a greased 1-qt. baking dish. Toss bread crumbs with paprika; sprinkle over the top. Bake, uncovered, at 350° for 30-35 minutes or until edges are bubbly. Serve warm with crackers. **Yield:** 3 cups.

## HAM TORTILLA STACK
### Andrea Leeds, Boise, Idaho

*This tasty appetizer is considered my specialty—I'm asked to make it whenever we have a sizable get-together. It has crunchy colorful peppers and a creamy ham filling tucked between tortillas.*

- 2 packages (8 ounces *each*) cream cheese, softened
- 1/2 cup mayonnaise
- 1 pound ground fully cooked ham
- 1 medium sweet red pepper, chopped

- 1 bunch green onions, chopped
- 1 can (2-1/4 ounces) chopped ripe olives, drained
- 12 flour tortillas (7 inches)
Salsa *or* picante sauce

In a mixing bowl, beat cream cheese and mayonnaise until smooth. Stir in the ham, red pepper, onions and olives. Spread over nine tortillas. Make three stacks of three tortillas each; top each stack with a plain tortilla. Cover and refrigerate for 8 hours or overnight. Cut into wedges. Serve with salsa. **Yield:** about 3-1/2 dozen.

## TANGY MOZZARELLA BITES
### Julie Wasem, Aurora, Nebraska

*I adapted this recipe from one I found years ago, substituting ingredients most people have on hand. I like to serve it with crackers or small bread slices.*

- 1/4 cup olive *or* vegetable oil
- 1 to 2 teaspoons balsamic *or* red wine vinegar
- 1 garlic clove, minced
- 1 teaspoon dried basil
- 1 teaspoon coarsely ground pepper
- 1 pound mozzarella cheese, cut into 1/2-inch cubes

In a bowl, combine the oil, vinegar, garlic, basil and pepper. Add cheese; toss to coat. Cover and refrigerate for at least 1 hour. **Yield:** about 3 cups.

## CHEESY MUSHROOM MORSELS
### Marian Platt, Sequim, Washington

*There's plenty of happy munching all around the table when I dish up these luscious morsels. Ideal for a large crowd, they taste like quiche without the crust or the fuss.*

- 1 pound fresh mushrooms, sliced
- 1 large onion, chopped
- 2 garlic cloves, minced
- 1/2 cup butter *or* margarine
- 1 large green pepper, chopped
- 10 eggs
- 4 cups (16 ounces) shredded Monterey Jack cheese
- 2 cups (16 ounces) small-curd cottage cheese
- 1/2 cup all-purpose flour
- 1 teaspoon baking powder
- 3/4 teaspoon salt
- 3/4 teaspoon dried basil
- 3/4 teaspoon ground nutmeg

In a large skillet, saute the mushrooms, onion and garlic in butter until tender. Add the green pepper; saute 1 minute longer. Remove from the heat; drain. In a large bowl, beat eggs. Stir in the cheeses, flour, baking powder, salt, basil and nutmeg. Add mushroom mixture. Pour into a greased 15-in. x 10-in. x 1-in. baking pan.

Bake, uncovered, at 350° for 30-35 minutes or until edges are golden and a knife inserted near the center comes out clean. Let stand for 15 minutes. Cut into squares; serve warm. **Yield:** about 12 dozen.

## SPINACH SPIRALS WITH MUSHROOM SAUCE
**Mrs. Archie Potts, San Antonio, Texas**
(Pictured below)

*I never thought I liked spinach until I tried these pretty spirals topped with a creamy mushroom sauce! It is a delicious dish to serve at a festive gathering.*

    3/4 pound fresh mushrooms, sliced
    1/4 cup butter *or* margarine
        3 tablespoons all-purpose flour
        1 cup chicken broth
        1 cup half-and-half cream
        2 tablespoons sherry *or* additional chicken broth
        1 teaspoon Dijon mustard
    1/2 teaspoon lemon juice
SPINACH ROLL:
    1/2 cup dry bread crumbs
        3 packages (10 ounces *each*) frozen chopped spinach, thawed and squeezed dry
        6 tablespoons butter *or* margarine, melted
    1/4 teaspoon salt
    1/8 teaspoon pepper
    1/8 teaspoon ground nutmeg
        4 eggs, *separated*
    1/4 cup grated Parmesan cheese

In a large skillet, saute mushrooms in butter for 2-3 minutes. Stir in flour until blended; cook 2-3 minutes longer or until liquid is absorbed. Gradually stir in broth and cream. Bring to a boil. Remove from the heat; stir in the sherry or additional broth, mustard and lemon juice. Cool for 15 minutes.

Grease and line a 15-in. x 10-in. x 1-in. baking pan with parchment paper; grease the paper. Sprinkle with bread crumbs; set aside. In a large bowl, combine spinach, butter, salt, pepper, nutmeg and egg yolks. In a small mixing bowl, beat egg whites on high speed until stiff peaks form. Gradually fold into spinach mixture. Gently spoon over bread crumbs; press down lightly. Sprinkle with Parmesan cheese.

Bake at 350° for 12-15 minutes or until center springs back when lightly touched. Cover with a piece of greased foil; immediately invert pan onto foil. Gently peel away parchment paper. Spread 1 cup mushroom sauce over spinach mixture to within 1 in. of edges. Roll up jelly-roll style, starting with a short side and peeling foil away while rolling. Cut into slices. Reheat remaining mushroom sauce; serve with spinach spirals. **Yield:** 12 servings.

## CARDAMOM CRESCENTS
**Mrs. Robert Garfield, Jamestown, New York**

*A hint of cardamom adds nice flavor to these tender golden rolls. They're my grandchildren's favorites, so I make the crescents all year long.*

        2 packages (1/4 ounce *each*) active dry yeast
    1/4 cup warm water (110° to 115°)
        1 teaspoon plus 1 cup sugar, *divided*
        2 cups warm milk (110° to 115°)
    3/4 cup butter *or* margarine, softened
1-1/2 teaspoons ground cardamom
        1 teaspoon salt
        2 eggs, lightly beaten
        7 to 8 cups all-purpose flour
Additional butter *or* margarine, melted

In a large mixing bowl, dissolve yeast in warm water. Add 1 teaspoon sugar; let stand for 5 minutes. Add the milk, butter, cardamom, salt and remaining sugar. Add the eggs and 2 cups flour; beat until smooth. Stir in enough remaining flour to form a soft dough. Turn onto a floured surface; knead until smooth and elastic, about 6-8 minutes. Place in a greased bowl, turning once to grease top. Cover and let rise in a warm place until doubled, about 1-1/2 hours.

Punch dough down. Turn onto a lightly floured surface; divide into six pieces. Roll each piece into a 10-in. circle; brush with melted butter. Cut each circle into 12 wedges. Roll up each wedge from the wide end; place pointed end down 2 in. apart on greased baking sheets. Curve ends down to form crescents. Cover and let rise until doubled, about 30 minutes. Bake at 400° for 12-15 minutes or until golden brown. Remove to wire racks. Brush with melted butter if desired. **Yield:** 6 dozen.

## CHRISTMAS DAY CHICKEN
### Marcia Larson, Batavia, Illinois

*I've been fixing this delicious chicken for Christmas dinner for over 10 years. It's convenient since you refrigerate it overnight, then simply coat with crumbs and bake. It comes out crispy on the outside and tender and juicy on the inside.*

        16 boneless skinless chicken breast halves
         2 cups (16 ounces) sour cream
     1/4 cup lemon juice
         4 teaspoons Worcestershire sauce
         2 teaspoons celery salt
         2 teaspoons pepper
         2 teaspoons paprika
         1 teaspoon seasoned salt
         1 teaspoon garlic salt
 1-1/2 to 2 cups finely crushed Waverly crackers
     1/2 cup vegetable oil
     1/2 cup butter *or* margarine, melted

Place the chicken in two large resealable plastic bags. In a bowl, combine the sour cream, lemon juice, Worcestershire sauce and seasonings. Pour over chicken; seal bags and refrigerate overnight.

Drain and discard marinade. Coat chicken with cracker crumbs; place in two greased 13-in. x 9-in. x 2-in. baking dishes. Combine oil and butter; drizzle over chicken. Bake, uncovered, at 350° for 50-60 minutes or until juices run clear. **Yield:** 16 servings.

## CHOCOLATE PARTY CAKE
### Cher Anjema, Kleinburg, Ontario

*This no-bake refrigerated cake, featuring angel food cake and chocolate, was my grandma's recipe. It has been on our Christmas menu ever since I can remember. As a child, I would have easily bypassed the turkey to get to this heavenly dessert.*

         1 envelope unflavored gelatin
         2 tablespoons cold water
         2 squares (1 ounce *each*) unsweetened chocolate
     1/2 cup sugar
     1/2 cup hot water
         4 egg yolks, lightly beaten
         1 teaspoon vanilla extract
         2 cups whipping cream, whipped
     1/2 cup chopped almonds, toasted
         1 prepared angel food cake (10 inches)
 FROSTING:
         1 cup whipping cream
         1 tablespoon confectioners' sugar
         1 teaspoon vanilla extract
     1/2 cup chopped almonds, toasted

In a small saucepan, sprinkle gelatin over cold water; let stand for 1 minute. Cook and stir over low heat until gelatin is dissolved; set aside.

In a heavy saucepan over low heat, cook and stir chocolate, sugar and hot water until chocolate is melted. Remove from the heat. Stir a small amount of hot chocolate mixture into egg yolks; return all to the pan, stirring constantly. Cook and stir over low heat until a thermometer reads 160°. Remove from the heat. Stir in gelatin mixture and vanilla until smooth. Cool to room temperature. Fold in whipped cream. Stir in almonds.

Using a serrated knife, cut cake into cubes. Arrange a third of the cubes in a greased 10-in. tube pan with removable bottom. Spoon a third of the chocolate mixture over top. Repeat layers twice. Tap pan on work surface so chocolate mixture fills in spaces. Cover and refrigerate for 8 hours or overnight.

For frosting, in a mixing bowl, beat cream until it begins to thicken. Add confectioners' sugar and vanilla; beat until stiff peaks form. Carefully run a knife around edge of pan to loosen. Invert cake onto serving plate; remove pan. Frost top and sides of cake. Sprinkle with almonds. Store in the refrigerator. **Yield:** 10-12 servings.

## MUSTARD-GLAZED HAM
### Dawn Wood, Machiasport, Maine

*Holiday ham gets a sweet and tangy taste from this honey of a glaze. I make sure to have extra on hand because my family likes to use it as a dipping sauce.*

         1 boneless fully cooked ham (about 5 pounds)
     3/4 cup honey mustard*
     1/4 cup packed brown sugar
         2 tablespoons orange juice
     1/8 teaspoon ground cloves
 Pinch allspice

Place ham on a rack in a shallow roasting pan. Bake at 325° for 1 hour. In a small bowl, combine the remaining ingredients. Spoon about 1/3 cup over ham. Bake 15 minutes longer or until a meat thermometer reads 140° and ham is heated through. Heat remaining glaze to serve with sliced ham. **Yield:** about 16 servings (1 cup sauce).

**\*Editor's Note:** As a substitute for honey mustard, combine 1/3 cup each honey and Dijon mustard.

## HOLIDAY HOMINY
### Sara Crowley, Tyler, Texas

*I was looking for an attractive holiday dish that didn't repeat the red of beets, the orange of yams or the green of broccoli. So I developed this one, featuring the glow of golden hominy.*

     1/2 cup butter *or* margarine
     1/2 cup all-purpose flour
         3 cups milk
         1 to 1-1/2 teaspoons seasoned salt
         1 to 1-1/2 teaspoons coarsely ground pepper
         2 cups cubed process cheese (Velveeta)
         5 cans (15-1/2 ounces each) yellow hominy, drained
 Paprika

In a large saucepan, melt butter; stir in flour until smooth. Gradually add milk, seasoned salt and pepper. Bring to a boil; cook and stir for 2 minutes or until thickened. Stir in cheese until melted. Place hominy in a greased 13-in. x 9-in. x 2-in. baking dish. Pour cheese sauce over hominy. Bake, uncovered, at 350° for 25 minutes. Sprinkle with paprika. Bake 10 minutes longer or until heated through. **Yield:** 12-14 servings.

**DELICIOUS DINING.** Shown clockwise fom top right: Herbed Beef Rib Roast (p. 28), Swiss Scalloped Potatoes (p. 29), Cranberry Applesauce (p. 28), Cherry Meringue Pie (p. 28), Vegetable-Stuffed Baked Onions (p. 28) and Pimiento Green Beans (p. 28).

## VEGETABLE-STUFFED BAKED ONIONS
**Ruth Andrewson, Peck, Idaho**
(Pictured on page 26)

*Stuffed with carrots, red pepper, diced bacon and bread crumbs, these elegant baked onions will dress up any special-occasion meal. My mother often pulled out this recipe when company was coming.*

        8 to 10 medium onions, peeled
        4 bacon strips, diced
      3/4 cup finely chopped carrots
      1/2 cup finely chopped sweet red pepper
    1-1/2 cups soft bread crumbs
      1/3 cup minced fresh parsley
        3 tablespoons butter *or* margarine, melted
    1-1/2 teaspoons salt
      1/2 teaspoon pepper
      3/4 cup beef broth

Cut 1/2 in. off the top of each onion; trim bottom so onion sits flat. Scoop out center, leaving a 1/2-in. shell. Chop removed onion; set 1/2 cup aside (discard remaining onion or save for another use). Place onion shells in a Dutch oven or large saucepan and cover with water. Bring to a boil; reduce heat and cook for 8-10 minutes.

Meanwhile, in a large skillet, cook bacon over medium heat until crisp. Remove to paper towels; drain, reserving 1 teaspoon drippings. In the drippings, saute chopped onion, carrots and red pepper for 8 minutes or until tender. Remove from the heat; stir in the bread crumbs, parsley, butter, salt, pepper and bacon.

Drain onion shells; fill each with about 1/3 cup vegetable mixture. Place in an ungreased shallow 3-qt. baking dish. Pour broth over onions. Cover and bake at 350° for 45-50 minutes or until heated through. **Yield:** 8-10 servings.

## CRANBERRY APPLESAUCE
**Trisha Czyz, Baldwinsville, New York**
(Pictured on page 27)

*Instead of the usual jellied cranberry sauce, I serve this refreshing alternative. It's not too sweet and not too sour...plus it's a snap to make.*

      1/2 cup plus 2 tablespoons water
      1/2 cup plus 2 tablespoons sugar
        5 medium Golden Delicious apples (about 2-1/2 pounds), peeled and chopped
    1-1/4 cups fresh *or* frozen cranberries
      1/2 teaspoon grated lemon peel
      1/4 teaspoon ground ginger *or* 1 teaspoon minced fresh gingerroot
      1/4 teaspoon ground cinnamon

In a large saucepan over medium heat, cook and stir water and sugar until sugar is dissolved. Add apples; cover and cook for 5 minutes, stirring often. Add cranberries; cover and cook until apples are tender and berries pop, about 15 minutes. Mash until sauce reaches desired consistency. Stir in lemon peel, ginger and cinnamon. Cook, uncovered, 5 minutes longer. Serve warm or refrigerate until serving. **Yield:** 3-1/2 cups.

## HERBED BEEF RIB ROAST
**Donna Conlin, Gilmour, Ontario**
(Pictured on page 27)

*This is one of my favorite ways to prepare a roast because it turns out so tender and flavorful. My husband and our six children just love it!*

        1 tablespoon garlic powder
        1 tablespoon ground mustard
        1 to 2 teaspoons salt
        1 to 2 teaspoons pepper
        1 beef rib roast (6 to 8 pounds)
      1/4 cup water
      1/4 cup beef broth
        1 tablespoon red wine vinegar *or* cider vinegar

Combine the garlic powder, mustard, salt and pepper; rub over entire roast. Place roast fat side up in a shallow roasting pan. Pour water, broth and vinegar into pan. Bake, uncovered, at 350° for 2-3/4 to 3 hours, basting frequently with pan juices, or until meat reaches desired doneness (for medium-rare, a meat thermometer should read 145°; medium, 160°; well-done, 170°). Let stand for 10-15 minutes before slicing. **Yield:** 10-12 servings.

## PIMIENTO GREEN BEANS
**Lyn McAllister, Mt. Ulla, North Carolina**
(Pictured on page 26)

*Here's an easy way to turn everyday green beans into a special side dish. Pimientos, Parmesan cheese and chicken broth add savory flavor and a dash of color.*

        2 pounds fresh green beans, cut into 2-inch pieces
        1 can (14-1/2 ounces) chicken broth
      1/2 cup chopped onion
        1 jar (2 ounces) chopped pimientos, drained
      1/2 teaspoon salt
      1/8 to 1/4 teaspoon pepper
      1/4 cup shredded Parmesan cheese

In a large saucepan, bring beans, broth and onion to a boil. Reduce heat; cover and cook for 10-15 minutes or until crisp-tender. Drain. Stir in the pimientos, salt and pepper. Sprinkle with Parmesan cheese. **Yield:** 10 servings.

## CHERRY MERINGUE PIE
**Irene Brill, Manassas, Virginia**
(Pictured on page 26)

*My mother always made cherry pie with a meringue topping— and I think her mother did, too. It's a nice way to finish off a holiday dinner or everyday meal.*

        1 can (21 ounces) cherry pie filling
        3 egg whites
      1/4 teaspoon cream of tartar
        6 tablespoons confectioners' sugar
      1/4 teaspoon almond extract
        1 pastry shell (9 inches), baked
      1/4 cup chopped walnuts

In a saucepan, heat pie filling on low. Meanwhile, in a mixing bowl, beat egg whites on medium speed until foamy. Add cream of tartar; beat until soft peaks form. Gradually beat in sugar, 1 tablespoon at a time, on high until stiff glossy peaks form.

Remove pie filling from the heat; stir in extract. Pour into pastry shell. Spread meringue over hot filling, sealing edges to crust. Sprinkle with walnuts. Bake at 350° for 15 minutes or until meringue is golden. Cool on a wire rack for 1 hour. Chill for at least 3 hours before serving. Refrigerate leftovers. **Yield:** 6-8 servings.

# SWISS SCALLOPED POTATOES
### Shirley Awood Glaab, Hattiesburg, Mississippi
(Pictured on page 27)

*If you're a fan of French onion soup, you'll love this layered potato casserole. My family really enjoys it with ham, turkey or pork roast.*

      5 medium potatoes (about 3 pounds), peeled and
         thinly sliced
      1 small onion, thinly sliced
      1 jar (4 ounces) diced pimientos, drained
      3 garlic cloves, minced
      2 cups (8 ounces) shredded Swiss cheese, *divided*
   3/4 teaspoon salt
   1/4 teaspoon pepper
      1 can (14-1/2 ounces) chicken broth
      2 tablespoons butter *or* margarine

In a greased shallow 3-qt. baking dish, layer a third of the potatoes, onion, pimientos, garlic and Swiss cheese; sprinkle with 1/4 teaspoon salt and a dash of pepper. Repeat layers once. Top with remaining potatoes, onion, pimientos, garlic, salt and pepper. Pour broth over the top; dot with butter. Bake, uncovered, at 375° for 1 hour.

Sprinkle with remaining cheese. Bake 30 minutes longer or until liquid is absorbed and cheese is melted. Let stand for 10 minutes before serving. **Yield:** 8 servings.

# FEATHER WHOLE WHEAT ROLLS
### Leann Swain, Orem, Utah

*My grandmother and mother have made this recipe famous in our family as well as our community. We never sit down to Thanksgiving or Christmas dinner without these melt-in-your-mouth rolls.*

         4 tablespoons active dry yeast
         2 tablespoons plus 2/3 cup sugar, *divided*
         2 cups warm water (110° to 115°)
         2 cups warm milk (110° to 115°)
         4 eggs
      2/3 cup vegetable oil
         2 teaspoons salt
         4 cups whole wheat flour
   4-1/2 to 5 cups all-purpose flour
   **Butter *or* margarine, melted**

In a mixing bowl, dissolve yeast and 2 tablespoons sugar in warm water; let stand for 5 minutes. Add the milk, eggs,

oil, salt and remaining sugar; beat until smooth. Stir in whole wheat flour and enough all-purpose flour to form a stiff batter (dough will be sticky). Do not knead. Cover and refrigerate for 8 hours.

Punch dough down. Divide into thirds. Cover and refrigerate two portions. Turn the remaining portion onto a lightly floured surface; roll to 1/2-in. thickness. Cut with a floured 2-1/2-in. biscuit cutter. Repeat with remaining dough. Place rolls 2 in. apart on greased baking sheets. Brush with butter. Cover and let rise in a warm place until doubled, about 2 hours. Bake at 425° for 8-12 minutes or until golden brown. Remove to wire racks. **Yield:** about 4 dozen.

# ELEGANT MUSHROOM SOUP
### Marjorie Jaeger, Enderlin, North Dakota

*This easy recipe turns commonplace ingredients into a wonderfully tasty soup. My family is delighted whenever they see it simmering on the stove.*

         1 large onion, chopped
      1/2 pound fresh mushrooms, sliced
         2 tablespoons butter *or* margarine
         2 tablespoons all-purpose flour
      1/4 teaspoon pepper
      1/8 teaspoon salt
         1 cup milk
         1 cup chicken broth
         1 tablespoon minced fresh parsley
   **Ground nutmeg, optional**
   **Sour cream**

In a large saucepan, saute onion and mushrooms in butter for 3 minutes or until onion is tender. Stir in flour, pepper and salt; gradually add milk and broth. Bring to a boil; cook and stir for 2 minutes or until thickened. Add parsley and nutmeg if desired. Top individual servings with a dollop of sour cream. **Yield:** 2-3 servings.

# CREAMY VEGETABLE CASSEROLE
### Maxine Simes, Sidney, Ohio

*Even kids will eat their veggies when you serve them this way, covered in a creamy cheese sauce and topped with crushed crackers. They just might ask for seconds!*

         1 package (24 ounces) frozen California-blend
            vegetables
         1 can (10-3/4 ounces) condensed cream of celery
            soup, undiluted
         1 jar (8 ounces) process cheese sauce
      1/2 cup finely crushed butter-flavored crackers
            (about 13 crackers)
         2 tablespoons butter *or* margarine, melted

Prepare vegetables according to package directions; drain. In a bowl, combine the soup and cheese sauce. Add vegetables and stir to coat. Transfer to a greased shallow 2-qt. baking dish. Toss cracker crumbs and butter; sprinkle over the top. Bake, uncovered, at 350° for 30 minutes or until heated through. **Yield:** 6 servings.

# Holiday Cookies

## TOFFEE CARAMEL SQUARES
### Karen Bourne, Magrath, Alberta

*Layers of caramel and chocolate cover a cookie crust, creating these rich treats. I made several pans for our son's wedding and received many requests for the recipe. The scrumptious bars are also perfect for cookie exchanges.*

    1-1/4 cups all-purpose flour
      1/4 cup sugar
      1/2 cup plus 2 tablespoons cold butter *or* margarine
FILLING:
      1/2 cup butter *or* margarine
      1/2 cup packed brown sugar
      1/2 cup sweetened condensed milk
        2 tablespoons light corn syrup
GLAZE:
        2 cups (12 ounces) semisweet chocolate chips
        1 tablespoon shortening

In a bowl, combine flour and sugar. Cut in butter until crumbly. Press into a greased 9-in. square baking pan. Bake at 350° for 18-20 minutes or until golden brown. Meanwhile, combine the filling ingredients in a saucepan. Bring to a boil over medium heat; boil and stir for 5 minutes. Pour over warm crust.
   In a microwave, melt chocolate chips and shortening. Spread over filling. Cool on a wire rack. Cut into squares. **Yield:** 3 dozen.

## GUMDROP COOKIES
### Carolyn Stromberg, Wever, Iowa

*These fun cookies are chock-full of chewy gumdrops. I use red and green ones at Christmas, black and orange for Halloween and pastel shades for Easter. I've made this recipe for years and find that kids really get a kick out of the cookies with a candy surprise inside!*

      3/4 cup shortening
        1 cup sugar, *divided*
      1/2 teaspoon almond extract
    1-3/4 cups all-purpose flour
      1/2 teaspoon baking soda
      1/4 teaspoon salt
        1 cup chopped fruit-flavored *or* spiced gumdrops
        2 egg whites

In a mixing bowl, cream shortening and 3/4 cup sugar. Beat in extract. Combine flour, baking soda and salt; gradually add to creamed mixture. Stir in gumdrops. In a small mixing bowl, beat egg whites until soft peaks form. Gradually add remaining sugar, beating until stiff peaks form. Fold into dough.
   Drop by heaping teaspoonfuls 2 in. apart onto ungreased baking sheets. Bake at 350° for 12-15 minutes or until golden brown. Cool for 1 minute before removing from pans to wire racks to cool completely. **Yield:** 3-1/2 dozen.

## CHOCOLATE-MINT SANDWICH COOKIES
### Monica Kneuer, Peconic, New York

*Refreshing mint filling sandwiched between two chocolate cookies makes for some tasty Noel nibbling.*

      3/4 cup butter (no substitutes), softened
        1 cup sugar
        1 egg
      1/2 teaspoon vanilla extract
        2 cups all-purpose flour
      3/4 cup baking cocoa
        1 teaspoon baking powder
      1/2 teaspoon baking soda
      1/2 teaspoon salt
      1/4 cup milk
FILLING:
        3 tablespoons butter, softened
    1-1/2 cups confectioners' sugar
        1 tablespoon milk
      1/4 teaspoon peppermint extract
        2 to 3 drops green food coloring, optional

In a mixing bowl, cream butter and sugar. Add egg and vanilla; mix well. Combine the flour, cocoa, baking powder, baking soda and salt; add to creamed mixture alternately with milk. Shape into two 10-1/2-in. rolls; wrap each in plastic wrap. Refrigerate overnight.
   Unwrap dough and cut into 1/8-in. slices. Place 2 in. apart on lightly greased baking sheets. Bake at 325° for 9-11 minutes or until edges are set. Remove to wire racks to cool. Combine filling ingredients; beat until smooth. Add food coloring if desired. Spread on the bottom of half of the cookies; top with remaining cookies. **Yield:** 5 dozen.

## PECAN LOGS
### Joyce Beck, Gadsden, Alabama

*Folks always expect to find these tender nutty logs on the cookie gift trays I give at Christmas. They're not overly sweet and go great with a steaming cup of coffee or tea.*

        1 cup butter (no substitutes), softened
        5 tablespoons confectioners' sugar
        2 teaspoons vanilla extract
        2 cups all-purpose flour
        1 cup finely chopped pecans
Confectioners' sugar

In a mixing bowl, cream butter and sugar. Beat in vanilla. Add flour, beating on low speed just until combined. Stir in pecans. Cover and refrigerate for 30 minutes.
   Shape 1/2 cupfuls into 1/2-in.-thick logs. Cut logs into 2-in. pieces. Place 2 in. apart on greased baking sheets. Bake at 350° for 15-18 minutes or until lightly browned. Roll warm cookies in confectioners' sugar; cool on wire racks. **Yield:** about 2-1/2 dozen.

# EGGNOG CUTOUT COOKIES
**Glenna Tooman, Boise, Idaho**
*(Pictured at right)*

*I created this cookie recipe because my sons liked eggnog so much. After frosting the cookies, you can add to their festive flair by sprinkling them with colored sugar.*

    1/2 cup butter (no substitutes), softened
    1 cup sugar
    2 eggs
    2 tablespoons plus 1 teaspoon eggnog*
2-1/2 cups all-purpose flour
    1/2 teaspoon salt
    1/4 teaspoon baking soda
    1/4 teaspoon ground nutmeg
ICING:
    2 cups confectioners' sugar
    1/4 teaspoon ground nutmeg, optional
    4 to 5 tablespoons eggnog*
Liquid *or* paste food coloring, optional

In a mixing bowl, cream butter and sugar. Beat in eggs. Stir in eggnog. Combine the flour, salt, baking soda and nutmeg; gradually add to creamed mixture. Cover and refrigerate for 1 hour or until easy to handle.

On a lightly floured surface, roll out dough to 1/8-in. thickness. Cut with 2-1/2-in. cookie cutters dipped in flour. Place 2 in. apart on greased baking sheets. Bake at 375° for 8-10 minutes or until edges begin to brown. Remove to wire racks to cool. In a mixing bowl, beat confectioners' sugar, nutmeg if desired and enough eggnog to achieve icing consistency. Add food coloring if desired. Spread over cooled cookies; let dry. **Yield:** about 4 dozen.

*\*Editor's Note*: This recipe was tested with commercially prepared eggnog.

# GINGER POPPY SEED COOKIES
**Mary Priesgen, Theresa, Wisconsin**

*Poppy seed and ginger pair up nicely in these popular treats. The refrigerated dough slices easily and bakes quickly.*

    3 cups butter (no substitutes), softened
1-1/2 cups sugar
1-1/2 cups packed brown sugar
    3 eggs
    2 teaspoons vanilla extract
7-1/2 cups all-purpose flour
    1/2 cup poppy seeds
    4 teaspoons ground cinnamon
    2 teaspoons ground ginger
1-1/2 teaspoons baking soda
    3/4 teaspoon salt

In a large mixing bowl, cream the butter and sugars. Add eggs and vanilla. Combine the remaining ingredients; add to creamed mixture. Shape into four 13-in. rolls. Wrap each in plastic wrap. Refrigerate for 2 hours or overnight.

Unwrap dough and cut into 1/4-in. slices. Place 2 in. apart on ungreased baking sheets. Bake at 375° for 9-11 minutes or until edges are golden brown. Remove to wire racks to cool. **Yield:** about 17 dozen.

# FROSTED PUMPKIN COOKIES
**Leona Luttrell, Sarasota, Florida**

*These family favorites taste so good, it's hard to eat just one! They freeze and travel well, especially if you let the icing completely dry, then layer the cookies between sheets of waxed paper.*

    1 cup shortening
    2 cups packed brown sugar
    2 cups cooked *or* canned pumpkin
    4 cups all-purpose flour
    2 teaspoons baking powder
    2 teaspoons baking soda
    2 teaspoons ground cinnamon
    1/8 teaspoon salt
    1 cup chopped pecans
    1 cup chopped dates
CARAMEL FROSTING:
    1/2 cup butter (no substitutes)
1-1/2 cups packed brown sugar
    1/4 cup milk
    1 teaspoon maple flavoring
    1/2 teaspoon vanilla extract
    2 to 2-1/2 cups confectioners' sugar

In a mixing bowl, cream shortening and brown sugar. Add pumpkin; mix well. Combine the flour, baking powder, baking soda, cinnamon and salt; gradually add to pumpkin mixture. Stir in pecans and dates. Drop by rounded teaspoonfuls 2 in. apart onto ungreased baking sheets. Bake at 375° for 13-15 minutes or until firm.

Meanwhile, for frosting, combine the butter, brown sugar and milk in a saucepan. Bring to a boil over medium heat, stirring constantly; boil for 3 minutes. Remove from the heat; stir in maple flavoring and vanilla. Cool slightly; beat in enough confectioners' sugar to achieve spreading consistency. Remove cookies to wire racks; frost while warm. **Yield:** 6-1/2 dozen.

**CREATIVE COOKIES.** Shown clockwise from top left: Coconut Fruitcake Cookies (p. 34), Crisp Sand Stars (p. 35), Walnut-Filled Pillows (p. 34), Mint Swirl Bars (p. 34) and Cream Cheese Spritz (p. 34).

## CREAM CHEESE SPRITZ
**Sarah Bedia, Lake Jackson, Texas**
(Pictured on page 32)

*A hint of orange and cinnamon highlights these Christmastime classics. I like to add colorful sprinkles before baking them. The recipe is from a booklet that came with a cookie press in the 1950s…and I still have the press!*

    1 cup shortening
    1 package (3 ounces) cream cheese, softened
    1 cup sugar
    1 egg yolk
    1 teaspoon vanilla extract
    1 teaspoon grated orange peel
2-1/2 cups all-purpose flour
  1/2 teaspoon salt
  1/4 teaspoon ground cinnamon
Green food coloring, decorator candies and colored
    sugar, optional

In a mixing bowl, beat shortening and cream cheese until blended. Add sugar; beat until creamy. Beat in egg yolk, vanilla and orange peel. Combine the flour, salt and cinnamon; gradually add to creamed mixture. Add food coloring if desired.

    Using a cookie press fitted with the disk of your choice, press dough 1 in. apart onto ungreased baking sheets. Decorate if desired. Bake at 350° for 9-12 minutes or until set (do not brown). Remove to wire racks to cool. **Yield:** about 9 dozen.

## WALNUT-FILLED PILLOWS
**Nancy Kostrej, Canonsburg, Pennsylvania**
(Pictured on page 33)

*These tender cookie pillows, filled with a delicious walnut mixture, are my husband's favorite. He says it wouldn't be Christmas without them.*

  1/2 cup cold butter (no substitutes)
    1 package (3 ounces) cold cream cheese
1-1/4 cups all-purpose flour
  3/4 cup ground walnuts
  1/4 cup sugar
    2 tablespoons milk
  1/2 teaspoon vanilla *or* almond extract
    1 egg, lightly beaten
Confectioners' sugar

In a large bowl, cut butter and cream cheese into flour until mixture resembles coarse crumbs. Using your hands, blend mixture together until a smooth dough forms, about 3 minutes. Pat into a rectangle; wrap in plastic wrap. Refrigerate for 1 hour or until firm. For filling, combine the walnuts, sugar, milk and vanilla.

    Unwrap dough and place on a lightly floured surface. Roll into a 17-1/2-in. x 10-in. rectangle; cut into 2-1/2-in. squares. Place a level teaspoonful of filling in the center of each square. Moisten edges with water; fold in half and seal with a fork. Place 1 in. apart on ungreased baking sheets. Brush with egg. Bake at 375° for 10-12 minutes or until edges are golden brown. Remove to wire racks to cool. Dust with confectioners' sugar. **Yield:** 28 cookies.

## COCONUT FRUITCAKE COOKIES
**Jolene Davis, Minden, Nevada**
(Pictured on page 32)

*Brimming with candied fruit, coconut and pecans, these sweet morsels resemble fruitcake. My grandmother would bake and serve the cookies in decorated miniature paper or foil muffin liners, and I have carried on the tradition.*

    3 cups chopped pecans
2-1/2 cups flaked coconut
1-1/4 cups chopped candied cherries
1-1/4 cups chopped candied pineapple
    1 cup chopped dates
    2 cups sweetened condensed milk

In a bowl, combine the first five ingredients. Stir in milk. Fill paper-lined miniature muffin cups two-thirds full. Bake at 300° for 20-25 minutes or until golden brown. Cool for 10 minutes before removing from pans to waxed paper to cool completely. Let stand for 24 hours in an airtight container at room temperature before serving. **Yield:** 8 dozen.

## MINT SWIRL BARS
**Debbie Devore, Fremont, Nebraska**
(Pictured on page 33)

*My folks love these cake-like bars, so I always make them for the holidays. The chocolaty mint squares look simply scrumptious and taste even better.*

    1 package (3 ounces) cream cheese, softened
  1/4 cup butter (no substitutes), softened
  3/4 cup sugar
    2 eggs
  2/3 cup all-purpose flour
  1/2 teaspoon baking powder
  1/2 teaspoon salt
  1/3 cup chopped walnuts
    1 square (1 ounce) semisweet chocolate, melted
  1/2 teaspoon peppermint extract
    2 to 3 drops green *or* red food coloring, optional
GLAZE:
    1 square (1 ounce) semisweet chocolate
    1 tablespoon butter
    1 cup confectioners' sugar
  1/2 teaspoon vanilla extract
    2 to 3 tablespoons boiling water

In a mixing bowl, beat cream cheese, butter and sugar. Add eggs, one at a time, beating well after each addition. Combine the flour, baking powder and salt; add to creamed mixture and mix well. Transfer half of the batter to another bowl; stir in nuts and chocolate. Spread into a greased 9-in. square baking pan.

    Stir peppermint extract and food coloring if desired into remaining batter. Spoon over chocolate layer; cut through batter with a knife to swirl. Bake at 350° for 15-20 minutes or until a toothpick inserted near the center comes out clean. Cool on a wire rack.

    In a saucepan, melt chocolate and butter. Remove from the heat; stir in confectioners' sugar, vanilla and enough water to achieve glaze consistency. Pour over brownies and spread evenly. Cut into bars. **Yield:** 2 dozen.

## CRISP SAND STARS
### Gladys Scharrer, Allenton, Wisconsin
(Pictured on page 33)

*With a subtle almond flavoring and a whole almond in the center, these thin crispy cookies should play a starring role on your Christmas cookie platter.*

1/2 cup butter (no substitutes), softened
1 cup sugar
2 egg yolks
1 tablespoon milk
1/2 teaspoon vanilla extract
1/4 teaspoon almond extract
1-1/2 cups all-purpose flour
1 teaspoon baking powder
1/2 teaspoon baking soda
1/2 teaspoon salt
Unblanched whole almonds
2 egg whites, lightly beaten
Additional sugar

In a mixing bowl, cream the butter and sugar. Beat in the egg yolks, milk and extracts. Combine the flour, baking powder, baking soda and salt; gradually add to creamed mixture. Cover and refrigerate dough for 1 hour or until easy to handle.

On a lightly floured surface, roll out dough to 1/8-in. thickness. Cut with a floured 3-in. star cutter. Place 1 in. apart on ungreased baking sheets. Press an almond in the center of each. Brush with egg white; sprinkle with sugar. Bake at 350° for 8-10 minutes or until lightly browned. Remove to wire racks to cool. **Yield:** about 5 dozen.

## TWO-TONE CHRISTMAS COOKIES
### Marie Capobianco, Portsmouth, Rhode Island

*I dreamed up this recipe using two of my favorite flavors, pistachio and raspberry. These pink and green cookies are tasty and eye-catching, too. They're perfect for formal or informal gatherings, and everybody likes them.*

1 cup butter (no substitutes), softened
1-1/2 cups sugar
2 egg yolks
2 teaspoons vanilla extract
1 teaspoon almond extract
3-1/2 cups all-purpose flour
1 teaspoon salt
1 teaspoon baking powder
1/2 teaspoon baking soda
9 drops green food coloring
1 tablespoon milk
1/3 cup chopped pistachios
9 drops red food coloring
3 tablespoons seedless raspberry preserves
2 cups (12 ounces) semisweet chocolate chips, melted
Additional chopped pistachios

In a mixing bowl, cream butter and sugar. Beat in egg yolks and extracts. Combine the flour, salt, baking powder and baking soda; gradually add to creamed mixture. Divide dough in half. Stir green food coloring, milk and nuts into one portion; mix well. Add red food coloring and jam to the other half.

Shape each portion between two pieces of waxed paper into an 8-in. x 6-in. rectangle. Cut in half lengthwise. Place one green rectangle on a piece of plastic wrap. Top with pink rectangle; press together lightly. Repeat. Wrap each in plastic wrap and refrigerate overnight.

Unwrap the dough and cut in half lengthwise. Return one of the rectangles to the refrigerator. Cut the remaining rectangle into 1/8-in. slices. Place 1 in. apart on ungreased baking sheets. Bake at 375° for 7-9 minutes or until set. Remove to wire racks to cool. Repeat with the remaining dough.

Drizzle cooled cookies with melted chocolate. Sprinkle with additional pistachios. **Yield:** 6-1/2 dozen.

## CARAMEL PECAN SHORTBREAD
### Dorothy Buiter, Worth, Illinois

*My grandchildren look for Grandma's "candy bar cookies" every Christmas. I recommend doubling the recipe for these sweet treats because they go so fast.*

3/4 cup butter (no substitutes), softened
3/4 cup confectioners' sugar
2 tablespoons evaporated milk
1 teaspoon vanilla extract
2 cups all-purpose flour
1/4 teaspoon salt
FILLING:
28 caramels*
2 tablespoons evaporated milk
2 tablespoons butter
1 cup confectioners' sugar
3/4 cup finely chopped pecans
ICING:
1 cup (6 ounces) semisweet chocolate chips
3 tablespoons evaporated milk
2 tablespoons butter
1/2 cup confectioners' sugar
1/2 teaspoon vanilla extract
Pecan halves

In a mixing bowl, cream the butter and confectioners' sugar. Beat in milk and vanilla. Combine flour and salt; gradually add to creamed mixture. Cover and refrigerate for 1 hour or until easy to handle. On a lightly floured surface, roll out the dough to 1/4-in. thickness. Cut into 2-in. x 1-in. strips. Place 1 in. apart on greased baking sheets. Bake at 325° for 12-14 minutes or until lightly browned. Remove to wire racks to cool.

For filling, combine caramels and milk in a saucepan. Cook and stir over medium-low heat until caramels are melted and smooth. Remove from the heat; stir in butter, sugar and pecans. Cool for 5 minutes. Spread 1 teaspoon over each cookie.

For icing, combine chocolate chips and milk in a saucepan. Cook and stir over medium-low heat until chips are melted and smooth. Remove from the heat; stir in butter, sugar and vanilla. Cool for 5 minutes. Spread over filling; top each with a pecan half. Store in an airtight container. **Yield:** about 4 dozen.

**\*Editor's Note**: This recipe was tested with Hershey caramels.

**CHRISTMAS CONFECTIONS.** Shown clockwise from top: Peanut Candy Popcorn Balls (p. 37), Old-Fashioned Molasses Candy (p. 37), Truffle Cherries (p. 37) and Brown Sugar Cashew Fudge (p. 37).

# *Seasonal Sweets*

## BROWN SUGAR CASHEW FUDGE
**Jennifer Adams, Plymouth, Massachusetts**
(Pictured on page 36)

*This creamy light-colored fudge, loaded with crunchy cashews, is a yummy variation on traditional chocolate...and it disappears just as fast!*

```
1-1/2 teaspoons plus 1/4 cup butter (no substitutes),
      softened, divided
    1 cup packed brown sugar
  1/2 cup evaporated milk
    2 tablespoons light corn syrup
2-1/2 cups confectioners' sugar
    2 cups coarsely chopped salted cashews
```

Line a 9-in. square pan with foil and grease the foil with 1-1/2 teaspoons butter; set aside. In a heavy saucepan, combine the brown sugar, milk, corn syrup and remaining butter. Cook and stir over medium heat until sugar is dissolved. Bring mixture to a rapid boil, stirring constantly for 5 minutes.

Remove from the heat. Gradually add confectioners' sugar; mix well. Fold in cashews. Immediately spread into prepared pan. Cool. Using foil, lift fudge out of pan. Cut into 1-in. squares. Refrigerate in an airtight container. **Yield:** 3 dozen.

## OLD-FASHIONED MOLASSES CANDY
**Laurie Pester, Colstrip, Montana**
(Pictured on page 36)

*This hard candy was always the first thing to sell out at fundraisers we held back when I was in high school. I still make the melt-in-your-mouth morsels every Christmas.*

```
3 tablespoons butter (no substitutes), softened,
    divided
1 cup sugar
3/4 cup light corn syrup
2 teaspoons cider vinegar
3/4 cup molasses
1/4 teaspoon baking soda
```

Grease a 15-in. x 10-in. x 1-in. pan with 1 tablespoon butter; set aside. In a heavy saucepan, combine sugar, corn syrup and vinegar. Cook over low heat until sugar is dissolved, stirring frequently. Increase heat to medium; cook until a candy thermometer reads 245° (firm-ball stage), stirring occasionally. Add molasses and remaining butter. Cook, uncovered, until a candy thermometer reads 260° (hard-ball stage), stirring occasionally. Remove from the heat. Add baking soda; beat well.

Pour into prepared pan. Let stand for 5 minutes or until cool enough to handle. Butter fingers; quickly pull candy until firm but pliable (color will be light tan). When candy is ready for cutting, pull into a 1/2-in. rope. Cut into 1-in. pieces. Wrap each in waxed paper or colored candy wrappers. **Yield:** 1-1/2 pounds.

## PEANUT CANDY POPCORN BALLS
**Alida Jaeger, Ixonia, Wisconsin**
(Pictured on page 36)

*Kids love these colorful novelties, concocted from popcorn, nuts, M&M's and marshmallows, so they make great stocking stuffers. Instead of balls, the salty-sweet recipe can be shaped into a cheery cake using a buttered angel food cake pan.*

```
    4 quarts popped popcorn
1-1/2 cups salted peanuts
1-1/2 cups chopped pecans
    1 package (16 ounces) green and red milk
      chocolate M&M's
  1/2 cup butter (no substitutes)
  1/2 cup vegetable oil
    1 package (16 ounces) miniature marshmallows
```

In a large bowl, combine the first four ingredients; mix well and set aside. In a large saucepan, combine the butter, oil and marshmallows; cook and stir until smooth. Pour over popcorn mixture; mix well. When cool enough to handle, shape into popcorn balls. Let stand at room temperature until firm before wrapping in plastic wrap or stacking. **Yield:** about 20 popcorn balls.

## TRUFFLE CHERRIES
**Anne Drouin, Dunnville, Ontario**
(Pictured on page 36)

*Chocolate is popular at our house, especially during the holidays, so these double-chocolate gems never last long!*

```
1/3 cup whipping cream
  2 tablespoons butter (no substitutes)
  2 tablespoons sugar
  4 squares (1 ounce each) semisweet chocolate
  1 jar (8 ounces) maraschino cherries with stems,
    well drained
```
COATING:
```
  6 squares (1 ounce each) semisweet chocolate
  2 tablespoons shortening
```

In a saucepan, bring cream, butter and sugar to a boil, stirring constantly. Remove from the heat; stir in chocolate until melted. Cover and refrigerate for at least 4 hours or until easy to handle. Pat cherries with paper towel until very dry. Shape a teaspoonful of chocolate mixture around each cherry, forming a ball. Cover and refrigerate for 2-3 hours or until firm.

In a small saucepan, melt chocolate and shortening over low heat. Dip cherries until coated; shake off excess. Place on waxed paper to harden. **Yield:** about 2 dozen.

> ● We recommend that you test your candy thermometer before each use by placing it in a pot of boiling water; the thermometer should read 212°. Adjust your recipe temperature up or down based on your test.

# COCONUT CHOCOLATE CREAMS
## Kelly-Ann Gibbons, Prince George, British Columbia

*My mom gave me the recipe for these tempting truffle-like candies. They make any occasion special for my family. I love to impress dinner guests by setting out a pretty plate of these treats at the end of the meal.*

2-1/2 cups flaked coconut
1 cup (6 ounces) semisweet chocolate chips
1/2 cup evaporated milk
2-1/2 cups confectioners' sugar
1/3 cup chopped pecans
1/3 cup chopped maraschino cherries

Place coconut in a blender or food processor; cover and process until finely chopped. In a microwave or heavy saucepan, melt chocolate chips and milk. Remove from the heat; stir in confectioners' sugar, 1-1/4 cups coconut, pecans and cherries. Cover and refrigerate for 2 hours or until firm. Set remaining coconut aside.

Shape chocolate mixture into 1-in. balls; roll in reserved coconut. Place on waxed paper-lined baking sheets. Refrigerate for 2 hours or until firm. Store in an airtight container in the refrigerator. **Yield:** about 3 dozen.

# APRICOT BONBONS
## Lois Oliver, Brooksville, Florida

*Chewy apricots paired with crispy rice cereal and pecans are an unbeatable combination. This recipe doesn't require a candy thermometer, plus the mixture stays pliable awhile, so you don't have to rush.*

1/2 cup butter (no substitutes), cubed
1 cup sugar
1 egg, beaten
1 package (7 ounces) dried apricots, finely chopped
1 teaspoon vanilla extract
Pinch salt
2 cups crisp rice cereal
1 cup finely chopped pecans
Confectioners' sugar

In a heavy saucepan, combine butter, sugar, egg, apricots, vanilla and salt. Bring to a boil over medium heat, stirring constantly. Cook and stir for 8 minutes or until thickened. Remove from the heat; stir in cereal and pecans. Let stand until cool enough to handle.

Shape into 1-in. balls; roll in confectioners' sugar. Place on baking sheets; let stand until completely cool. Reroll in sugar if desired. Refrigerate in airtight containers. **Yield:** about 3-1/2 dozen.

# PECAN FONDANT
## Melanie Johnson, Newsoms, Virginia

*I love to cook and was well-taught by my mother, who always made cute confections for Christmas. These candies are a holiday tradition in my home. It seems I can never make enough, so it's a good thing they're simple to assemble.*

1/3 cup butter (no substitutes), softened
1/3 cup light corn syrup
1/8 teaspoon salt
3-1/2 cups confectioners' sugar, *divided*
Additional confectioners' sugar
About 180 pecan halves, toasted (about 3/4 pound)

In a bowl, stir the butter, corn syrup and salt with a wooden spoon until smooth. Add 1 cup sugar; stir until completely blended. Gradually add remaining sugar, stirring until completely blended.

Dust work surface with additional sugar. Knead dough until smooth, about 5 minutes. Shape into 1/2-in. balls. Place each ball between two pecan halves; gently press together. Place on waxed paper-lined baking sheets. Cover and chill for 3 hours or until set. Keep refrigerated until serving (candies will be soft). **Yield:** about 7-1/2 dozen.

# SPEARMINT CRUNCH
## Rose Randall, Derry, Pennsylvania

*I love getting food ready for the holidays, so I start planning early. This is one of my favorite recipes, and it's so easy to make. Kids can have fun crushing the spearmint candies.*

1 pound white candy coating, coarsely chopped
3/4 cup crushed spearmint candy (4 ounces)

In a microwave-safe bowl, melt candy coating at 70% power for 1 minute; stir. Microwave at additional 30-second intervals, stirring until smooth. Stir in spearmint candy. Spread onto a waxed paper-lined baking sheet. Chill for 8-10 minutes. Break into small pieces; store in airtight containers. **Yield:** 1-1/4 pounds.

# MAPLE PRALINES
## Mary Beth Cool, Canajoharie, New York

*This recipe rekindles memories of my grandfather and his love for making maple syrup. When I was in college, my mother would send me a package of her pralines during sugaring season. They were so popular with my friends, I barely managed to tuck away a few for myself.*

1 cup sugar
2/3 cup milk
1/2 cup maple syrup
2 tablespoons butter (no substitutes)
3/4 cup coarsely chopped pecans, toasted

In a heavy 1-qt. saucepan, combine sugar, milk and syrup. Cook and stir over medium heat until mixture boils. Reduce heat to medium-low. Cook, uncovered, until a candy thermometer reads 234° (soft-ball stage), stirring occasionally.

Remove from the heat. Add butter; do not stir. Cool, without stirring, to 160°. Stir in pecans. Beat vigorously with a wooden spoon until mixture just begins to thicken but is still glossy. Quickly drop by spoonfuls onto waxed paper. Cool. Store in an airtight container. **Yield:** about 1 pound.

**Editor's Note:** This recipe should not be doubled. Make one batch at a time. See the box on page 37 for information about testing your candy thermometer.

# PEANUT BUTTER COCOA BONBONS
### Debbie Downs, Steens, Mississippi

*I'm a minister's wife and also have a candy-making business. This yummy pairing of peanut butter and chocolate produced terrific treats for a recent fellowship. Everyone commented on the flavor and quickly emptied my tray.*

    2 packages (3 ounces *each*) cream cheese,
      softened
    4 cups confectioners' sugar
  1/3 cup baking cocoa
    1 teaspoon vanilla extract
    1 cup chopped peanuts
    1 package (10 ounces) peanut butter chips
    1 tablespoon shortening

In a large mixing bowl, beat cream cheese, confectioners' sugar, cocoa and vanilla until smooth. Stir in peanuts. Cover and refrigerate for 2 hours or until firm. Drop by heaping teaspoonfuls onto a waxed paper-lined baking sheet. Refrigerate, uncovered, for 1 hour. Shape into 1-in. balls; return to baking sheet. Refrigerate, uncovered, for 3 hours or until firm.

In a microwave or heavy saucepan, melt peanut butter chips and shortening; stir until smooth and blended. Dip balls and place on waxed paper-lined baking sheets. Chill until firm. Store in an airtight container in the refrigerator. **Yield:** about 3 dozen.

# CHOCOLATE PEANUT CANDY SQUARES
### Karen Lester, Des Moines, Iowa

*Several years ago, I took this recipe to my sister's annual Christmas cookie- and candy-making party. Everyone still tells me that their families beg them to make these decadent delights for their holiday festivities.*

    1 tablespoon plus 1 cup butter *or* margarine,
      *divided*
    1 package (12 ounces) semisweet chocolate chips
    1 package (10 to 11 ounces) butterscotch chips
    1 jar (18 ounces) peanut butter
    1 can (16 ounces) salted peanuts
    1 can (14 ounces) sweetened condensed milk
    1 package (3 ounces) cook-and-serve vanilla
      pudding mix
    1 teaspoon maple flavoring
    1 package (2 pounds) confectioners' sugar

Grease a 15-in. x 10-in. x 1-in. pan with 1 tablespoon butter; set aside. In a saucepan over low heat, cook and stir chips and peanut butter until chips are melted and mixture is smooth. Spread half into prepared pan; refrigerate. Add peanuts to the remaining mixture; set aside.

In a saucepan, combine the milk, pudding mix and remaining butter; cook and stir until mixture comes to a boil. Cook and stir for 1 minute. Remove from the heat; stir in maple flavoring. In a mixing bowl, beat confectioners' sugar and pudding mixture until smooth. Carefully spread over bottom layer. Carefully spread with reserved peanut mixture. Chill for at least 24 hours. Cut into 1-in. squares. Refrigerate in airtight containers. **Yield:** 12 dozen.

# MARSHMALLOW FUDGE
### Mary Peltz, Glen Ullin, North Dakota

*My mom has made this fast-to-fix fudge at Christmas for as long as I can remember. Pretty pastel marshmallows add a colorful twist to the candy.*

    1 tablespoon plus 2 cups butter (no substitutes),
      *divided*
    1 package (10-1/2 ounces) pastel miniature
      marshmallows
    1 package (12 ounces) semisweet chocolate chips
    1 package (11 ounces) butterscotch chips
    1 cup peanut butter

Line a 13-in. x 9-in. x 2-in. pan with foil; grease the foil with 1 tablespoon butter. Place marshmallows in prepared pan. In a saucepan over low heat, melt the chips, peanut butter and remaining butter, stirring constantly. Pour over marshmallows. Tap pan lightly on work surface. Refrigerate. Using foil, lift fudge out of pan. Cut into squares. Store in an airtight container in the refrigerator. **Yield:** 5 dozen.

# DOUBLE-DECKER FUDGE
### Jennifer Russell, Mt. Ulla, North Carolina

*Everyone loves peanut butter and chocolate, so this layered fudge is always a hit with family and friends. I found the recipe about 15 years ago and have been making it for the holidays ever since.*

    1 tablespoon plus 1/2 cup butter (no substitutes),
      *divided*
4-1/2 cups sugar
    1 can (12 ounces) evaporated milk
    1 jar (7 ounces) marshmallow creme
    2 cups peanut butter chips, *divided*
  1/2 cup baking cocoa
    1 teaspoon vanilla extract

Line a 9-in. square pan with foil and grease the foil with 1 tablespoon butter; set aside. In a heavy saucepan, combine the sugar, milk, marshmallow creme and 1/4 cup butter. Cook and stir over medium heat until sugar is dissolved. Bring to a rapid boil; boil for 5 minutes, stirring constantly. Remove from the heat.

Pour 3 cups of hot mixture into a bowl; add 1 cup peanut butter chips. Stir until chips are melted and mixture is smooth. Pour into prepared pan. To the remaining hot mixture, add cocoa, vanilla, and remaining chips and butter; stir until chips and butter are melted and mixture is smooth. Pour evenly over peanut butter layer in pan. Cool. Using foil, lift fudge out of pan. Cut into 1-in. squares. Refrigerate in airtight containers. **Yield:** 3-1/2 pounds.

> • Don't let your guests leave empty-handed this holiday season. Put homemade goodies such as fudge, seasoned nuts and fancy cookies into inexpensive mugs, decorative tins, small canisters or boxes. Wrap the containers with clear or colored plastic and place in a pretty box. Place the gifts on a tray near the door, and let everybody choose one as they leave your house.

**DELECTABLE DESSERTS.** Shown clockwise from top left: Drummer Boy Cake (p. 41), Cherry Pineapple Fruitcake (p. 42) and French Vanilla Cream Puffs (p. 41).

# Festive Desserts

## DRUMMER BOY CAKE
(Pictured on page 40)

*Looking for an impressive finale to your holiday dinner? This spectacular dessert, drummed up by our Test Kitchen, features a sweet-tart cranberry topping paired with a tangy orange cake and filling.*

    1 envelope unflavored gelatin
1/4 cup cold water
    3 cups fresh *or* frozen cranberries
    1 cup sugar
1/2 cup red currant jelly
CAKE/FILLING:
    1 medium navel orange, unpeeled and quartered
    1 package (18-1/4 ounces) yellow cake mix
1-1/2 cups water, *divided*
1/3 cup vegetable oil
    3 eggs
3/4 cup sugar
    5 teaspoons cornstarch
1/8 teaspoon salt
    2 tablespoons butter *or* margarine, cubed
Yellow liquid food coloring
FROSTING:
    1 cup shortening
1-1/2 teaspoons vanilla extract
1/2 teaspoon orange extract
4-1/2 cups confectioners' sugar
1/4 cup milk
Yellow and red liquid food coloring
  28 fresh *or* frozen cranberries

For topping, sprinkle gelatin over cold water in a microwave-safe bowl; let stand for 1 minute. Microwave on high for 40 seconds; stir. Let stand for 1 minute or until gelatin is completely dissolved; set aside. In a saucepan over medium-low heat, cook cranberries and sugar, uncovered, for 7 minutes or until slightly thickened, stirring occasionally. Cool slightly. Stir in jelly and gelatin mixture. Cover and chill for 5 hours or overnight.

For cake, process orange in a blender or food processor until finely chopped; set aside. In a mixing bowl, beat cake mix, 1 cup water, oil and eggs on low speed until moistened. Add 1/3 cup chopped orange; beat for 2 minutes on medium. Set remaining orange aside for filling. Pour batter into two greased and floured 9-in. round baking pans. Bake at 350° for 28-31 minutes or until a toothpick comes out clean. Cool for 10 minutes; remove from pans to wire racks.

For filling, combine sugar, cornstarch, salt and remaining water in a saucepan until smooth. Add butter and 1/3 cup chopped orange (discard any remaining orange or save for another use). Bring to a boil; cook and stir for 2 minutes or until thickened. Stir in a few drops yellow food coloring; cool.

Split each cooled cake into two horizontal layers. Place bottom layer on serving plate; spread with a third of the filling. Repeat layers twice. Top with remaining cake layer. Spread the cranberry topping over top to within 1/2 in. of edges.

In a mixing bowl, cream shortening and extracts. Add sugar, 1/2 cup at a time, alternately with milk, beating until frosting is light and fluffy. Using 2/3 cup of frosting, frost cake sides. Tint remaining frosting gold with yellow and red food coloring. Cut a hole in a pastry or plastic bag; insert round tip #8. Fill with gold frosting. Pipe connecting diagonal stripes around side of cake; add cranberries at end points. With star tip #21, pipe a shell border around top and bottom of cake. **Yield:** 12-15 servings.

**Editor's Note:** This recipe was prepared with Duncan Hines yellow cake mix. Use of a coupler ring will allow you to easily change pastry tips for different designs.

## FRENCH VANILLA CREAM PUFFS
Lena Haines, Lawrenceville, Georgia
(Pictured on page 40)

*French vanilla filling dotted with mini chocolate chips is sandwiched in puffy pastry for this elegantly sweet dessert. You could substitute white chocolate or chocolate pudding for the vanilla if you like.*

    1 cup water
1/2 cup butter (no substitutes)
    1 cup all-purpose flour
1/4 teaspoon salt
    4 eggs
FILLING:
1-1/2 cups cold milk
    1 package (3.4 ounces) instant French vanilla pudding mix
    1 cup whipped topping
    1 package (12 ounces) miniature semisweet chocolate chips
Confectioners' sugar

In a saucepan, bring water and butter to a boil. Add flour and salt all at once; stir until a smooth ball forms. Remove from the heat; let stand for 5 minutes. Add eggs, one at a time, beating well after each addition. Beat until mixture is smooth and shiny.

Drop by rounded teaspoonfuls 2 in. apart onto greased baking sheets. Bake at 400° for 20-25 minutes or until golden brown. Remove puffs to wire racks. Immediately cut a slit in each for steam to escape. Cool. Split puffs and remove soft dough.

For filling, in a mixing bowl, beat milk and pudding mix on low speed for 2 minutes. Refrigerate for 5 minutes. Fold in whipped topping and chips. Fill cream puffs just before serving; replace tops. Dust with confectioners' sugar. **Yield:** about 2-1/2 dozen.

> • Make it easy for guests to identify the foods you're serving at a holiday buffet. Write the name of the food or recipe on a small card. Then cut a slit in small pears or apples, lemons or limes, and insert a card in each slit. For a fancier touch, you can spray paint the fruits silver or gold.

# CHERRY PINEAPPLE FRUITCAKE
### SueAnn Bunt, Painted Post, New York
(Pictured on page 40)

*This is the finishing touch to our Christmas dinner. My family always claimed they didn't like fruitcake, but they love this one! For the best flavor, let it sit overnight before slicing.*

- 1 cup chopped candied cherries
- 1 cup chopped candied pineapple
- 2 cups chopped pecans
- 4 cups all-purpose flour, *divided*
- 2 cups butter *or* margarine, softened
- 2 cups sugar
- 6 eggs
- 2 teaspoons vanilla extract
- 1 teaspoon baking powder

In a bowl, combine the cherries, pineapple, pecans and 1 cup flour; set aside. In a mixing bowl, cream butter and sugar. Add eggs, one at a time, beating well after each. Beat in vanilla. Combine baking powder and remaining flour; gradually add to creamed mixture. Fold in fruit mixture.

Spoon into a greased and waxed paper-lined 10-in. tube pan. Bake at 300° for 1-3/4 to 2 hours or until a toothpick inserted near the center comes out clean. Cool for 10 minutes before removing from pan to a wire rack. Remove waxed paper while warm; cool completely before slicing. **Yield:** 12-16 servings.

# PISTACHIO CHERRY SQUARES
### Kathy Zielicke, Fond du Lac, Wisconsin

*This dessert's Christmas colors really add to the festivity of a buffet table, but it's the creamy, cool taste that keeps people coming back for more. Kids will enjoy helping when you make this no-bake treat.*

- 2 cups graham cracker crumbs (about 32 squares)
- 1/2 cup butter *or* margarine, melted
- 1/4 cup sugar

CREAM CHEESE LAYER:
- 1 package (8 ounces) cream cheese, softened
- 2/3 cup confectioners' sugar
- 1 carton (8 ounces) frozen whipped topping, thawed

PUDDING LAYER:
- 2-1/2 cups cold milk
- 2 packages (3.4 ounces *each*) instant pistachio pudding mix

TOPPING:
- 1 carton (8 ounces) frozen whipped topping, thawed
- 2 cans (21 ounces *each*) cherry pie filling

Combine the cracker crumbs, butter and sugar; press into an ungreased 13-in. x 9-in. x 2-in. dish. Refrigerate. In a mixing bowl, beat cream cheese and sugar; fold in whipped topping. Spread over crust. In a mixing bowl, beat milk and pudding mixes on low speed for 2 minutes. Spread over cream cheese layer; chill until firm, about 1 hour.

Spread whipped topping over pudding layer. Top with pie filling. Refrigerate overnight. Cut into squares. **Yield:** 12-15 servings.

# GINGERSNAP ICE CREAM TORTE
### Cary Schulte, Broadway, Virginia

*My husband and I developed this sweet frozen treat featuring gingersnaps, caramel and ice cream. Since a little of this rich cake goes a long way, it'll easily feed a crowd.*

- 2 cups finely crushed gingersnaps (about 40 cookies)
- 1/2 cup packed brown sugar
- 1/2 cup butter *or* margarine, melted
- 1 package (14 ounces) caramels
- 1/3 cup half-and-half cream *or* milk
- 1-1/2 cups cold milk
- 2 packages (3.4 ounces *each*) instant vanilla pudding mix
- 1/2 gallon vanilla ice cream, softened
- 1/2 cup chopped pecans

In a bowl, combine the gingersnaps, brown sugar and butter; set half aside. Press remaining mixture onto the bottom of a greased 9-in. springform pan. Bake at 350° for 10 minutes. Cool completely. In a microwave or heavy saucepan, melt caramels. Stir in cream until smooth; set aside.

In a mixing bowl, beat milk and pudding mixes on low speed for 2 minutes. Stir in ice cream until blended. Spoon half into the crust. Top with half of the reserved gingersnap mixture. Drizzle with half of the caramel sauce; sprinkle with half of the pecans. Repeat layers. Cover and freeze for at least 4 hours or until firm. Remove from the freezer 15 minutes before serving. **Yield:** 16-20 servings.

# FESTIVE MINT CREAM DESSERT
### Sally Hook, Houston, Texas

*Mint ice cream and colorful sprinkles make this cool concoction perfect for holiday parties or meals. For a chocolaty dessert, use rocky road or chocolate ice cream instead.*

- 3/4 cup butter *or* margarine, *divided*
- 1 package (16 ounces) chocolate cream-filled sandwich cookies, crushed
- 2 quarts mint ice cream
- 1-1/2 cups milk chocolate chips
- 1 cup confectioners' sugar
- 3/4 cup evaporated milk
- 1 carton (16 ounces) frozen whipped topping, thawed

Chocolate syrup and red and green sprinkles, optional

In a saucepan or microwave, melt 1/2 cup butter. Stir in cookie crumbs; mix well. Press into a 13-in. x 9-in. x 2-in. dish. Freeze for 30 minutes or until firm. Meanwhile, remove ice cream from freezer to soften. Spread ice cream over crust; return to the freezer until firm.

In a saucepan, combine chocolate chips, confectioners' sugar, milk and remaining butter. Bring to a boil, stirring frequently. Cook and stir for 3-5 minutes or until thickened. Cool to room temperature. When cool, spread over ice cream; return to freezer.

When chocolate layer has hardened, spread with whipped topping (dish will be full). Cover and freeze. Remove from the freezer 20-30 minutes before serving. If desired, drizzle with chocolate syrup and top with sprinkles. **Yield:** 24 servings.

## SWEET POTATO CAKE ROLL
### Bernice Taylor, Wilson, North Carolina

*Smooth cream cheese filling is all rolled up in the cinnamony sweet potato flavor of a sponge cake. This tantalizing change-of-pace dessert makes an attractive conclusion to a holiday meal.*

        2 eggs
        1 cup sugar
    2/3 cup mashed cooked sweet potatoes
        1 cup self-rising flour*
        1 teaspoon ground cinnamon
        2 tablespoons confectioners' sugar
CREAM CHEESE FILLING:
        1 package (8 ounces) cream cheese, softened
        1 cup confectioners' sugar
        1 tablespoon butter *or* margarine, melted
        1 teaspoon vanilla extract
    1/3 cup chopped pecans
Additional confectioners' sugar, optional

Line a greased 15-in. x 10-in. x 1-in. baking pan with waxed paper and grease the paper; set aside. In a mixing bowl, beat eggs on high speed for 5 minutes. Gradually beat in sugar until thick and lemon-colored. Add sweet potatoes; mix well. Combine flour and cinnamon; fold into sweet potato mixture. Spread into prepared pan.

Bake at 350° for 10-15 minutes or until cake springs back when lightly touched. Cool for 5 minutes; invert cake onto a kitchen towel dusted with confectioners' sugar. Gently peel off waxed paper. Roll up cake in the towel jelly-roll style, starting with a short side. Cool on a wire rack.

For filling, in a mixing bowl, beat cream cheese, confectioners' sugar, butter and vanilla until fluffy. Fold in nuts. Unroll cake; spread filling evenly over cake to within 1/2 in. of edges. Roll up again. Cover and refrigerate until serving. Dust with confectioners' sugar if desired. **Yield:** 8-10 servings.

*Editor's Note: As a substitute for 1 cup self-rising flour, place 1-1/2 teaspoons baking powder and 1/2 teaspoon salt in a measuring cup. Add all-purpose flour to measure 1 cup.

## MINCEMEAT CHERRY PIE
### Kathleen Tucker, Huachuca City, Arizona

*Cherries and orange marmalade give a nice twist to traditional mincemeat pie. It's sure to add some old-fashioned flavor to your Yuletide festivities.*

Pastry for double-crust pie (9 inches)
        1 can (21 ounces) cherry pie filling
1-3/4 cups prepared mincemeat
    1/3 cup orange marmalade
    1/4 cup chopped walnuts
        1 tablespoon all-purpose flour

Line a 9-in. pie plate with bottom pastry. Trim evenly with edge of plate. In a bowl, combine the remaining ingredients. Pour into crust. Roll out remaining pastry to fit top of pie; place over filling. Trim, seal and flute edges. Cut slits in top. Cover edges loosely with foil. Bake at 400° for 40-45 minutes or until crust is golden brown and filling is bubbly. Cool on a wire rack. **Yield:** 6-8 servings.

## EGGNOG CREAM PIE
### Susan Williams, Reno, Nevada

*I discovered this easy recipe on the back of an eggnog carton, then modified it slightly to simplify things. I can whip up the pie and still have time to devote to guests.*

        1 package (5.1 ounces) cook-and-serve vanilla
            pudding mix
    1/8 to 1/4 teaspoon ground nutmeg
1-1/2 cups eggnog*
        2 cups whipping cream, whipped
        1 pastry shell (9 inches), baked
Additional whipped cream and ground nutmeg,
    optional

In a saucepan, combine the pudding mix, nutmeg and eggnog. Cook and stir over medium heat until mixture comes to a boil. Cook and stir 1-2 minutes longer or until thickened. Remove from the heat. Cool. Fold in whipped cream. Pour into crust. Garnish with whipped cream and nutmeg if desired. **Yield:** 6-8 servings.

*Editor's Note: This recipe was tested with commercially prepared eggnog.

## GLITTER GELATIN TORTE
### June Deere, Urbana, Ohio

*This fluffy torte is a nice alternative to heavy holiday desserts. Bright cubes of gelatin shimmer in every slice.*

1-1/2 cups graham cracker crumbs (about 24 squares)
    1/3 cup plus 1/4 cup sugar, *divided*
    1/2 cup butter *or* margarine, melted
        1 package (3 ounces) strawberry gelatin
        3 cups boiling water, *divided*
1-1/4 cups cold water, *divided*
        1 package (3 ounces) lime gelatin
        1 package (3 ounces) lemon gelatin
        1 can (8 ounces) crushed pineapple, drained
        3 tablespoons lemon juice
Dash salt
1-1/2 cups whipping cream, whipped
    1/4 cup chopped walnuts

In a bowl, combine the cracker crumbs, 1/3 cup sugar and butter; press onto the bottom and 2 in. up the sides of a greased 9-in. springform pan. Refrigerate.

In a small bowl, dissolve strawberry gelatin in 1 cup boiling water; stir in 1/2 cup cold water. Pour into an 8-in. square dish coated with nonstick cooking spray; chill until firm. Repeat with lime gelatin, pouring into another 8-in. square dish.

In a large mixing bowl, dissolve lemon gelatin and remaining sugar in remaining boiling water. Add pineapple, lemon juice, salt and remaining cold water. Refrigerate until partially set, about 1 hour. Beat on medium speed until foamy, about 2 minutes.

Cut strawberry and lime gelatin into 1/2-in. cubes; set aside 1/4 cup of each for garnish. Fold remaining cubes into lemon gelatin. Fold in whipped cream. Spoon into crust. Top with walnuts and reserved gelatin cubes. Cover and refrigerate for at least 6 hours. Remove sides of pan. Cut into wedges. **Yield:** 12-14 servings.

**GREAT GIFTS.** Shown clockwise from to
Cookie Ornaments (p. 45), Cajun Spi
Mix (p. 45) and Cranberry Chutney (p. 45

# Gifts from the Kitchen

## CRANBERRY CHUTNEY
**Karyn Gordon, Rockledge, Florida**
(Pictured on page 44)

*You can serve this chunky chutney over cream cheese or Brie with crackers, or as a condiment with roast pork or poultry. Either way, its slightly tart flavor and deep red hue lend a festive flair to the table.*

      4 cups (1 pound) fresh *or* frozen cranberries
      1 cup sugar
      1 cup water
  1/2 cup packed brown sugar
      2 teaspoons ground cinnamon
1-1/2 teaspoons ground ginger
  1/2 teaspoon ground cloves
  1/4 teaspoon ground allspice
      1 cup chopped tart apple
  1/2 cup golden raisins
  1/2 cup diced celery

In a large saucepan, combine the first eight ingredients. Bring to a boil. Reduce heat; simmer, uncovered, for 20 minutes, stirring occasionally. Add the apple, raisins and celery. Simmer, uncovered, until thickened, about 15 minutes. Cool. Refrigerate until serving. **Yield:** 3 cups.

## COOKIE ORNAMENTS
**Patricia Slater, Baldwin, Ontario**
(Pictured on page 44)

*What a welcome gift these fun frosted ornaments will make. But beware...the ginger-flavored cookies are so appetizing, they might never make it to the tree!*

  1/3 cup butter (no substitutes), softened
  1/3 cup shortening
  3/4 cup sugar
      1 egg
      1 teaspoon vanilla extract
      2 cups all-purpose flour
1-1/2 teaspoons baking powder
      1 teaspoon ground ginger
  1/4 teaspoon salt
  1/8 teaspoon ground cloves
FROSTING:
1-1/2 cups confectioners' sugar
      3 tablespoons butter, softened
  1/2 teaspoon vanilla extract
      1 to 2 tablespoons milk
Food coloring and colored sprinkles, optional

In a mixing bowl, cream the butter, shortening and sugar. Beat in egg and vanilla. Combine the flour, baking powder, ginger, salt and cloves; gradually add to creamed mixture. Cover and refrigerate for 1 hour or until easy to handle.
    Divide dough in half. On a lightly floured surface, roll out each portion to 1/8-in. thickness. Cut with floured 2-1/2-in. cookie cutters. Using a floured spatula, place cookies 1 in. apart on ungreased baking sheets. With a straw, make a hole about 1/2 in. from the top of each cookie. Bake at 375° for 7-9 minutes or until edges are lightly browned. Remove to wire racks to cool.
    In a small mixing bowl, combine confectioners' sugar, butter, vanilla and enough milk to achieve frosting consistency. Frost cookies. Decorate with tinted frosting and colored sprinkles if desired. Let dry completely. Thread ribbon or string through holes. **Yield:** about 4 dozen.

## CAJUN SPICE MIX
**Coleen Deon, Dover Plains, New York**
(Pictured on page 44)

*You can give fish, beef, pork or poultry a zesty boost with this spicy seasoning. I like to sprinkle the mix on catfish fillets before broiling them.*

      2 tablespoons paprika
      1 tablespoon chili powder
      2 teaspoons onion powder
      2 teaspoons garlic powder
1-1/2 teaspoons salt
1-1/2 teaspoons white pepper
1-1/2 teaspoons pepper
      1 teaspoon dried oregano
      1 teaspoon dried thyme

In a bowl, combine all ingredients. Store in an airtight container in a cool dry place for up to 6 months. **Yield:** about 1/3 cup.

## CANDY SNACK MIX
**Mary Newsom, Grand Ridge, Florida**

*Chock-full of raisins, peanuts and M&M's, this crunchy salty-sweet mix stays fresh for weeks. I keep it on hand to serve to unexpected guests or to fill decorative containers to give as last-minute gifts.*

      1 package (24 ounces) roasted peanuts
      1 package (18 ounces) Golden Grahams cereal
      1 package (15 ounces) raisins
  1/2 cup butter (no substitutes)
    12 ounces white candy coating
      2 cups creamy peanut butter
      1 package (2 pounds) confectioners' sugar
      1 package (15 ounces) red and green milk
         chocolate M&M's

In a large bowl, combine the peanuts, cereal and raisins. In a heavy saucepan over low heat, melt butter, candy coating and peanut butter; stir until smooth. Pour over cereal mixture and toss to coat. Place sugar in a large bag; add coated mixture. Close bag and shake to coat. Spread onto baking sheets; sprinkle with M&M's. When cool, store in airtight containers. **Yield:** 25 cups.

## BANANA FRUIT MINI LOAVES
### Jean Engle, Pella, Iowa

*Plenty of goodies come in these little breads. The recipe is from my aunt, who always baked homemade treats for my sister and me when we visited her. Several of her recipes remain favorites of mine.*

    2 eggs
    2/3 cup sugar
    1 cup mashed bananas (about 2 medium)
1-3/4 cups all-purpose flour
    3 teaspoons baking powder
    1/2 teaspoon salt
    1 cup mixed candied fruit
    1/2 cup raisins
    1/2 cup chopped walnuts

In a mixing bowl, beat eggs and sugar. Add bananas; mix well. Combine the flour, baking powder and salt; gradually add to egg mixture. Fold in the fruit, raisins and walnuts. Transfer to three greased 5-3/4-in. x 3-in. x 2-in. loaf pans. Bake at 350° for 30-35 minutes or until a toothpick comes out clean. Cool for 10 minutes before removing from pans to wire racks to cool completely. **Yield:** 3 mini loaves.

**Editor's Note:** Bread can be baked in one 9-in. x 5-in. x 3-in. loaf pan for 55-60 minutes.

## CANDIED PECANS
### Opal Turner, Hughes Springs, Texas

*I package these crispy pecans in jars, tied with pretty ribbon, for family and friends. My granddaughter gave some to a doctor at the hospital where she works, and he said they were too good to be true!*

2-3/4 cups pecan halves
    2 tablespoons butter (no substitutes), softened, *divided*
    1 cup sugar
    1/2 cup water
    1/2 teaspoon salt
    1/2 teaspoon ground cinnamon
    1 teaspoon vanilla extract

Place pecans in a shallow baking pan in a 250° oven for 10 minutes or until warmed. Grease a 15-in. x 10-in. x 1-in. baking pan with 1 tablespoon butter; set aside. Grease the sides of a large heavy saucepan with remaining butter; add sugar, water, salt and cinnamon. Cook and stir over low heat until sugar is dissolved. Cook and stir over medium heat until mixture comes to a boil. Cover and cook for 2 minutes to dissolve sugar crystals.

Cook, without stirring, until a candy thermometer reads 236° (soft-ball stage). Remove from the heat; add vanilla. Stir in warm pecans until evenly coated. Spread onto prepared baking pan. Bake at 250° for 30 minutes, stirring every 10 minutes. Spread on a waxed paper-lined baking sheet to cool. **Yield:** about 1 pound.

**Editor's Note:** We recommend that you test your candy thermometer before each use by placing it in a pot of boiling water; the thermometer should read 212°. Adjust your recipe temperature up or down based on your test.

## THICK 'N' SPICY SAUCE
### Vicki Atkinson, Kamas, Utah

*With raisins for sweetness and pepper for kick, this spicy sauce is excellent with ham but also lends a nice barbecue flavor to burgers and roast beef. Prepare a batch for the outdoor chefs on your list.*

    1 small onion, cut into wedges
    1 garlic clove
    1 cup ketchup
    1/3 cup butter *or* margarine, melted
    1/2 cup raisins
    2 to 4 teaspoons pepper
    3 tablespoons brown sugar
    2 tablespoons white vinegar
    2 tablespoons lemon juice
    1 teaspoon salt
    1 teaspoon ground mustard
    1/2 teaspoon dried basil
    1/4 teaspoon *each* dried marjoram, tarragon and thyme
    1/4 teaspoon dried rosemary, crushed

In a blender or food processor, combine all ingredients. Cover and process until smooth. Pour into a saucepan. Cook and stir over medium heat for 8-10 minutes or until heated through. Refrigerate leftovers. **Yield:** 2-1/2 cups.

## HONEY FUDGE SAUCE
### Amy Kraemer, Hutchinson, Minnesota

*This velvety sauce will sweeten the season for any ice cream lover. The honey and chocolate blend can be drizzled warm or cold over ice cream, fruit and other desserts.*

    1 cup (6 ounces) semisweet chocolate chips
    1/2 cup honey
    2 tablespoons butter (no substitutes)
    1/2 teaspoon salt
    3/4 cup evaporated milk
    1 tablespoon vanilla extract

In a heavy saucepan, combine the chips, honey, butter and salt. Cook and stir over low heat until chips are melted; stir until smooth. Gradually stir in milk and vanilla; heat through, about 2 minutes (do not boil). **Yield:** 1-2/3 cups.

## CHERRY STREUSEL SQUARES
### TerryAnn Moore, Oaklyn, New Jersey

*I don't think food should take longer to make than it does to eat, so I love these time-saving bar cookies. At Christmas, I like to use red and green cherries.*

    1 cup butter (no substitutes), softened
    1/3 cup packed brown sugar
    1 teaspoon vanilla extract
    1/4 teaspoon almond extract
    2 cups all-purpose flour
    1 cup chopped pecans

    1 cup finely chopped candied *or* maraschino
        cherries
STREUSEL:
    1 cup all-purpose flour
    1/2 cup sugar
    6 tablespoons cold butter
    1/2 cup chopped pecans

In a mixing bowl, cream butter and brown sugar. Add extracts. Gradually add flour. Stir in pecans and cherries.
Spread into an ungreased 13-in. x 9-in. x 2-in. baking
pan. In a small bowl, combine the flour and sugar; cut in
butter until mixture resembles coarse crumbs. Add pecans.
Sprinkle over dough. Bake at 350° for 30-35 minutes or until very light brown. Cool on a wire rack. Cut into 1-1/2-
in. squares. **Yield:** 4 dozen.

# OVEN-DRIED BEEF JERKY
### Patti Murphy, Wilmington, Ohio

*These satisfying snack strips are perfect for lunch boxes, road
trips or late-night snacks. Make enough to give as gifts and
to freeze for your family, too.*

1-1/2 to 2 pounds lean beef round steak
    1/4 cup soy sauce
    1 tablespoon Worcestershire sauce
    1/2 teaspoon onion salt
    1/4 teaspoon garlic powder
    1/4 teaspoon pepper

Trim and discard all fat from meat. Cut meat into 5-in. x
1/2-in. strips. In a large resealable plastic bag, combine
the remaining ingredients; add meat. Seal bag and toss to
coat. Refrigerate for 8 hours or overnight.
    Place wire racks on foil-lined baking sheets. Drain and
discard marinade. Place meat strips 1/4 in. apart on racks.
Bake, uncovered, at 200° for 6-7 hours or until meat is dry
and leathery. Remove from the oven; cool completely. Refrigerate or freeze in an airtight container. **Yield:** about
3/4 pound.

# SPICED CEREAL CRUNCH
### Janet Burkholder, Harrisonburg, Virginia

*My mother gave me the recipe for this irresistible party pleas-
er. I receive compliments every time I serve it.*

    3 cups Cheerios
    2 cups *each* Wheat Chex, Rice Chex and
        Corn Chex
1-1/2 cups pecan halves
1-1/3 cups packed brown sugar
    1/2 cup butter (no substitutes)
    1/4 cup light corn syrup
    2 teaspoons ground cinnamon
    1/2 teaspoon salt

Combine the cereals and nuts in a large roasting pan; set
aside. In a saucepan, combine the brown sugar, butter, corn
syrup, cinnamon and salt; bring to a boil over medium heat,
stirring occasionally. Boil and stir for 3 minutes. Pour over

cereal mixture and stir to coat. Bake at 250° for 1 hour, stirring every 15 minutes. Spread onto waxed paper. When
cool, break apart and store in an airtight container. **Yield:**
about 3 quarts.

# BREAK-APART COOKIE BITES
### Marcia Wolff, Rolling Prairie, Indiana

*These crisp treats lend a different shape to a cookie tray.
And they're easy to prepare—just press into a pan, bake
and break. My family enjoys them during the holidays and all
year long.*

    1/2 cup butter *or* margarine, softened
    1/2 cup shortening
    1 cup sugar
    1 teaspoon vanilla extract
    2 cups all-purpose flour
    1 teaspoon salt
    1 cup miniature semisweet chocolate chips
    1 cup finely chopped walnuts, *divided*

In a mixing bowl, cream butter, shortening and sugar. Beat
in vanilla. Combine flour and salt; gradually add to creamed
mixture. Stir in chocolate chips and 3/4 cup walnuts.
Spread into a greased 15-in. x 10-in. x 1-in. baking pan.
Sprinkle with remaining nuts; press down gently. Bake at
375° for 20-25 minutes or until golden brown. Cool completely. Break into pieces. **Yield:** about 8-1/2 dozen.

# CHOCOLATE
# PEPPERMINT PINWHEELS
### Ellen Johnson, Hampton, Virginia

*My cookie-loving family is never satisfied with just one batch
of these minty pinwheels, so I automatically double the
recipe each time I bake them.*

    1/2 cup shortening
    3/4 cup sugar
    1 egg
    1 tablespoon milk
    1 teaspoon peppermint extract
1-1/4 cups all-purpose flour
    1/4 teaspoon salt
    1/4 teaspoon baking powder
    1 square (1 ounce) unsweetened chocolate,
        melted

In a mixing bowl, cream shortening and sugar. Add egg,
milk and extract; mix well. Combine the flour, salt and baking powder; gradually add to creamed mixture. Divide
dough in half. Add chocolate to one portion; mix well.
Roll each portion between waxed paper into a rectangle
about 1/2 in. thick. Remove top sheet of waxed paper;
place plain dough over chocolate dough. Roll up jelly-roll
style, starting with a long side. Wrap in plastic wrap; refrigerate for 2 hours or until firm.
    Unwrap dough and cut into 1/4-in. slices. Place 2 in.
apart on greased baking sheets. Bake at 375° for 8-10
minutes or until lightly browned. Remove to wire racks to
cool. **Yield:** about 3 dozen.

# Meringue Snowflakes Sweeten Holiday Decor

THE FORECAST calls for a flurry of fun when you fashion these frosty snowflakes. The quick-to-fix meringue icing and easy instructions provided by *CW*'s creative kitchen staff make the delicate ornaments a cinch to shape. Even the kids can lend a hand, dusting them with cheery glitter or other sprinkles once the flakes have been formed.

Although they aren't meant for munching, the flakes will find favor as decorations wherever you hang them. You can follow the pretty patterns we show here, or design your own snappy snowflakes.

We predict that one batch won't be enough…you'll want an entire blizzard!

## MERINGUE SNOWFLAKE ORNAMENTS

**2 egg whites**
**2-2/3 cups confectioners' sugar**
 **1/4 teaspoon cream of tartar**
**Pastry bag *or* heavy-duty**
   **resealable plastic bags**
**Pastry tip—#7 round**
**White craft *or* edible glitter, silver**
   **dragees *and/or* nonpareils,**
   **optional**
**Waxed paper**
**Snowflake patterns on next page**

Photocopy patterns or trace them onto paper; cut out around the patterns.

Place them on baking sheets and cover them with waxed paper; tape the waxed paper in place.

In a mixing bowl, beat egg whites, confectioners' sugar and cream of tartar on low speed for 1 minute. Beat on medium for 6-8 minutes or until very stiff. Cut a small hole in the corner of a pastry or plastic bag; insert #7 round tip. Place 1 cup meringue in bag. Press plastic wrap over the surface of unused meringue and refrigerate.

Making continuous lines and tracing the longest lines of the pattern first, pipe meringue onto waxed paper over the patterns. Sprinkle with glitter, dragees or nonpareils if desired. Let dry overnight.

Carefully peel off the waxed paper, and turn over snowflakes with flat side up. Place remaining meringue in a mixing bowl and beat until very stiff. Fill pastry or plastic bag and pipe meringue over each line of snowflake. Minor breaks can be repaired at this time.

Let snowflakes dry. When completely dry, use fishing line, ribbon or cord as a hanger. **Yield:** about 7 snowflakes (4 inches each).

Accent your holiday decor with the snowflakes or give them as gifts!

**Editor's Note:** Snowflakes should be used only as decoration.

Meringue powder may be substituted for the egg whites. Use 1 tablespoon powder with 3 tablespoons plus 1/2 teaspoon water for 2 egg whites.

Meringue powder and white edible glitter can be ordered from Wilton Industries. Call 1-800/794-5866 or check out the company's Web site at *www.wilton.com.* ♥

### Handy Hints
Follow these pointers for turning out picture-perfect snowflakes:
 • The meringue is best when it's used immediately after beating. If it begins to soften, beat the frosting until it is stiff.
 • To smooth irregularities as you pipe the meringue, use a small paintbrush dipped in water.

**MERINGUE SNOWFLAKE
ORNAMENT PATTERNS**
Photocopy or trace and cut out

**CHOCK-FULL OF CHOCOLATE.** Ann Okun (behind counter at left) and assistant Jen Michaud (below) stock shop with seasonal sweets.

# Noel Season Is the Sweetest Time of Year for Candy Maker

CHRISTMAS just isn't complete without sweets. So, as the holiday aproaches, Ann Okun devotes her days to rolling out luscious chocolate treats by the dozens.

The creamy confections are concocted in a renovated barn on the 140-year-old farm she and her husband, Peter, own in Dracut, Massachusetts.

"Starting in September, we pull out recipes I've developed and begin fashioning candy by hand, using fresh local ingredients," Ann says.

"There's no high-speed equipment used here…except for me when a customer is waiting for an order!"

Jolly gingerbread men from a nearby baker get gussied up in hand-dipped chocolate pants and hats. "While the hat is wet, it's dipped in nonpareils," Ann details. "Then we add suspenders and a belt using a squeeze bottle filled with colored chocolate."

She treats candy canes sweetly by dunking them in chocolate and nonpareils. Pretzel rods are wrapped in caramel, dipped in chocolate and rolled in chopped almonds.

Chocolate lollipops and baskets are formed in plastic molds. To give the pops pizzazz, Ann hand-paints the inside of the mold with colored chocolate before pouring in white or milk chocolate. The top pop this time of year is a reindeer with chocolate antlers, brown eyes and a red nose.

Ann bolsters her seasonal stock with mouth-watering mainstays such as turtles, peanut butter cups, coconut drops, white chocolate-covered popcorn and some 30 flavors of fudge.

Her candy-coated enterprise took shape 15 years ago when Ann molded Easter lollipops for her children, Nathan and Rachel. Her husband was so impressed, he suggested she sell them.

Nowadays, when Peter isn't taking a moment to sample her efforts, he's busy running their Christmas tree business and tending four greenhouses filled with annuals and perennials they sell each spring.

To kick off the Yuletide season, the couple hosts an open house. Visitors can sip cider and sample sweets while shopping for assorted holiday gifts, trees, wreaths and chocolates galore.

But Christmas isn't the only time crowds crave Ann's candy. "Easter is our second busiest time," she shares. "Valentine's Day, Halloween and Mother's Day also stir up sales."

Ann produces over 3,000 pounds of fudge and 2,000 pounds of assorted chocolates a year plus hundreds of holiday novelties. She also satisfies sweet tooths from all over, even as far away as New Zealand.

"It is hard work," she admits. "But having folks tell me this is the best candy they've ever tasted makes it all worthwhile!"

**Editor's Note:** *Ann's candies are available at Broken Wheel Farm, 702 Broadway Rd., Dracut MA 01826; by calling 1-888/211-7713; or on the Internet at www.bwfarm.com.* ♥

# Grandma's 'Brag' Page

**SPICE OF HER LIFE.** Janie Weverka loves having the grandkids visit her Sargent, Nebraska farm all at once. She benched the cute cousins long enough to snap them in the sweet gingerbread sweatshirts she stitched. From left are Chelsea, Michaela, Jamison, Emma, Jayden and Savannah.

**THREE'S COMPANY.** Santa's sleepy sidekicks are all sacked out, but triplets Ryan, Adam and Michael don't wear out Grandma JoAnn Akin of Frederick, Oklahoma. "They're three times the fun!"

**GOOD CHEER.** Grandkids Mackenzie and Jack were all smiles for Marjorie Murray of Bridgewater, New Jersey when she took their photo on Christmas.

**SEASON'S REASON** is played out perfectly by Kay Mickelson's costumed crew—her seven grandchildren. "Grandpa constructed the scene, manger and all, and I captured the memorable moment to use as our Yuletide card," pens the proud Kokomo, Indiana grandma.

**GLORIOUS GIFT.** The festivities caught up with 3-week-old Morgan Rae Whalthall (left). But elated Grandma Jane Smith of Rossiter, Pennsylvania won't tire of this precious present.

**PLUSH PAL.** A stuffed St. Nick lights up 5-month-old Kaitlyn's face. "She was so excited to share the chair with him," says Great-Grandma Marcella Griepentrog, Wahpeton, North Dakota.

**SEASON'S GREETINGS.** Jennie McInturff (at left with grandchildren Gracen and Hogan) dresses up the front door in holiday finery.

# She Hangs Merry Memories On Her Flock of Family Trees

A TRIMMED TREE is a tradition with most folks at Christmas. But at Jennie McInturff's, one tree just isn't enough.

Her spacious home in Fair Oaks Ranch, Texas is trimmed top to bottom in firs—13 at last count. There are trees for her daughter, Jamie, her son, Jason, and for his children, Hogan, 4, and Gracen, 2. There's even a pine for her pets.

"The tabletop tree for the dogs is one of my favorites," Jennie says. "It's filled with canine knickknacks from relatives and doggie biscuits with ribbon hangers.

"On my son's tree, I hung the little toy cars he played with as a child. And daughter Jamie's tree sports the golfing medals she won from the age of 10 through her college career."

Jennie's own personal pine is garnished with tiny shoes and purses and necklaces strung like garland.

While the trees might change places from year to year, the tall family fir is always the main attraction in the living room. It's a virtual scrapbook, covered with festively framed photos of relatives and friends.

"It started as a 2-foot tree when Jamie was in kindergarten," Jennie notes. "She's 24 now."

**Rooted in Memories**

There's even more memorabilia among her other Yuletide creations.

"For my husband, Ron, I fashioned a wreath with the ornaments he receives each year from the company he works for," she says.

Running up the railing to the second floor loft is an evergreen garland embellished with Santas, stockings, bears and other baubles.

"They're the Christmas ornaments Jason and Jamie collected during their school years," Jennie explains. "It real-

ly brings back fun memories for all of us when we see this trim."

One of her own special memories is preserved in a picture frame on the second floor.

"I framed the letter I wrote to Santa in 1959 asking for a doll," she points out. "Alongside the letter is a photo of me with that doll, which I still have. I bring her out every Christmas."

In addition to the precious pieces of family history hung all through the house, Jennie wraps each room in greenery.

"I twist lights around 9-foot garlands and add berries, blooms and bows wher-

**MERRY MEMORIES** abound throughout the McInturff house at Christmas. Jennie hangs family photos and mementos on trees, keepsake ornaments on wreaths and railings and even framed a long-ago letter to St. Nick. Evergreen garland completes the festive look.

ever my imagination might take me," she explains.

"I drape the garlands over the front entrance and on the fireplace mantels. I double up garland and wrap it around my floor lamps, adding raffia, tassels, pinecones or ornaments."

Leftover greens, ribbon, berries or birds might end up accenting a chandelier, an ivy plant, a stack of antique books or the front door wreaths.

"It's different each Christmas. I'm always trying to do something new. I'd change the wallpaper every year if I could," Jennie says with a grin.

### Christmas Clues

One thing that hasn't changed is the McInturffs' annual holiday "hunt".

"Ron and I started this tradition when the children were young and we needed time to bring out a big present like a bike or a computer," Jennie says.

"The kids would open a box and find a note telling them to look in the garage, the mailbox or even at a neighbor's house, where they'd receive another clue. They would continue the search until they found the gift, usually in a bedroom or back under the tree.

"Every year I hint that we might not have the hunt because the kids are too old, but they wouldn't think it was Christmas if we didn't!"

The holiday hunt also makes wonderful memories, the kind Jennie likes to preserve on trees, in frames and just about anywhere else she can think of.

"I had such wonderful Christmases when I was a child," she says. "I want to continue that feeling for my children and grandchildren…and decorating makes it all the more enjoyable." ♥

## I'll Never Forget...

# Papa's Handmade Skis Made My Christmas the Best Ever

*By Marvel Stephen of Cottage Grove, Oregon*

THE YEAR Papa decided I should learn to ski, deep snows covered the land, the buildings, even the towering trees on our small farm.

Our rustic house was bursting with excitement and activity. Christmas was only a few weeks away, and there was much to do before aunts, uncles and cousins filled our home for the annual holiday celebration.

December's early sunsets urged us to finish our chores and supper fast so we could get to work on our Christmas gifts. Having recently mastered the art of making French knots, I chose to embroider dish towels cut from flour sacks. Mother was tatting lovely lace to trim her presents, and Papa was creating a pair of skis for me.

Working close together in our cozy kitchen made it impossible not to be aware of what each other was making—but we were clever at pretending we didn't know.

No one mentioned anything about Papa crafting skis for me, but I knew that's what he was doing.

### Big Buildup

One day, he came home with two long boards tied to the side of our car. He spent the next few evenings sketching the shape of the front ends of the skis onto the boards.

When he was satisfied with the shape, he cut away the excess lumber with hand tools, rounded the edges, sanded the surfaces and made small corrections to the pointed ends.

My excitement soared as I watched him soak the ends in the large boiler Mother used to heat water for the laundry. After soaking and steaming the wood for several days, the skis were placed in braces to draw the softened ends up in a graceful curve. In between additional soakings and steamings, Papa tightened the braces.

To make the leather straps that would fit over my boots, he cut the tops off a pair of his old work shoes, then cut each top into two pieces and fastened them

securely to the sides of each wooden ski.

With the braces in place, Papa propped the skis against the wall behind the kitchen stove, where I could admire them daily. I imagined myself flying down the hill near our house as if I had wings.

Finally, Christmas Eve arrived. Mother and I rushed to finish washing up the supper dishes, while Papa removed the skis from their braces and placed them behind the fragrant fir tree we'd cut down and brought home to decorate.

With more than his usual enthusiasm, Papa passed out the gifts from beneath the tree, and we all shared the joy as each package was opened.

After all the presents were distributed, Papa appeared ready to relax. Then suddenly, he "remembered" those carefully crafted strips of wood behind the Christmas tree.

I beamed as he gently placed the skis on my lap. If the tips didn't look quite as curved as I thought they had been, I still believed they were the most beautiful things on earth.

"We'll try them out on the hill tomorrow," Papa promised.

### Practice Run

Christmas Day dawned bright and sunny. Snow mounded around the house, and winter birds flitted about in search of food.

We trudged through drifts to the hill above the slough. If Papa noticed the diminishing curves on the tips of the skis he had tucked under his arm, he didn't say anything.

When we reached the top, he rubbed an extra coat of wax on the skis, then secured my boots under the leather straps.

"Ready, Chicky? Fly like an angel," directed Papa with a smile.

"Ready," I replied and took my first hesitant steps on the skis. I slipped over the edge, then gathered speed until I felt like I was soaring over the snow...but not for long.

Those tips *had* straightened out. The

points of the skis, no longer curved, pierced a slight snowdrift halfway down the hill, and I tumbled head over galoshes. I giggled as I carved a body-size path all the way down to the slough.

At first, Papa laughed, too. Then he became serious.

"I'm sorry about the skis, Chicky. I'll make you another pair," he apologized.

"Oh, Papa," I sighed. "This is the best Christmas I've ever had."

I wanted to say more as I put my small mittened hand in his large gloved one, but I couldn't find the words to tell him he'd already given me the greatest gift of all...his love. ♥

# Colorful Christmas Crop Spruces Up the Holly-days

**HEAPS OF HOLLY.** Linda Morrelli (above left) and Nonnie Hotchkiss (below) help out with the annual holly harvest. Nonnie's husband, Burt, designed a slide-along frame and bag to ease the prickly process. Linda's husband, Frank, selects the best of what they prune to sell as boughs or fashion into wreaths.

WHEN you live in Holley, Oregon, decking halls with boughs of holly is only natural. And Nonnie Hotchkiss has plenty of the prickly greenery to assure a *berry* merry Christmas.

Nonnie and her husband, Burt, tend 5 to 6 acres of English holly bushes on their 40-acre farm. "English or standard green holly is the variety that is ready early enough to harvest for Christmas," she explains.

The mail-order venture they run with longtime friends Linda and Frank Morrelli ships boughs and handmade holly wreaths to customers across the country and as far away as India.

"Initially, Burt and I bought 1,000 holly bushes...and then we waited," Nonnie details.

"After a few years, the bushes can be pruned and shaped. But it takes 10 years, when the plant has grown 8 to 12 feet tall, before serious harvesting can begin."

When their Web site sprouted in 1997, the first order was for a whopping 85 boxes of boughs.

"That first year, Burt proved to be the best at harvesting," Nonnie recalls.

"I fashioned the greeting cards and care notes that accompanied the orders and helped with Web page design. Frank was meticulous about selecting and packaging the boughs. And Linda handled the shipping, banking and bookkeeping with ease.

"Greg Downs, who runs the 9-hole golf course on our property, and Mary Bate, another friend, showed a real knack for wreath making."

The circle of pals gets firmly planted in their roles just after Thanksgiving. First the prickly holly is cut, using pruning clippers and a good pair of gloves. Stilts or a three-legged ladder come in handy for taller bushes.

"To preserve freshness, we dip the holly sprigs in a fixative solution," Nonnie notes. "Then we get them ready for shipping."

The Hotchkisses' horse barn houses the growing business. There, wreaths are carefully shaped and trimmed with berries and bows, and boxes are filled with boughs. Linda prepares the boxes for mailing before stacking them in a room kept at 34° to wait for delivery.

"Customers use our holly boughs and wreaths to decorate mantels, mirrors and tables, to accent centerpieces or embellish Yuletide presents," describes Nonnie. "Some like to dress up mailboxes with holly or decorate the back window of their cars."

The Christmas rush lasts only about 3 weeks, but it's an intense period, Nonnie says. "And, as soon as it's over, we start talking about what we can do to

make it even better next year."

**Editor's Note:** *For more information, write to Holley Holly, P.O. Box 264, Sweet Home OR 97386, call toll-free (888) 652-9297 or visit their Web site at www.christmasholly.com.*

# Her Jolly Bottle Santas Pour on Plenty of Charm!

THERE'S no keeping Susan Blomenberg's Christmas spirit bottled up. Her enthusiasm for the holiday spills out year-round, filling this Nebraska crafter's workshop with sacks full of Santas.

"I have them everywhere," says Susan, who lives with her husband, John, in a restored turn-of-the century home outside the small town of Seward. "I've always adored Santa, mainly because of my father. He loved the magical story of St. Nick."

To mold her merry old souls, Susan relies on papier-mache. At first, she shaped her figures around Styrofoam cones, then switched to colorful bottles.

"I had plenty of bottles on hand, so instead of tossing them out, I began to use them as bases. Plus, the bottles are stronger and more stable than the foam cones," she explains.

"Now, when I go to the grocery store, I often find myself looking at the shape of the bottle rather than what's in it! Mainly I use soda pop, soy sauce and vinegar bottles.

"I find inspiration in these containers, too. They help determine what a Santa will look like. Plain bottles get completely covered with papier-mache robes, while more colorful versions peek out from under open cloaks and actually become part of the clothing."

Susan models expressive faces from clay and adds textured papier-mache beards. She uses wire and foil to form hats and arms, then covers those with papier-mache. Most of her festive fellows stand about 15 inches tall.

Once a character is created, she lets it dry for about 2 weeks before brushing on color with acrylic paints. Finally, each crafty Claus gets two protective coats of varnish.

"No two St. Nicks are alike. Some carry American flags, others hold a wreath or a string of lights," says Susan. "My country Santas tote wood, apples and oranges. But most are dressed in red and haul a bag of toys or gifts."

On request, Susan adds personal touches to the jolly gents. For an artist friend, she designed a Santa carrying a brush and a bag of paints. Some folks even provide a bottle that holds precious memories to form a figure around.

Although she pours many hours into those bottles, Susan considers making Santas a hobby and works full-time.

"Building my Christmas characters is a great way to get away from work stress," she shares. "It is so rewarding to create something out of nothing and to make people smile."

**Editor's Note:** *Contact Susan for more information on her Santas at Blomenberg Studio, 1627 336th Rd., Seward NE 68434-7849; 1-402/643-4838. Or you can send Susan an E-mail at sm02308@navix.net.* ♥

**TOUCH OF GLASS.** Susan Blomenberg (at top) adds a splash of fun to Christmas with papier-mache Santas she shapes around bottles.

# Merry Miniature Ornaments Trim the Season with Smiles

JACKIE HASKELL'S holiday designs might be small in size…but they are big on charm. In fact, the tiny clay ornaments she shapes are widely appreciated in and around her Jamestown, North Dakota home.

The trims elicit a little questioning, too. "People always ask, 'How do you make them so small? Do you use a magnifying glass?'" says Jackie. "Sometimes a magnifying glass wouldn't be such a bad idea, especially when I'm working long hours!

"I craft a variety of Yuletide characters and scenes, including Nativities, Santas, reindeer and elves. They are the right height for hanging on a table-top Christmas tree or perching in a printer's box," details the self-taught crafter.

She also shapes decorations for Thanksgiving, Easter and Halloween as well as birdhouses, flowers and animals, including her tallest, a 3-inch giraffe.

Jackie cooks up her miniature menagerie with just a few tools—a ruler, straight pin, pair of scissors, oven-proof plate and a pasta maker—to produce even strips of clay.

"I don't use molds, except to make gingerbread men, hearts and stars," she says. "Each part of a figure starts as a ball of polymer clay. Once I've formed the pieces, they are pressed together and shaped until I like the overall look.

"I usually make 10 to 20 of the same design at once. Since the clay can be 'fired' in the oven, I bake them on a plate. When they're cool, I add feathers, yarn, curly hair, bells, glitter and other embellishments.

"To get just the right color, I combine different shades of clay, mixing them to get the desired hue," Jackie adds. "There is no painting involved, unless I brush letters on a clay sign or freckles on my little people."

Ideas for her wee whimsies just pop into her head, she says. "Many come from my rural upbringing. I love to make miniatures with a country touch."

The fun starts to multiply as she gets ready for fall craft shows. "That's when my family pitches in," Jackie says.

"My husband, Clark, builds displays for the shows, while son Colton, 7, tries his hand at clay crafting. My mother and oldest son Chase, 10, come and work at the events.

"Our youngest son, Jaden, 2, just likes to get hold of whatever's in sight. Maybe someday he can make a small contribution, too!"

**Editor's Note:** *For details on Jackie's designs, write to JH Miniatures, 515 2nd St. NE, Jamestown ND 58401. Or visit her Web site at www.jhminiatures.com.* ♥

**TINY BAUBLES.** In the hands of Jackie Haskell (at top right), small balls of brightly colored clay shape up into merry miniatures perfect for wee trees and printer's boxes. From angels and bears to a Nativity, teeny trims make a big impression at craft shows.

# Santa Claus and His Perky Elf Deliver Miles of Smiles

WANT to work a little elfin magic around your home for the holidays? Give this jolly St. Nick and his sprightly sidekick a try. They'll add Christmas character anywhere you put them!

"My trims add a festive touch to doorknobs, trees and even gifts," says Janet Best of Dover, Tennessee. And with Janet's easy, no-sew instructions, you'll have the delightful duo spreading good cheer in a flash.

## Materials Needed (for both):
*Patterns at right and on next page*
*Tracing paper and pencil*
*Felt—3-inch x 8-inch piece each of green and red, 4-inch square of white, 3-inch x 4-inch piece of flesh for Santa and 3-inch x 6-inch piece of flesh for elf*
*24 inches of 1/2-inch-wide pre-gathered white eyelet trim for Santa*
*24 inches of 1/2-inch-wide pre-gathered white lace trim for elf*
*24 inches of 1/4-inch-wide red satin ribbon*
*Two 3-inch x 4-inch pieces of lightweight cardboard*
*Glue gun and glue stick*
*Powdered cosmetic blush*
*Cotton swab*
*3/8-inch buttons—two blue buttons for Santa's eyes, two gray buttons for elf's eyes and two white buttons for tips of hats*
*Scissors*

**Finished Size:** Each trim measures about 4-1/2 inches across x 6-3/4 inches high without hanger.

## Directions:
Trace patterns onto tracing paper as directed on patterns. Cut out patterns on traced lines.

Trace around patterns onto felt and cardboard as directed on patterns. Cut out each shape just inside traced lines.

Glue a felt face onto one side of each piece of cardboard with edges matching.

Starting at bottom and following dashed lines on pattern, glue four rows of eyelet trim onto Santa's face for beard. Trim excess as needed. In same way, glue lace trim to elf's face.

Glue hat trim centered across top of each face, covering ends of trim along top edge of face.

Apply a thin bead of glue to edge of each hat where shown on pattern. Glue red hat along top edge of cardboard on back of Santa's face and green hat along top edge of cardboard on back of elf's face. Apply glue to hat at dot on pattern. Fold hat to front and glue hat to

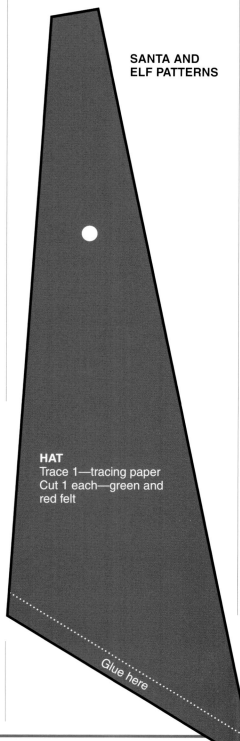

SANTA AND ELF PATTERNS

HAT
Trace 1—tracing paper
Cut 1 each—green and red felt

Glue here

hat trim to hold.

Cut ribbon into two 12-in. lengths. Glue ends of one piece to back of Santa at sides of hat for hanger. Repeat with other piece to make hanger for elf.

Glue blue buttons to Santa's face and gray buttons to elf's face for eyes. Glue a white button to tip of each hat.

Fold each ear along dashed line on pattern and spot-glue at dots. With folded edges toward face, glue ears to elf where shown on pattern.

Place a small amount of cosmetic blush onto cotton swab and add to cheek area, using a circular motion.

Hang in your home for the holidays!

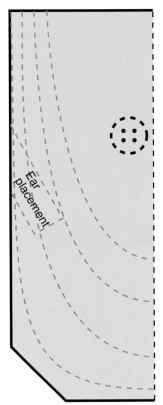

Ear placement

Trace, flop and repeat for complete pattern

**FACE**
Trace 1—tracing paper
Cut 2—flesh felt
Cut 2—lightweight cardboard

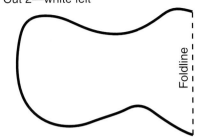

**HAT TRIM**
Trace 1—folded tracing paper
Cut 2—white felt

Foldline

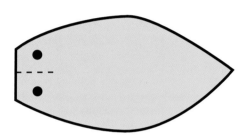

**EAR**
Trace 1—tracing paper
Cut 2—flesh felt

# Bell Trim Winds Up in a Jiffy

CLEVER crafter Patricia Klesh of Martinsville, New Jersey wound up with this coiled ornament after recycling the white spiral wire from an old calendar. It's so easy even pint-size crafters will have fun making it—so let the good "chimes" roll!

**Materials Needed:**
*White spiral wire approximately 10 inches long from discarded calendar or notebook*
*One red pipe cleaner (chenille stem)*
*1-inch gold liberty bell*
*Red satin ribbon—16 inches of 1/8-inch-wide and 12 inches of 1/4-inch-wide*
*Small artificial holly leaves, red berries and tiny pinecones*
*White acrylic craft paint and small paintbrush*
*Glue gun and glue stick*
*Craft scissors*

**Finished Size:** Spiral bell trim measures about 5 inches across x 7-1/2 inches long including hanger.

**Directions:**
Lightly paint tips of scales on pinecones white. Let dry.

Thread pipe cleaner through spiral wire. Cut off excess pipe cleaner.

Hook ends of wire together and form into a teardrop shape as shown in photo.

Thread 1/8-in.-wide ribbon through top of bell. Keeping ends of ribbon even, tie a knot about 1-1/2 in. from top of bell. Then thread ends of ribbon through top of wire where joined and knot again. Tie another knot about 3 in. from top of wire for hanging loop. Cut away excess ribbon.

Glue the holly leaves, berries and pinecones to center top of the wire as shown in photo.

Tie remaining ribbon in a bow. Glue bow to top of ornament. Trim ends of ribbon to desired length. ♥

# Baby's Cuddly and Cute In Pint-Sized Santa Suit

COLD winds may blow, but Santa's little helper will stay toasty warm in this snugly knit suit!

Helle Hill of Thornton, Colorado lent a fluffy feel to the jacket, pants and hat by using textured yarn on the cuffs and trim. "Experienced knitters will really have fun stitching this one," she assures.

## Materials Needed:

*4-ply worsted-weight yarn—two 8-ounce skeins of red and one 3-ounce skein of black (Helle used Red Heart Super Saver yarn in Hot Red and Black)*

*White textured bulky weight yarn—one 6-ounce skein (Helle used Red Heart Baby Clouds yarn in Cloud #9113—white)*
*Knitting needles—set of double-pointed size 4, set of double-pointed size 6 and circular size 6 or size needles needed to obtain correct gauge*
*Three stitch holders*
*Eight stitch markers*
*Tapestry needle*
*Six large snap fasteners*
*All-purpose thread—black, red and white*
*Hand-sewing needle*
*6-inch square of cardboard*
*Scissors*

**Gauge:** When working in St st on size 6 needles, 18 sts and 28 rows = 4 inches.

**Finished Size:** Jacket chest measurement is about 20 inches around. Back length of jacket measures about 13-1/2 inches. Waist on pants measures about 17 inches and length from waist to heel is about 15 inches. Hat circumference measures about 18 inches.

## KNITTING REMINDERS:

**Changing colors:** To avoid holes when changing colors, always pick up new color of yarn from beneath dropped yarn.

**Working in rounds:** Place sts evenly on three dp needles. Place a marker between sts at beginning of round and move marker with each round worked. Being careful not to twist sts, join last st to first st by pulling up yarn firmly and making first st with fourth needle.

**Stockinette stitch:** St st
  **Row 1 (WS):** Purl across row.
  **Row 2 (RS):** Knit across row.
  Repeat Rows 1 and 2.
**Ribbing:**
  **Every Round:** K 1, p 1.

## Directions:

**PANTS:** With red yarn, cast on 90 sts onto smaller dp needles.
  Working in rounds, work in k 1, p 1

ribbing until the piece measures about 1 in.: 90 sts.

Change to larger dp needles, working in rounds, k all sts until piece measures about 7 in. or desired length from waist to crotch: 90 sts.

K 40, bind off 5 sts for front of crotch, k 40, bind off 5 sts for back of crotch. Place last 40 sts on stitch holder. Separate the remaining 40 sts onto three dp needles for leg. Add stitch marker.

**Leg:** Working in rounds, k all sts on needles until leg is about 4 in. long (adjust length of leg here as needed, keeping in mind that the white trim and boot will add approximately 5 in. to the length of the leg): 40 sts. Fasten off.

**White trim:** With white yarn, * k 3, k 2 tog; repeat from * around: 32 sts.

Working in rounds, k all sts until white trim measures about 1 in.: 32 sts. Fasten off.

**Boot: Rounds 1-16:** With black yarn, k all sts around: 32 sts.

**HEEL: Row 1:** K 16, making sure these sts are centered on back side of leg, turn, keeping remaining 16 sts on two other needles and working in rows.

  **Row 2:** P 15, turn.
  **Row 3:** K 14, turn.
  **Row 4:** P 13, turn.
  **Row 5:** K 12, turn.
  **Row 6:** P 11, turn.
  **Row 7:** K 10, turn.
  **Row 8:** P 9, turn.
  **Row 9:** K 8, turn.
  **Row 10:** P 7, turn.
  **Row 11:** K 7, pick up a new st from previous row, k 2 tog, turn.
  **Row 12:** P 8, pick up a new st from previous row, p 2 tog, turn.
  **Row 13:** K 9 and continue as in Row 11.
  **Row 14:** P 10 and continue as in Row 12
  **Row 15:** K 11 and continue as in Row 11.
  **Row 16:** P 12 and continue as in Row 12.
  **Row 17:** K 13 and continue as in Row 11.
  **Row 18:** P 14 and continue as in Row 12.
  **Row 19:** K 15 and continue as in Row 11.
  **Row 20:** P 16 and continue as in Row 12.

  **Round 1:** Working in rounds, k 17, pick up a new st from previous row, k 2 tog, k 14, pick up a new st from previous row, k 2 tog: 32 sts.
  **Rounds 2-17:** K all sts: 32 sts.
  **Round 18:** K 2, k 2 tog around: 24 sts.
  **Round 19:** K all sts: 24 sts.
  **Round 20:** K 1, k 2 tog around: 16 sts.
  **Rounds 21-22:** K 2 tog around. Cut

yarn at end of Round 21, leaving a tail of yarn. Run yarn through sts when working Round 22. Draw up yarn tightly and fasten off.

For second leg, pick up sts from stitch holder. Attach red yarn and work as before except at Row 1 of heel k until end of row, turn and work heel as before, making sure heel sts are centered on back side of leg so both heels will face in the same direction.

Use tapestry needle and matching yarn to sew crotch seam together and to weave in all loose ends.

**JACKET: SLEEVES (make two):** With white yarn and larger dp needles, cast on 24 sts.

Working in rounds, k all sts until piece measures about 1-1/2 in. Fasten off.

With red yarn, k all sts while inc 16 sts evenly around: 40 sts.

Working in rounds, k all sts until piece measures about 8 in. or desired length to underarm: 40 sts.

**Arm shaping: Row 1:** Bind off first 2 sts, k 38: 38 sts.

**Row 2:** Bind off first 2 sts, p 36: 36 sts.
**Row 3:** Bind off first 2 sts, k 34: 34 sts.
**Row 4:** Bind off first 2 sts, p 32: 32 sts. Place remaining sts on stitch holder. Repeat for second sleeve.

**BACK:** With white yarn and larger needles, cast on 40 sts.

**Rows 1-5:** Work in St st: 40 sts. Fasten off yarn at end of Row 5.

**Row 6:** With red yarn, k 2, inc 1, * k 4, inc 1; repeat from * across row until last 2 sts, k 2: 50 sts.

**Rows 7-41:** Work in St st.

**Row 42:** K 4, k 2 tog, * k 8, k 2 tog; repeat from * until last 4 sts, k 4. Drop red yarn: 45 sts.

**Rows 43-48:** With black yarn, work in St st. Fasten off black yarn at end of Row 48: 45 sts.

**Row 49:** With red yarn, p across row: 45 sts.

**Row 50:** K 5, inc 1, * k 9, inc 1; repeat from * across row to last 4 sts, k 4: 50 sts.

**Rows 51-59:** Work in St st: 50 sts.
**Row 60:** Bind off 3 sts, k remaining sts: 47 sts.

**Row 61:** Bind off 3 sts, p remaining sts: 44 sts.

**Row 62:** Bind off 2 sts, k remaining sts: 42 sts.

**Row 63:** Bind off 2 sts, p remaining sts: 40 sts.

Place sts on stitch holder.

**FRONT: Right Front:** With white yarn and larger needles, cast on 24 sts.

**Rows 1-5:** Work in St st: 24 sts. Fasten off yarn at end of Row 5.

**Row 6:** With red yarn, [k 4, inc 1] five times across to last 4 sts, k 4: 29 sts.

**Row 7:** P 23, [k 1, p 1] three times: 29 sts.

**Rows 8-41:** K the k sts and p the p sts: 29 sts.

**Row 42:** [K 1, p 1] three times, * k 4, k 2 tog; repeat from * across to last 5 sts, k 5. Drop red yarn: 26 sts.

**Rows 43-48:** With black yarn, work in St st. Fasten off black yarn at end of Row 48: 26 sts.

**Row 49:** With red yarn, p across row: 26 sts.

**Row 50:** [K 1, p 1] three times, [k 5, inc 1] three times, k 5: 29 sts.

**Rows 51-60:** K the k sts and p the p sts: 29 sts.

**Row 61:** Bind off 3 sts, p across row until last 6 sts, [k 1, p 1] three times: 26 sts.

**Row 62:** K the k sts and p the p sts: 26 sts.

**Row 63:** Bind off 2 sts, p across row until last 6 sts, [k 1, p 1] three times. Place 24 sts on stitch holder. Fasten off.

**Left Front:** With white yarn and larger needles, cast on 24 sts.

**Rows 1- 5:** Work in St st: 24 sts. Fasten off yarn at end of Row 5.

**Row 6:** With red yarn, [k 4, inc 1] four times, k 4, pick up white yarn and k last 4 sts: 28 sts.

**Rows 7-41:** Work in St st, working the last 4 sts on all even rows and the first 4 sts on all odd rows with white yarn.

**Row 42:** K 6, k 2 tog, [k 4, k 2 tog] twice, k 4, with white yarn k last 4 sts. Drop white yarn: 25 sts.

**Row 43:** With black yarn, p 1, p 2 tog, p across row: 24 sts.

**Rows 44-48:** Work even in St st. Fasten off black yarn at end of Row 48: 24 sts.

**Row 49:** With white yarn, p 2, [p 2 tog] twice, with red yarn p across row: 22 sts.

**Row 50:** K 6, inc 1, [k 5, inc 1] twice, k 5, with white yarn k 4: 25 sts.

**Rows 51-63:** Work in St st, keeping in color pattern and binding off first 3 sts of Row 60, and first 2 sts of Row 62. Fasten off yarn at end of Row 63. Place 20 sts on stitch holder.

With right sides facing, place pieces from left to right onto circular needle in the following order: left front, sleeve, back, sleeve, right front. Use stitch markers to mark the last and first sts of each piece as they are added. Do not mark outside sts. Continue to work in rows: 148 sts.

**Rows 64-65:** K the k sts and p the p sts, keeping front band in white and other pieces in red as before: 148 sts.

**Rows 66-89:** Working in established pattern, k the k sts and p the p sts, while k 2 tog before and after marked sts on all even rows: 52 sts at end of Row 89.

**Row 90:** K 1, p 1, [k 2 tog] twice, k remaining sts. Fasten off red yarn: 50 sts.

**Row 91:** With white yarn, p across row.

**Rows 92-93:** Work in St st.

**Row 94:** Bind off all sts in k. Fasten off white yarn.

Use tapestry needle to weave in all loose ends. Sew underarm seams with right sides together using a narrow seam and matching yarn.

Use matching thread and hand-sewing needle to sew snaps evenly spaced down wrong side of white front band and onto right side of left front band.

**HAT:** With white yarn, cast on 60 sts onto larger dp needles.

**Rounds 1-6:** K around. Fasten off white yarn at end of Round 6.

**Round 7:** With red yarn, k 2, inc 1, * k 4, inc 1; repeat from * to last 2 sts, k 2: 75 sts.

**Rounds 8-30:** K around: 75 sts.

**Round 31:** * K 3, k 2 tog; repeat from * around: 60 sts.

**Round 32:** K around: 60 sts.

**Rounds 33 and 35:** * K 2, k 2 tog; repeat from * around.

**Rounds 34 and 36:** K around.

* K 2 tog; repeat from * around until 6 sts remain. Cut yarn, leaving a tail of yarn. Run yarn through remaining sts. Remove sts from needle, draw up yarn tightly and fasten off.

Use tapestry needle to weave in all loose ends.

**Pom-pom:** Wrap cardboard piece with about 3 yards of white yarn. Slip yarn from cardboard, leaving yarn looped. Tie another piece of white yarn centered across all the loops. Cut loops open. Shake to fluff pom-pom. Use tapestry needle to hand-sew pom-pom to top of hat. Trim ends as needed.

Dress up your favorite little fellow in this merry suit! ♥

---

### ABBREVIATIONS

| | |
|---|---|
| dp | double-pointed |
| inc | increase |
| k | knit |
| p | purl |
| RS | right side |
| st(s) | stitch(es) |
| tog | together |
| WS | wrong side |
| * [ ] | Instructions following asterisk or within brackets are repeated as directed. |

# Cheery Stenciled Vest Covers Christmas in Festive Fashion

YOU'LL have a holly-jolly Christmas in this stenciled Yuletide vest! Joanne Bembry of Jasper, Florida stenciled green holly leaves and red berries along the edges of the casual cover-up, which pairs nicely with a bright turtleneck.

Don it for a festive celebration or work it into your weekly wardrobe. However you choose to use it, this vest will spread cheer year after year!

## Materials Needed:
*Pattern below*
*Commercial lined vest pattern with straight front and bottom edges*
*100% cotton or cotton-blend fabrics—white-on-white print for outside of vest and coordinating solid or print for lining in amounts required for pattern*
*Matching all-purpose thread*
*Iron-on fleece—amount required for two vest fronts*
*Gold metallic thread*
*Stencil plastic or freezer paper*
*Permanent fine-line marker*
*Stencil cutter or X-Acto knife*
*Acrylic fabric paints (or acrylic craft paints and fabric medium)—green and red*

*Stencil brush or small piece of household sponge*
*Paper plate or palette*
*Paper towels*
*Waxed paper*
*Transparent tape*
*Quilter's ruler*
*Quilter's marking pen or pencil*
*1/4-inch round paper punch*
*Standard sewing supplies*

**Finished Size:** Size will vary depending on size of garment and number of design repeats used.

## Directions:
Trace pattern as shown onto corner of stencil plastic or freezer paper with permanent marker.

Cut out holly leaves and alignment points on traced lines with stencil cutter or X-Acto knife. Use paper punch to cut out holly berries.

Pre-wash fabrics using detergents without fabric softeners or built-in stain resistors, washing each color separately. If the water is discolored, wash again until the rinse water runs clear. Dry and

press the fabrics.

Cut out vest pieces as instructed in pattern.

Place stencil pattern on right side of one lower vest front corner with holly leaves positioned as shown in photo. Position dashed lines of pattern on seamlines of vest. Use quilter's marking pen or pencil to mark alignment points.

Reposition pattern so only two leaves and the berries are on the bottom of vest front. Mark alignment points. Continue to reposition stencil pattern and mark alignment points along center front of vest front.

Repeat on right side of remaining vest front, making a mirror image of the design.

**STENCILING:** Cover flat work surface with waxed paper. Place a vest front right side up on covered surface. Tape stencil pattern in place, matching first set of alignment marks.

Place small amounts of each paint on paper plate or palette as needed. If necessary, mix paints with fabric medium prior to use.

Dip the stencil brush or sponge into green paint and wipe off excess on paper towel until it is almost dry. Apply paint in an up-and-down motion in cutout areas of holly leaves. Carefully remove the stencil. Holly berries will be stenciled later.

Clean stencil and tape it to vest, matching second set of alignment marks. Stencil this set of holly leaves as before. Continue the stenciling process until holly leaf design is complete on both vest fronts. Let dry.

Clean stencil and tape it to right side of a vest front, positioning the berry portion of the design as desired. Stencil berries red.

Continue stenciling process, adding number of berries desired. Repeat on other vest front, making a mirror image. Let dry.

Set paints as directed by manufacturer's instructions.

## STENCILED HOLLY CHRISTMAS VEST PATTERN
Trace 1—stencil plastic or freezer paper
Cut out and stencil as directed
▲ = alignment points

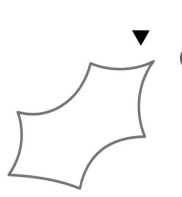

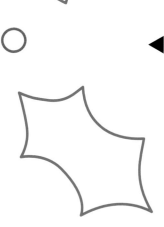

From iron-on fleece, cut two front vest pieces, reversing one. Apply iron-on fleece to wrong side of vest fronts following manufacturer's instructions.

Follow pattern directions to construct the vest.

**QUILTING:** Use quilter's ruler and quilter's marking pen or pencil to mark quilting lines about 2-1/2 in. from center front and bottom edge of vest fronts. Machine-stitch on these lines using gold metallic thread in the needle and thread to match lining in bobbin.

In same way, mark quilting lines parallel to front edge, spacing them about 1-1/2 in. apart. Machine-stitch on these lines with matching thread.

Pull all loose threads to inside of vest and fasten off.

Wear your vest for any festive occasion—and enjoy! ♥

# Knit Stocking Cap Heads Off Old Man Winter

FOLKS of all ages will appreciate this head warmer! "It's a one-size-fits-most kind of cap," details Amy Albert Bloom of Shillington, Pennsylvania.

"The cap is nice and stretchy, which makes it suitable for almost any size. And, thanks to the seam that runs up the back, I've taken it in to make the cap smaller, too," she adds. "The design is especially nice for crafters who have done some knitting before."

**Materials Needed:**
*4-ply worsted-weight yarn—two 3-ounce skeins each of green and white*
*Size 8 knitting needles or size needed to obtain correct gauge*
*Size H (5mm) crochet hook*
*Tapestry needle*
*6-inch square of cardboard for winding pom-pom*
*Scissors*

**Finished Size:** Stocking cap is about 27 inches long with pom-pom.

**Gauge:** Working in St st, 16 sts and 24 rows = 4 inches.

**Stitches Used/General Instructions:**
**STOCKINETTE STITCH: St st**
    **Row 1 (RS):** K across row.
    **Row 2 (WS):** P across row.
    Repeat rows 1 and 2 as directed, changing colors as instructed and leaving a 10-in. tail of yarn at the end of each color change to use later to sew seam of cap.

**Directions:**
**STOCKING CAP:** Make a provisional cast-on by using crochet hook and white yarn to make 91 chains (loop on hook does not count as a chain). Cut yarn and pull a tail of yarn through the final loop on hook.

With green yarn and knitting needle, pick up 90 sts in back loop only of each chain, starting with back loop of first chain made and leaving last chain made unused.

Work in St st for 6-1/2 in., ending with a WS row. Fasten off, leaving a 15-in. tail of yarn.

Change to white yarn and work in St st for 2 in., ending with a RS row. Fasten off. Fold cast-on edge to wrong side for hem, bringing provisional cast-on row to needle.

Change to green yarn. Pull back loop of final chain of cast-on to ravel cast-on chain, leaving a green loop free. Pick up and purl free loop and first loop of row on needle as one. Continue in this way across row, forming the hem.

Work in St st for 1-1/2 in., ending with a WS row. Fasten off.

In same way, work a band of white yarn, green yarn and then white yarn. Fasten off.

Change to green yarn. * K 1, k 2 tog; repeat from * across row. Work in St st for 1-1/2 in., ending with a WS row. Fasten off.

In same way, work a band of white yarn, green yarn, white yarn and then green yarn. Fasten off.

Change to white yarn. Work in St st for 2 in.

Run yarn through sts remaining on needle. Draw up yarn tightly.

Fold stocking cap with right sides together, matching ends of rows. Thread needle with white yarn and sew seam of last white band. Sew remainder of back seam, using matching tails of yarn. Tuck seam to inside of hem and stitch seam with green yarn.

**POM-POM:** Working with a green strand and a white strand of yarn as one, wind yarn around 6-in. piece of cardboard 50 times. Cut yarn at opposite edges of cardboard to make yarn pieces 6 in. long. Tie a 24-in. piece of yarn tightly around center of stack.

Make another stack of yarn in the same way.

Place second stack of yarn on top of

first stack. Tie the two stacks of yarn together tightly.

Holding long ends of yarn, shake the pom-pom to fluff yarns. Use scissors to trim ends and make a ball measuring about 5 in. across. Do not cut long yarn ends.

Thread long yarn ends onto tapestry needle and sew pom-pom to tip of hat. Fasten off and trim excess yarn.

Keep someone special warm with this nifty knit cap! ♥

---

### ABBREVIATIONS

| | |
|---|---|
| k | knit |
| p | purl |
| RS | right side |
| st(s) | stitch(es) |
| tog | together |
| WS | wrong side |
| * | Instructions following asterisk are repeated as directed. |

# 'Endeering' Critter Will Rein in Grins

ANYONE would be amused to find this clever Christmas critter under the tree. Pat Reid of Newcastle, Oklahoma crafted her soft-sculpture Rudolph from felt and velour, then dolled him up holiday-style in a bell-trimmed vest and red scarf.

The lanky animal's suited to sit on a shelf, windowsill or package, thanks to the uncooked rice Pat added to his stuffing. Wherever you tuck him, he's sure to corral some festive fun!

### Materials Needed:
*Patterns on next page*
*Tracing paper and pencil*
*10-inch x 18-inch piece of tan velour fabric*
*9-inch x 12-inch piece or scraps of brown felt for hooves, antlers and hair of reindeer*
*4-inch x 10-inch piece of green and white print fabric for vest*
*2-inch x 12-inch piece of red and white print fabric for scarf*
*Matching all-purpose thread*
*Black six-strand embroidery floss*
*Needles—embroidery and hand-sewing*
*Two 10mm glue-on wiggle eyes*
*1/2-inch red pom-pom for nose*
*Three 9mm gold jingle bells*
*One 1/2-inch red pom-pom*
*1/2 cup of uncooked rice or plastic doll pellets*
*Polyester stuffing*
*White (tacky) glue*
*Powdered cosmetic blush*
*Cotton swab*
*Standard sewing supplies*

**Finished Size:** Soft-sculpture reindeer measures about 4 inches across x 16 inches tall.

### Directions:
Trace patterns onto tracing paper as directed on patterns. Cut out. Open folded patterns for complete patterns.

From tan velour, cut two 2-in. x 9-in. pieces for the front legs and two 2-in. x 10-in. pieces for the back legs. Then cut pattern pieces from fabrics as directed on patterns.

Sew all seams with right sides of fabrics together and edges of fabric matching, using matching thread and 1/4-in. seams unless instructions state otherwise.

Fold each leg lengthwise with right sides together. Then sew long edges of each together to make a tube. Turn each right side out through opening at one end. Center seam along length of each tube.

Pin one end of each front and back leg with raw edges matching to right side of one body piece where shown on pattern. Pin other body piece on top with edges matching and legs sandwiched between layers.

Sew body pieces together, catching ends of legs in stitching and leaving opening for turning where indicated on pattern. Clip curves and turn right side out through opening.

Pour uncooked rice or plastic doll pellets into bottom of the body. Stuff remainder of body with stuffing and set aside.

Sew two head pieces together, leaving opening for turning where indicated on pattern. Clip curves. Turn right side out and stuff head.

Thread hand-sewing needle with a double strand of matching thread and sew around opening with a running stitch. See Fig. 1 for stitch illustration. Pull threads to gather neck edge slightly.

Place head on top of body and hand-sew head to body, tucking all raw edges in.

Sew a pair of ears together, leaving opening where indicated on pattern. Turn ear right side out through opening. Turn raw edge in and hand-sew opening closed, leaving thread attached. Pull thread to gather edge slightly. Hand-sew ear to head where indicated on pattern. Repeat for other ear.

Sew a pair of hooves together, leaving opening for turning where indicated on pattern. Turn hoof right side out through opening. Thread a hand-sewing needle with a double strand of matching thread. Hand-sew around opening, leaving thread attached. Turn raw edge in and slip an end of a leg into opening. Draw thread to gather edge slightly and hand-sew hoof to end of leg, tucking all raw edges in. Repeat with remaining pairs of hooves.

With matching thread, hand-tack ends of antlers to top of head between ears so antlers stand as shown in photo. Then hand-tack edges of hair to top of head as shown.

Press 1/4 in. to wrong side on all edges of vest. Topstitch around vest with matching thread to hold. Cut a slit in each side of the vest where shown on

pattern.

Slip vest onto reindeer and pull front legs through slits.

Overlap front edges of vest slightly and hand-sew jingle bells to front of vest for buttons.

Fold fabric for scarf in half lengthwise with wrong sides together. Wrap scarf around neck as shown in photo and tie ends in an overhand knot. Hand-tack scarf as needed to hold.

Glue wiggle eyes and pom-pom nose to head where shown on pattern

Separate six-strand embroidery floss. Thread embroidery needle with two strands of black floss. Add two long straight stitches to head for mouth where shown on pattern. See Fig. 2 for stitch illustration.

Use cotton swab and a circular motion to apply cosmetic blush to reindeer's cheeks.

Tie an overhand knot in each leg as shown in photo.

Round up smiles with your merry reindeer! ♥

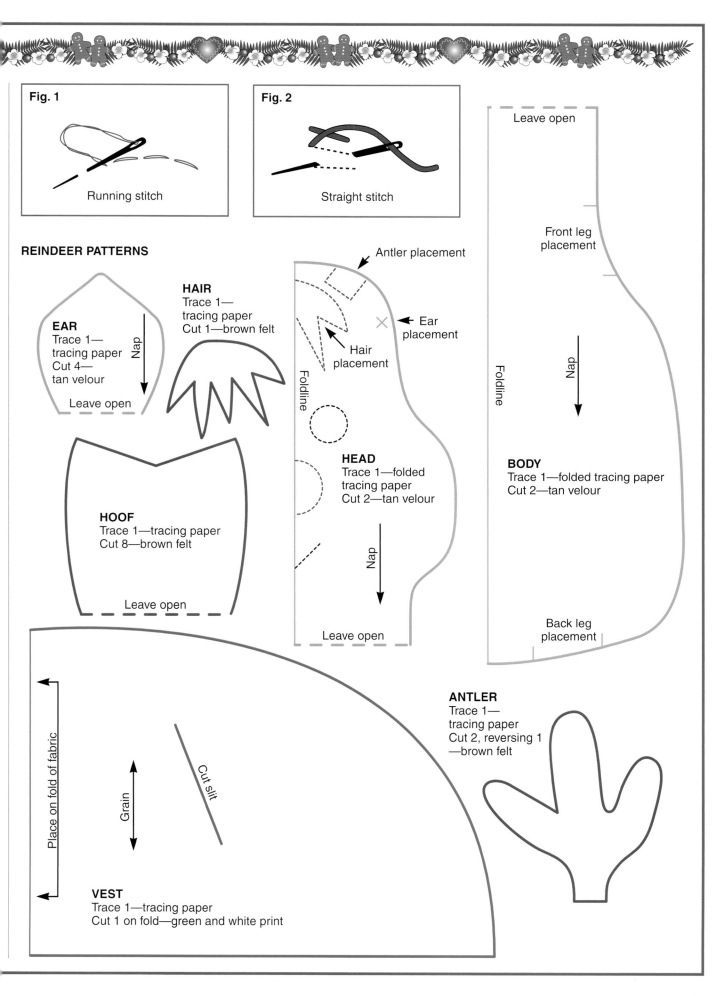

**Fig. 1**

Running stitch

**Fig. 2**

Straight stitch

**REINDEER PATTERNS**

**EAR**
Trace 1—
tracing paper
Cut 4—
tan velour
Leave open

**HAIR**
Trace 1—
tracing paper
Cut 1—brown felt

**HOOF**
Trace 1—tracing paper
Cut 8—brown felt
Leave open

Antler placement

Ear placement

Hair placement

Foldline

**HEAD**
Trace 1—folded
tracing paper
Cut 2—tan velour

Nap

Leave open

Leave open

Front leg placement

Foldline

Nap

**BODY**
Trace 1—folded tracing paper
Cut 2—tan velour

Back leg placement

**ANTLER**
Trace 1—
tracing paper
Cut 2, reversing 1
—brown felt

Place on fold of fabric

Grain

Cut slit

**VEST**
Trace 1—tracing paper
Cut 1 on fold—green and white print

# Round Out Your Noel Decor With a Dainty Doily Design

WITH its lacy look, Ruth Shepherd's delicate doily will lend a warm, old-fashioned feel to any room in the house. "It's a quick 15-round design that uses a combination of basic crochet stitches," says the Chickasaw, Alabama crafter.

This pretty doily's so easy you'll want to hook one for yourself and more for all of the folks on your Christmas list!

**Materials Needed:**
*Size 10 crochet cotton—approximately 175 yards of red and 25 yards of green*
*Size 5 (1.5mm) steel crochet hook or size needed to obtain correct gauge*
*Tapestry needle*
*Scissors*

**Gauge:** End of Round 3 = 2-1/4 inches across.

**Finished Size:** Doily measures about 12 inches across.

**Directions:**
With red, ch 8, join with sl st to form ring.

**Round 1:** Ch 3 (counts as first dc), work 19 dcs in ring, join with sl st in the top of beginning ch-3: 20 dcs.

**Round 2:** Ch 4 (counts as first dc plus 1 ch), [dc in next dc, ch 1] 19 times, join with sl st in third ch of beginning ch-4: 20 dcs.

**Round 3:** Ch 3, work 2 dcs in same st, work 3 dcs in each dc around, join with sl st in top of beginning ch-3: 60 dcs.

**Round 4:** Sc in same st, * ch 10, sk 1 dc, sc in each of next two dcs; repeat from * around, ending with ch 10, sk 1 dc, sc in next dc: 20 ch-10 sps. Fasten off.

**Round 5:** With sl knot on hk, red thread and right side facing, ch 3 for first dc in any ch-10 sp, work 2 dcs in same sp, * ch 3, work 3 dcs in next ch-10 sp; repeat from * around, ch 3, join with sl st in top of beginning ch-3.

**Round 6:** Sc in same st, * ch 10, sk

1 dc, sc in next dc, work 3 scs in next ch-3 sp, sc in next dc; repeat from * around, ending last repeat with a sl st in beginning sc: 20 ch-10 sps.

**Round 7:** Sl st to fifth ch of next ch-10 sp, ch 3 for first dc, work 2 dcs in same ch-10 sp, * ch 5, work 3 dcs in next ch-10 sp; repeat from * around, ending last repeat with ch 5, join with sl st in top of beginning ch-3.

**Round 8:** Sc in same st, * ch 10, sk 1 dc, sc in next dc, work 5 scs in next ch-5 sp, sc in next dc; repeat from * around, ending last repeat with sl st in beginning sc.

**Round 9:** Sl st to fifth ch of next ch-10 sp, ch 3 for first dc, work 2 dcs in same ch-10 sp, * ch 6, work 3 dcs in next ch-10 sp; repeat from * around, ending last repeat with ch 6, join with sl st in top of beginning ch-3.

**Round 10:** Sc in same st, ch 10, work (1 sc, ch 10, sc) in next dc, ch 10, sc in next dc, * work 6 scs in next ch-6 sp, sc in next dc, ch 5, sl st in last ch-10 sp made, ch 5, work (1 sc, ch 10, sc) in next dc, ch 10, sc in next dc; repeat from * around, ending last repeat with 6 scs in next ch-6 sp, sc in next dc, ch 5, sl st in last ch-10 sp made, ch 5, work (1 sc, ch 10, sc) in next dc, ch 5, sl st in first ch-10 sp of round, ch 5, join with sc in last dc. Fasten off.

**Round 11:** With sl knot on hk, red thread and right side facing, ch 3 for first dc in center of any ch-10 sp, work 2 dcs in same sp, * ch 8, sc in next sl st joining ch-10 sps, ch 8, work 3 dcs in next ch-10 sp; repeat from * around, ending last repeat with ch 8, join with sl st in top of beginning ch-3.

**Round 12:** Sc in same st, * ch 10, sk 1 dc, sc in next dc, work 5 scs in

## ABBREVIATIONS

| | |
|---|---|
| ch(s) | chain(s) |
| dc(s) | double crochet(s) |
| hk | hook |
| sc(s) | single crochet(s) |
| sk | skip |
| sl | slip |
| sl st | slip stitch |
| st | stitch |
| sp(s) | space(s) |
| * or [ ] | Instructions following an asterisk or within brackets are repeated as directed. |
| ( ) | Instructions in parentheses are all worked in one stitch or space as indicated. |

next ch-8 sp, ch 3, work 5 scs in next ch-8 sp, sc in next dc; repeat from * around, ending last repeat with sl st in beginning sc.

**Round 13:** Sl st to fifth ch of ch-10 sp, ch 3 for first dc, work 2 dcs in same ch-10 sp, * ch 6, work 3 dcs in next ch-3 sp, ch 6, work 3 dcs in next ch-10 sp; repeat from * around, ending last repeat with ch 6, join with sl st in top of beginning ch-3. Fasten off.

**Round 14:** With sl knot on hk, green thread and right side facing, ch 3 for first dc in first dc of any 3-dc group in a ch-10 sp, work 3 dcs in same st, ch 3, sk 1 dc, work 4 dcs in next dc, * ch 5, sc in center dc of next 3-dc group, ch 5, work 4 dcs in next dc, ch 3, sk 1 dc, work 4 dcs in next dc; repeat from * around, ending last repeat with ch 5, sc in center dc of next 3-dc group, ch 5, join with sl st in top of beginning ch-3.

**Round 15:** * Ch 4, work (1 sc, ch 3, sc) in next ch-3 sp, ch 4, sk 3 dcs, sc in next dc, ch 3, dc in each of next ch-5 sps, ch 3, sc in next dc; repeat from * around, join with sl st in beginning ch. Fasten off.

Use a tapestry needle to weave in loose ends.

Give one or two as a gift or display your colorful doily in a merry way on an end table or shelf! ♥

# Holly Barrette Lends Festive Look to Locks

NEED to dress up your tresses for a seasonal celebration? Hold your hair in place with this eye-catching embellishment that's a cinch to make—and inexpensive, too.

"All you need is a few red pom-poms, a scrap of green felt and a store-bought barrette," says Jan York of Grass Valley, California. "In no time, you'll have an attractive sprig of holly to highlight your hairdo."

### Materials Needed:
*Patterns below right*
*Tracing paper and pencil*
*4-inch x 7-inch scrap of green felt*
*Green all-purpose thread*
*Hand-sewing needle*
*3-inch barrette (available in the jewelry findings section of most craft stores)*
*Three 1/4-inch red pom-poms*
*Glue gun and glue stick*
*Scissors*

**Finished Size:** Holly barrette measures about 5-1/2 inches long x 2 inches high.

### Directions:
Trace patterns onto folded tracing paper. Cut out each on traced lines and open for complete patterns.

Cut holly from felt as directed. From green felt also cut a 1/4-in.-wide x 3-in.-long strip.

Thread hand-sewing needle and knot ends together. Center small holly leaf on top of large holly leaf and hand-tack center to hold. Leave thread attached.

Wrap strip of green felt snugly over

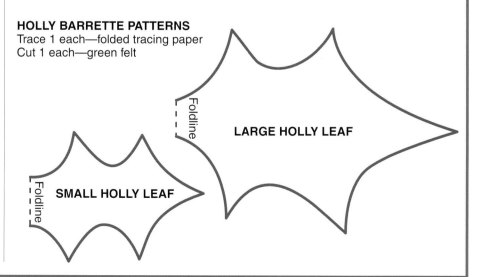

center of holly leaves to pleat felt slightly. Hand-sew felt strip together in back to hold. Fasten off thread and trim excess felt close to stitching.

Glue wrong side of holly centered along top of barrette. Glue pom-poms to center of holly as shown in photo.

Wear in your hair during the holidays!

**HOLLY BARRETTE PATTERNS**
Trace 1 each—folded tracing paper
Cut 1 each—green felt

Foldline

**LARGE HOLLY LEAF**

Foldline

**SMALL HOLLY LEAF**

# Christmas Tree Crochet Spruces Up Rooms

CABIN FEVER hit Deanna Dison when she dreamed up her attractive evergreen wall hanging. Deanna built her ribbon-trimmed tree with blocks done in the popular log cabin quilt design.

"I first made the Yuletide pattern as a quilt using 6-inch blocks," explains the Spearsville, Louisiana crafter. "For this crocheted version, I added the ribbons, but you could also trim it with buttons or ornaments."

**Materials Needed:**
*4-ply worsted-weight yarn—10 ounces each of light blue and green variegated; 6 ounces of navy blue; and 4 ounces each of white and gold*
*Size G (4.25mm) crochet hook or size needed to obtain correct gauge*
*Size 16 tapestry needle*
*Ribbon—1 yard of 1-inch-wide gold mesh wire-edge ribbon and 6 yards each of 1/2-inch-wide red satin ribbon and 1/2-inch-wide white wire-edge ribbon*
*Scissors*
*36-inch length of 1/2-inch wooden dowel*

**Gauge:** Each completed block measures about 3-1/4 inches square.

**Finished Size:** Wall hanging measures about 31-1/2 inches across x 45 inches long.

**Directions:**
**WHITE BLOCK (make 8):** With white, ch 2, (lp on hk does not count as a ch).

**Round 1:** Work 6 scs in second ch from hk, join with sl st in first sc: 6 scs. Mark this side as the right side of the block.

**Round 2:** Ch 1, work 2 scs in each sc around, join with sl st in first sc, ch 1: 12 scs.

**Row 1:** Work 1 sc in same sp and in each of next three scs, ch 1, turn: 4 scs.

**Rows 2-4:** Work 1 sc in each sc of previous row, ch 1, turn: 4 scs.

**Row 5:** Work 1 sc in each of next three scs, work 3 scs in last sc, do not turn, work 1 sc in each st at ends of Rows 4, 3 and 2, work 1 sc in same st as last st on Row 1, work 1 sc in each of next 3 scs on Round 2, ch 1, turn: 13 scs.

**Rows 6-8:** Work 1 sc in each of next 9 scs, ch 1, turn: 9 scs.

**Row 9:** Work 1 sc in each of next 8

scs, work 3 scs in last sc, do not turn, work 1 sc in each st at ends of Rows 8, 7 and 6, work 1 sc in same st as last st on Row 1, work 1 sc in each of next 3 scs on Round 2, ch 1, turn: 18 scs.

**Rows 10-12:** Work 1 sc in each of next 9 scs, ch 1, turn: 9 scs.

**Row 13:** Work 1 sc in each of next 8 scs, work 3 scs in last sc, do not turn, work 1 sc in each st at ends of Rows 12, 11 and 10, work 1 sc in same st as last st on Row 9, work 1 sc in each of next 2 scs on Round 2, work 1 sc in

same st as first st on Row 1 and 1 sc in each st at ends of Rows 1, 2, 3, 4 and 5, ch 1, turn: 23 scs.

**Rows 14-17:** Work 1 sc in each of next 14 scs, ch 1, turn, at end of Row 17, fasten off, leaving 10 in. of yarn for sewing blocks together later.
**WHITE AND LIGHT BLUE BLOCK (make 34):** With white yarn, ch 2.

Repeat Rounds 1 and 2 of White Block. Fasten off at end of Round 2.

With light blue yarn and sl knot on hk, sc in any st of Round 2, work 1 sc in

each of next 3 scs, ch 1, turn: 4 scs.

Repeat Rows 2-17 of White Block.

**GOLD AND VARIEGATED GREEN BLOCK (make 34):** With gold yarn, ch 2.

Repeat Rounds 1 and 2 of White Block. Fasten off at end of Round 2.

With variegated green yarn and sl knot on hk, sc in any st of Round 2, work 1 sc in each of next 3 scs, ch 1, turn: 4 scs.

Repeat Rows 2-17 of White Block.

**GOLD, LIGHT BLUE AND VARIEGATED GREEN BLOCK (make 18):** With gold yarn, ch 2.

Repeat Rounds 1 and 2 of White Block. Fasten off at end of Round 2.

With light blue yarn and sl knot on hk, sc in any st of Round 2, work 1 sc in each of next 3 scs, ch 1, turn: 4 scs.

Repeat Rows 2-8 of White Block.

Work Row 9 as follows: Work 1 sc in each of next 8 scs, work 1 sc, in last sc, drop light blue yarn and pick up variegated green yarn, work 2 scs in same st, do not turn, work 1 sc in each st at ends of Rows 8, 7 and 6, work 1 sc in same st as last st on Row 1, work 1 sc in each of next 3 scs in Round 2, ch 1, turn: 18 scs.

Repeat Rows 10-17 of White Block.

**WHITE, LIGHT BLUE AND GOLD BLOCK (make 2):** With white yarn, ch 2.

Repeat Rounds 1 and 2 of White Block. Fasten off at end of Round 2.

With light blue yarn and sl knot on hk, sc in any st of Round 2, work 1 sc in each of next 3 scs, ch 1, turn: 4 scs.

Repeat Rows 2-8 of White Block.

Work Row 9 as follows: Work 1 sc in each of next 8 scs, work 1 sc, in last sc, drop light blue yarn and pick up gold yarn, work 2 scs in same st, do not turn,

work 1 sc in each st at ends of Rows 8, 7 and 6 and 1 sc in same st as last st on Row 1, work 1 sc in each of next 3 scs in Round 2, ch 1, turn: 18 scs.

Repeat Rows 10-17 of White Block.

**ASSEMBLY:** Lay out blocks in 12 rows with eight blocks in each row as shown in photo, making sure right sides of each block are up.

Using tails of yarn and tapestry needle, hand-sew blocks together to make rows. Then sew rows together.

Use tapestry needle to weave in all loose ends.

**BORDER: Round 1:** With sl knot on hk, gold yarn and right side facing, * work 3 scs in corner, work 13 scs evenly spaced across each block to next corner; repeat from * around, ending with a sl st in beginning st.

**Round 2:** Ch 1, do not turn, * work 3 scs in center st of corner, work 1 sc in each st around to next corner; repeat from * around, ending with a sl st in beginning st. Fasten off.

**Round 3:** With sl knot on hk, navy blue yarn and right side facing, * work 3 scs in center st of corner, work 1 sc in each st around to next corner; repeat from * around, ending with a sl st in beginning st.

**Rounds 4-8:** Ch 1, * work 3 scs in center st of corner, work 1 sc in each st around to next corner; repeat from * around, ending with a sl st in beginning st. Fasten off at end of Round 8.

**Round 9:** With right side facing, attach navy blue yarn in front lp of top right-hand corner st, * working in front lps only, work (1 sc, ch 2, 1 dc in same st), sk two sts; repeat from * across top to next corner; ** working in both lps,

work (1 sc, ch 2, 1 dc in same st), sk two sts; repeat from ** around, ending with a sl st in beginning st.

**Row 1:** Ch 1, work 1 sc in back lp of each sc of Round 8 (working across top only for hanging sleeve), ch 1, turn.

**Rows 2-6:** Sk first sc, work 1 sc in each sc to last sc, sk last sc, ch 1, turn. At end of Row 6, fasten off.

Thread tapestry needle with matching yarn and sew long edge only of Row 6 to back of Round 2 of border for hanging sleeve.

**FINISHING:** Cut red and white ribbon into 12-in. lengths. Thread the ribbon through stitches from back where desired and tie ribbon into bows on front.

Tie gold ribbon into bow and hand-sew bow to top of tree. Insert dowel into hanging sleeve.

Deck your walls with this fine pine!

---

### ABBREVIATIONS

| | |
|---|---|
| ch(s) | chain(s) |
| dc(s) | double crochet(s) |
| hk | hook |
| lp(s) | loop(s) |
| sc(s) | single crochet(s) |
| sl st | slip stitch |
| sp | space |
| sk | skip |
| st(s) | stitch(es) |
| ( ) | Instructions in parentheses are all worked in one stitch or space as indicated. |
| * | Instructions following asterisk are repeated as directed. |

# Follow These Helpful Hints to Make Your Crafting Merry

MAKING merry Yuletide crafts adds to the joy of the season, whether you're knitting a colorful stocking cap, painting ornate ornaments or working leaves and berries into a wreath.

Without a little planning, however, those fun endeavors can become frustrating burdens. Try these easy ideas to help keep your projects a joy to make… and a joy to behold!

● Establish a gift-giving theme. For example, you could craft wearables or photo albums for everyone or pot holders and oven mitts for the ladies or stuffed toys for the tots, etc.

● Jot down a list of supplies you'll need and take it with you when you shop. Check off items as you buy them.

● Buy extras, such as an additional yard of lace or another basket, to allow for a last-minute gift.

● Keep a calendar that shows start and end dates for each project and try to stick to it!

● Have at least one take-along project (knitting, crocheting and cross-stitch all work well) to pass the time at the doctor's office, while traveling, etc.

● Work in assembly-line fashion when making multiples of one item.

That might not sound creative, but it's a real time-saver!

● Take frequent breaks to stretch, relax or simply change positions, and you'll reduce stress and muscle strain.

● Tackle several different crafts at once to avoid boredom.

● Strive to finish projects at various intervals, perhaps one each week, to give yourself a sense of accomplishment.

● Take notes throughout the year on gift ideas for others.

● And, most importantly, start early so you don't feel rushed and can enjoy yourself! ♥

# Winsome Reindeer Hang Around for Holidays

IT'S a sure sign of the season when you hitch Rudolph and his North Pole pals to your wall. But this whimsical woodcraft is not only fun to look at, it's functional, too.

"I originally gave these signs as pot holder hangers," points out Sandy Rollinger of Apollo, Pennsylvania. "Then I learned that my friends were using them for other items…candles, keys, mittens and Christmas stockings.

"You can make the board longer to accommodate all of Santa's flight crew and more handy hooks," Sandy suggests.

## Materials Needed:
*Pattern on next page*
*Tracing paper and pencil*
*5-1/2-inch x 12-inch piece of 1-inch-thick pine for sign*
*Three 1/2-inch wooden dome-top furniture plugs*
*Drill with 1/8-inch bit*
*Sandpaper and tack cloth*
*Paper plate or palette*
*Paper towels*
*Small container of water*
*Acrylic craft paints—brown, cream, dark green, red and dark red*
*Paintbrushes—small flat and small sponge brush*
*Small piece of household sponge*
*Powdered cosmetic blush*
*Cotton swab*
*Dimensional paints—green, red and white*
*Three white cup hooks*
*24 inches of 16-gauge green or black craft wire*
*Black fine-line permanent marker*
*Several pieces of natural raffia*
*Artificial holly*
*Glue gun and glue stick*
*Clear acrylic spray sealer*
*Scissors*

**Finished Size:** Reindeer sign measures 12 inches across x 5-1/2 inches high without hanger.

## Directions:
Drill a hole through sign 1/2 in. from each corner along one long edge. Sand piece smooth and wipe with tack cloth to remove sanding dust.

Place small amounts of paint on paper plate or palette as needed. Paint as directed, extending paint around side edges of sign. Apply additional coats of paint as needed for complete coverage, allowing drying time between coats.

Using sponge brush, paint entire sign cream. Let dry.

Trace reindeer pattern onto tracing paper. Turn tracing paper pattern over and rub flat side of pencil lead over traced lines to darken.

Center pattern on sign. Trace over pattern with dry ballpoint pen or stylus to transfer pattern onto wood. Transfer another pattern on each side of center reindeer, reversing and positioning one as shown in photo.

Use small flat brush to paint two furniture plugs black and one red for reindeer noses. Let dry.

Mix a bit of cream into brown paint to make a light brown. Use flat brush to paint each head light brown.

Add a bit more cream paint to brown paint to make a lighter brown and use flat brush to paint all antlers and insides of each ear.

While paint is still wet, make light brown again and use flat brush to shade edges of each antler. Add a bit of water to brown paint and use flat brush to shade edges of each head. Let dry.

Use flat brush to paint all bows red. While paint is still wet, shade each bow as shown in photo with dark red paint.

Use household sponge and an up-and-down motion to dab dark green paint onto outside edges of sign, allowing some cream color to show through.

Glue red nose onto center reindeer and a black nose onto the others. Let dry.

Spray with sealer. Let dry.

Use cotton swab and a circular motion to apply cosmetic blush to cheek areas.

Use black marker to outline each reindeer and to add details to each as shown on pattern and in photo.

Use white dimensional paint to add eyes to each reindeer where shown on pattern. Then add random white dots to front of sign for snow. Also add a small white dot to each nose.

Use green dimensional paint to add a tiny dot to each eye and to paint holly leaves on the top of each reindeer's head. When dry, use red dimensional paint to add tiny berries to the center of each group of holly leaves. Let dry.

Attach cup holders along bottom of sign where desired.

Coil craft wire loosely around pencil, leaving about 4 in. on each end straight. Remove pencil and thread straight ends of wire through holes on top of sign from back to front. Wrap ends back around coiled wire to hold. Shape wire into an arc for hanger.

Tie raffia into a small bow. Trim ends as desired. Glue bow to top of hanger and artificial holly onto front of bow.

Hang in your kitchen or hall and enjoy!

**REINDEER SIGN PATTERN**

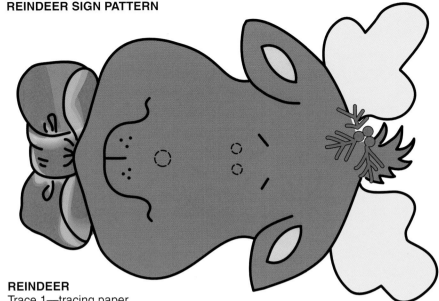

**REINDEER**
Trace 1—tracing paper
Paint 3 as directed

# Cowboy Claus Brightens Boughs

LASSO this Western Santa for your homespun holiday tree. He'll round up smiles for miles!

Cyndee Kromminga of Winfield, Kansas started with a standard lightbulb that she painted white to create her Christmas cowpoke. "My ranch-hand elf in his festive straw hat will fit into any country setting," she says with a smile.

**Materials Needed:**
*Standard lightbulb*
*Acrylic craft paints—black, flesh, red and white*
*Small flat paintbrush*
*Small piece of household sponge*
*Paper towels*
*4-inch natural straw hat*
*8 inches of 1/4-inch-wide green satin picot ribbon*
*Small artificial poinsettia*
*Three small artificial holly leaves*
*White oven-bake polymer clay for nose (Cyndee used Sculpey)*
*White curly doll hair*
*10 inches of 20-gauge craft wire*
*White (tacky) glue*
*Scissors*

**Finished Size:** Lightbulb Santa measures about 3-3/4 inches across x 5 inches tall without hanger.

**Directions:**
Roll a bit of polymer clay to make a pea-size nose for Santa. Bake according to manufacturer's directions. Let cool.

Dip piece of household sponge into white paint. Dab the sponge on a paper towel to evenly distribute paint. With an up-and-down motion, paint entire lightbulb white. Let dry.

Use flat brush and flesh to paint a 1-1/2-in. circle centered on one side of lightbulb for Santa's face. Paint polymer clay nose flesh. Let dry.

Glue nose to center of face. Let dry.

Hold lightbulb vertically with socket end facing up. Dip handle of paintbrush into black paint and dab on two small dots above nose for eyes. Let dry.

Dip flat brush into red paint and wipe on paper towel until nearly dry. Dab a circle of color on each side of nose for cheeks. Let dry.

Stretch and rub a palm-size wad of curly doll hair until fluffy. Make a hole in center of hair. Spread a 1-in.-wide band of glue around outside edge of face and press hair firmly into glue, leaving face exposed. Let dry.

Cut a hole in top of straw hat large enough for socket end of lightbulb. Use tip of scissors to pierce small holes in crown of hat on opposite sides below hole.

Thread an end of craft wire through small holes, leaving ends about 2 in.

long and a loop for hanger. Wrap ends around wire to hold. Then wrap ends around handle of paintbrush to coil.

Slip hat over socket end and glue as needed to hold to lightbulb. Let dry.

Glue ribbon around crown of hat with ends overlapped in front. Trim excess.

Glue holly leaves and poinsettia to front of hat. Let dry.

Turn up sides of straw hat as shown in photo.

Trim your tree with this playful cowboy Claus!

# Evergreen Forest Branches Out Across Quick Country Quilt

PINING for something special to spruce up your Yuletide decor? Then you'll want to piece together this striking patchwork, rooted in holiday hues.

Julie Todd of Aurelia, Iowa used red and green fabric strips and no-sew tree appliques to fashion her field of firs. It's so inviting you can almost smell that fresh balsam fragrance!

## Materials Needed:

*Pattern on next page*
*Tracing paper and pencil*
*44-inch-wide 100% cotton fabrics—1/2 yard of white print for blocks; 1/4 yard each of green solid and red solid for piecing; 1/2 yard of green print for binding; 1 yard of coordinating fabric for backing; and 1/4 yard each of several different green prints for trees or ten 5-inch x 3-1/2-inch scraps*
*Matching all-purpose thread*
*Clear nylon thread for quilting*
*1/2 yard of no-sew paper-backed fusible web*
*28-inch x 34-inch piece of lightweight*

*quilt batting*
*Quilter's marking pen or pencil*
*Quilter's ruler*
*Rotary cutter and mat (optional)*
*Standard sewing supplies*

**Finished Size:** Quilt measures about 24-1/2 inches wide x 30 inches long.

## Directions:

Pre-wash fabrics, washing each color separately. If water is discolored, wash again until rinse water runs clear. Dry and press all fabrics.

**CUTTING:** Cut fabrics using rotary cutter and quilter's ruler, or mark fabrics using ruler and marker of choice and cut with scissors. Cut strips crosswise from selvage to selvage.

From green solid, cut four 1-1/2-in. x 44-in. strips.

From red solid, cut four 1-1/2-in. x 44-in. strips.

From white print, cut four 4-in. x 44-in. strips.

From green print, cut four 2-1/2-in. x 44-in. strips for binding. For borders, cut two 1-1/2-in. x 22-1/2-in. strips and two 1-1/2-in. x 30-in. strips.

From coordinating fabric, cut a 28-in. x 34-in. piece for backing.

**PIECING:** Do all piecing with accurate 1/4-in. seams and right sides of fabrics together. Press seams toward darker fabrics unless otherwise directed.

Sew a 44-in.-long green solid strip to one long edge of a 44-in.-long white print strip. Sew a 44-in.-long red solid strip to other long edge of the white strip, making a 6-in.-wide x 44-in.-long pieced strip. The width of the white (center) strip should be an accurate 3-1/2 in. along its entire length.

In the same way, sew the remaining 44-in.-long strips together, making a total of four red, white and green pieced strips.

Referring to Fig. 1 on next page, cut pieced strips to make 20 accurate red, white and green 6-1/2-in. pieced squares.

Lay out two rows of pieced squares with four blocks in each row as shown

in Fig. 2. Lay out the rest of the blocks to make a total of five rows with Rows 1, 3 and 5 alike and Rows 2 and 4 alike.

Sew blocks in each row together in planned order and press seams of each row in opposite directions. Then sew rows together in planned order, carefully matching corners. Press the seams in one direction.

Sew one 1-1/2-in. x 22-1/2-in. green print border strip to top edge of pieced wall quilt and a matching border strip to bottom edge. Press seams. Then sew a 1-1/2-in. x 30-in. border strip to each side edge. Press seams.

**APPLIQUES:** Trace tree pattern onto tracing paper as directed on pattern and cut out.

Trace tree pattern 10 times onto paper side of fusible web, leaving 1/2 in. between shapes. Cut shapes apart.

With the grain lines matching, fuse the trees onto the wrong side of different green print fabrics following manufacturer's directions. Cut out the trees on traced lines.

Remove paper backing from trees. Center and fuse each tree onto a white print block following the pattern shown in the photo.

**QUILTING:** Place backing wrong side up on a flat surface and smooth out. Place batting centered over backing, smoothing out wrinkles. Center pieced top right side up on top of batting.

Hand-baste all layers together, stitching from center to corners, then horizontally and vertically every 4 in.

With thread to match backing in the bobbin and clear nylon thread in needle, sew in a continuous step pattern along seams on left and bottom edges of each green strip. Then in same way, sew in a continuous step pattern along seams of red strips.

Baste around the outside edges of pieced top. Trim the edges of the batting and backing even with the edges of the pieced top.

**BINDING:** Sew the short edges of the binding strips together to make one long strip.

Press 1/2 in. of short edge of binding to wrong side. Fold strip in half lengthwise with wrong sides together and press.

Starting with folded end, sew binding to front of quilt with raw edges matching. Miter corners. Trim excess, leaving a 1/2-in. overlap.

Fold binding to back, encasing raw edges. Hand-sew fold of binding to backing, covering seam.

Remove basting.

Hang your festive fir quilt to be enjoyed by all! ♥

## TREE QUILT PATTERN

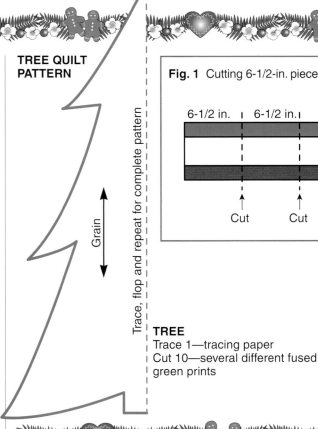

Trace, flop and repeat for complete pattern

Grain

**TREE**
Trace 1—tracing paper
Cut 10—several different fused green prints

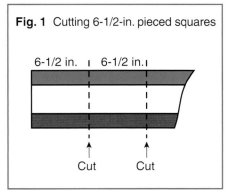

**Fig. 1** Cutting 6-1/2-in. pieced squares

6-1/2 in. | 6-1/2 in.

Cut      Cut

**Fig. 2** Layout

Row 1

Row 2

Row 3

Row 4

Row 5

# Pin Makes a Meaningful Memento

GET to the point with this simple Nativity pin! Verlyn King of Tremonton, Utah used plywood, a craft stick and wooden cutouts that she sanded and painted to put together the attractive accessory. The little pin is big on effect when it's attached to a sweater or lapel.

**Materials Needed:**
*2-inch x 3-inch piece of 1/8-inch-thick birch plywood*
*1/16-inch-thick purchased wooden cutouts—3/8-inch circle and 1-inch-long oval (Verlyn used Woodsies shapes)*
*1/2-inch-high x 1/4-inch-thick wooden star*
*Craft stick*
*Scroll or band saw*
*Sandpaper and tack cloth*
*Paper plate or palette*
*Paper towels*
*Acrylic craft paints—brown, flesh, dark flesh, gold metallic, navy blue and white*
*Paintbrushes—small flat and liner*
*Clear acrylic sealer*
*Black fine-line permanent marker*
*1-1/4-inch pin back*
*White (tacky) glue*

**Finished Size:** Nativity pin measures 2 inches across x 3-1/4 inches high.

**Directions:**
Use scroll or band saw to cut a 1-1/4-in. x 2-1/2-in. rectangle from birch plywood for background of pin and a 1-in. x 1/4-in. piece from craft stick for manger.

Sand pieces smooth and wipe with tack cloth to remove sanding dust.

Place small amounts of paint on paper plate or palette as needed. Paint as directed, extending paint around side edges of each piece. Apply additional coats of paint as needed for complete coverage, allowing drying time between coats.

Use flat brush to paint the pin background navy blue. Let dry.

Use flat brush to paint circle flesh for head and oval white for body. Also paint star gold metallic and manger brown. Let dry.

Glue manger centered across narrow end of pin with long edge about 1/4 in. from bottom of pin as shown in photo. Glue body above manger and head to left end of body. Let dry.

Glue star centered on top of pin with tip of star extending about 1/4 in. above

top edge of pin. Let dry.

Use liner and gold metallic paint to add rays from star and straw to manger as shown in photo. Let dry.

Dip flat brush into dark flesh paint and wipe on paper towel until no brush strokes show. Then use a circular motion to add a cheek to head.

Apply sealer to entire pin. Let dry.

Referring to photo for position, use black marker to add eye, mouth and details to baby and blanket.

Glue pin back centered vertically onto back of pin.

Brighten up holiday outfits with this spirited trim that reminds us all of the true meaning of Christmas! ♥

# Felt Mosaic Tops Table in Snowy Splendor

EXPECT a flurry of "oohs" and "aahs" when friends catch a glimpse of this frosty table topper that's pieced together with bright bits of felt.

"It's sized right to add festive flair to a small round table or a sideboard," Sharlene Smith writes from her home in Branchville, Virginia. "It's even prettier on top of a colorful tablecloth."

## Materials Needed:
*Patterns on next page*
*Tracing paper and pencil*
*1 yard of no-sew paper-backed fusible web*
*Felt—19-1/2-inch circle of off-white for backing; three 9-inch x 12-inch pieces of dark blue for background*
*and scraps or one 9-inch x 12-inch piece each of black, green, light blue, orange, red, tan, white and yellow for snowman, tree and holly*
*Sixteen 1/2-inch red pom-poms*
*White (tacky) glue*
*Textured snow paint and small paintbrush*
*Iron and ironing surface*
*Scissors*

**Finished Size:** Snowman table topper measures 19 inches across.

## Directions:
Use copy machine to enlarge pattern to 200%, or mark tracing paper with a 1-in. grid and draw pattern as shown onto tracing paper. Trace individual patterns onto paper side of fusible web, leaving 1/2 in. between shapes.

Cut shapes apart. Fuse shapes onto color of felt shown on patterns following manufacturer's directions. Cut out shapes on traced lines.

**HOLLY:** Remove paper backing from holly leaves and stems and place them fused side down around outside of off-white felt circle, referring to photo for placement. Fuse shapes in place.

**SNOWMAN:** Remove paper backing from all shapes that make up the broom and snowman except nose, eyes and mouth of snowman.

Place shapes fused side down onto felt circle, referring to photo for placement and leaving space as shown between all pieces. Fuse shapes in place.

74

Remove paper backing from the nose, eyes and mouth and fuse onto snowman where shown on pattern.

**TREE:** Remove paper backing from each section of tree and place next to snowman as shown in photo, again leaving space as shown between each section of the tree and the snowman. Fuse shapes in place.

**BACKGROUND:** Center and fuse an 8-in. x 11-in. piece of no-sew paper-backed fusible web onto each piece of dark blue felt.

Randomly cut the paper-backed felt into a variety of sizes and shapes to fill in the background of the off-white felt circle as shown, leaving space between all pieces to create a mosaic look.

When pleased with the arrangement, remove paper backing and fuse the pieces onto the background, leaving spaces between pieces as planned.

**FINISHING:** Trim 1/4 in. from outside edge to make the finished piece a 19-in. circle.

Glue pom-poms to holly in groups of two and three as shown in photo.

Use small paintbrush to apply textured snow paint to each section of tree as shown in photo.

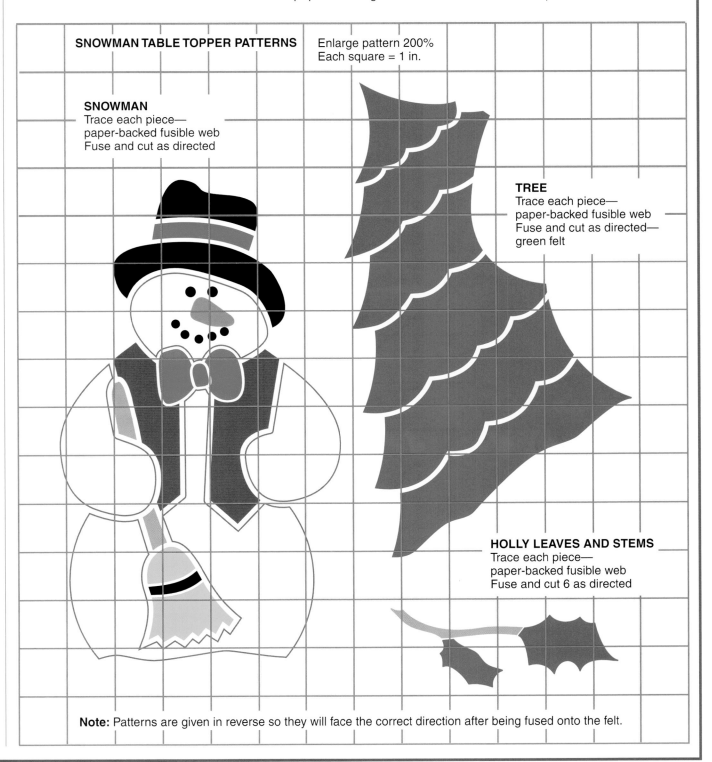

**SNOWMAN TABLE TOPPER PATTERNS**
Enlarge pattern 200%
Each square = 1 in.

**SNOWMAN**
Trace each piece—
paper-backed fusible web
Fuse and cut as directed

**TREE**
Trace each piece—
paper-backed fusible web
Fuse and cut as directed—
green felt

**HOLLY LEAVES AND STEMS**
Trace each piece—
paper-backed fusible web
Fuse and cut 6 as directed

**Note:** Patterns are given in reverse so they will face the correct direction after being fused onto the felt.

# Snip Fun Foam Trims in a Snap

White (tacky) glue
Small flat paintbrush
Six-strand embroidery floss
   —gold, green, red and
   white
Embroidery needle
Two 12mm gold jingle bells
One 1/2-inch red pom-pom
Scissors

**Finished Size:** Tree measures about 3-1/8 inches across x 4 inches high. Candy cane measures about 2-3/4 inches across x 4-1/8 inches high. Bell measures about 4-1/4 inches across x 4-1/2 inches high. Stocking measures about 3-1/4 inches across x 3-3/4 inches high.

**Directions:**
Trace patterns onto tracing paper as directed on patterns. Cut out each on traced lines.

**TREE:** Cut a 4-in. x 5-in. piece of green-and-white check fabric. Use paintbrush to apply a thin even coat of glue to one side of a same-size section of craft foam.

Place fabric right side up over glue and smooth out all wrinkles. Let dry.

Place pattern onto fabric side of glued piece with grain lines matching. Trace around pattern. Remove pattern and cut out shape, cutting just inside traced lines.

Thread embroidery needle with red six-strand floss. Whipstitch around entire tree, starting and stopping at top of tree. See Fig. 1 for stitch illustration.

Cut a 6-in. length of rickrack. Glue ends together to form a loop for hanger. Glue ends to top of right side of tree.

Cut a 3-in., 4-in. and 5-in. length of red satin ribbon. Tie each piece into a bow. Glue the smallest bow to the top of the tree, covering the ends of the hanging loop. Glue the medium and large bows below the small bow where shown in photo. Trim ends of bows to desired length.

**CANDY CANE:** Cut a 3-1/2-in. x 5-in. piece of red-and-white stripe fabric with stripes running parallel to the long edge. Apply glue to a same-size section of craft foam.

Glue fabric to craft foam and cut out candy cane as directed for the tree.

Thread embroidery needle with white six-strand floss. Whipstitch around the entire candy cane, starting and stopping at the top.

Cut a 6-in. length of rickrack. Glue ends together to form a loop. Glue ends to top of right side of candy cane.

Cut a 5-in. and 7-in. length of red satin ribbon.

Thread a jingle bell onto center of longer ribbon and tie ribbon in a bow. Glue bow to top of candy cane, covering the ends of hanging loop.

Tie remaining piece of ribbon into a small bow and glue bow centered on top of larger bow. Trim ends of bows to desired length.

**BELL:** Cut a 5-in. square of green Christmas print fabric. Apply glue to a same-size section of craft foam.

Glue fabric to craft foam and cut out bell as directed for the tree.

Thread embroidery needle with gold six-strand floss. Whipstitch around the entire bell, starting and stopping at the top of the bell.

Cut a 6-in. length of rickrack. Glue ends together to form a loop. Glue ends to top of right side of bell.

Cut a 3-1/2-in. and 4-in. length of rickrack and glue pieces to fabric side of bell where shown on pattern.

Cut a 6-in. and a 9-in. length of red satin ribbon.

Thread a jingle bell onto center of longer ribbon and tie ribbon in a bow. Glue bow to bottom of bell.

Tie remaining piece of ribbon in a small bow and glue bow to top of bell, covering ends of hanging loop. Trim ends of bows to desired length.

**STOCKING:** Cut a 4-1/2-in. square of green, red and white print fabric. Apply glue to a same-size section of craft foam.

Glue fabric to craft foam and cut out stocking as directed for the tree.

Thread embroidery needle with green six-strand floss. Whipstitch around entire stocking, starting and stopping at the top of stocking.

Cut a 6-in. length of rickrack. Glue ends together to form a loop. Glue ends to top of right side of stocking.

Cut a 9-in. length of red ribbon and tie ribbon in a bow. Glue the bow to top of stocking, covering the ends of hanging loop. Trim ends of the bow to desired length.

Glue rickrack to heel, toe and top of stocking where shown on pattern. Trim excess. Glue pom-pom to toe where shown on pattern.

Hang on your Christmas tree or trim a gift box!

THESE charming little trinkets can be whipped up in a jiffy with quick-to-craft art foam and Yule-inspired fabric. Lana Condon of Jupiter, Florida supplies the patterns for the merry motifs.

Just cut out the shapes, glue fabric to foam, add rickrack and whipstitch a decorative edging. You'll have them hanging on the family fir in no time!

**Materials Needed (for all):**
Patterns on next page
Tracing paper and pencil
One 9-inch x 12-inch sheet of red or
   green craft foam
100% cotton or cotton-blend fabrics—
   1/8 yard each or scraps of green-
   and-white check for tree, red-and-
   white stripe for candy cane, green
   Christmas print for bell and green,
   red and white print for stocking
40 inches of red baby rickrack
1-1/3 yards of 1/4-inch-wide red satin
   ribbon

**FOAM/FABRIC ORNAMENT PATTERNS**

**Fig. 1**

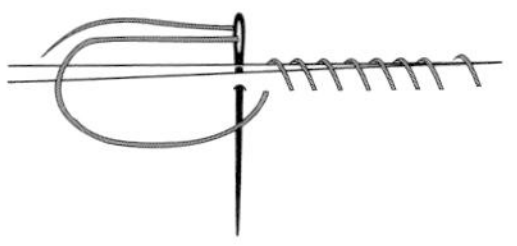

Whipstitch

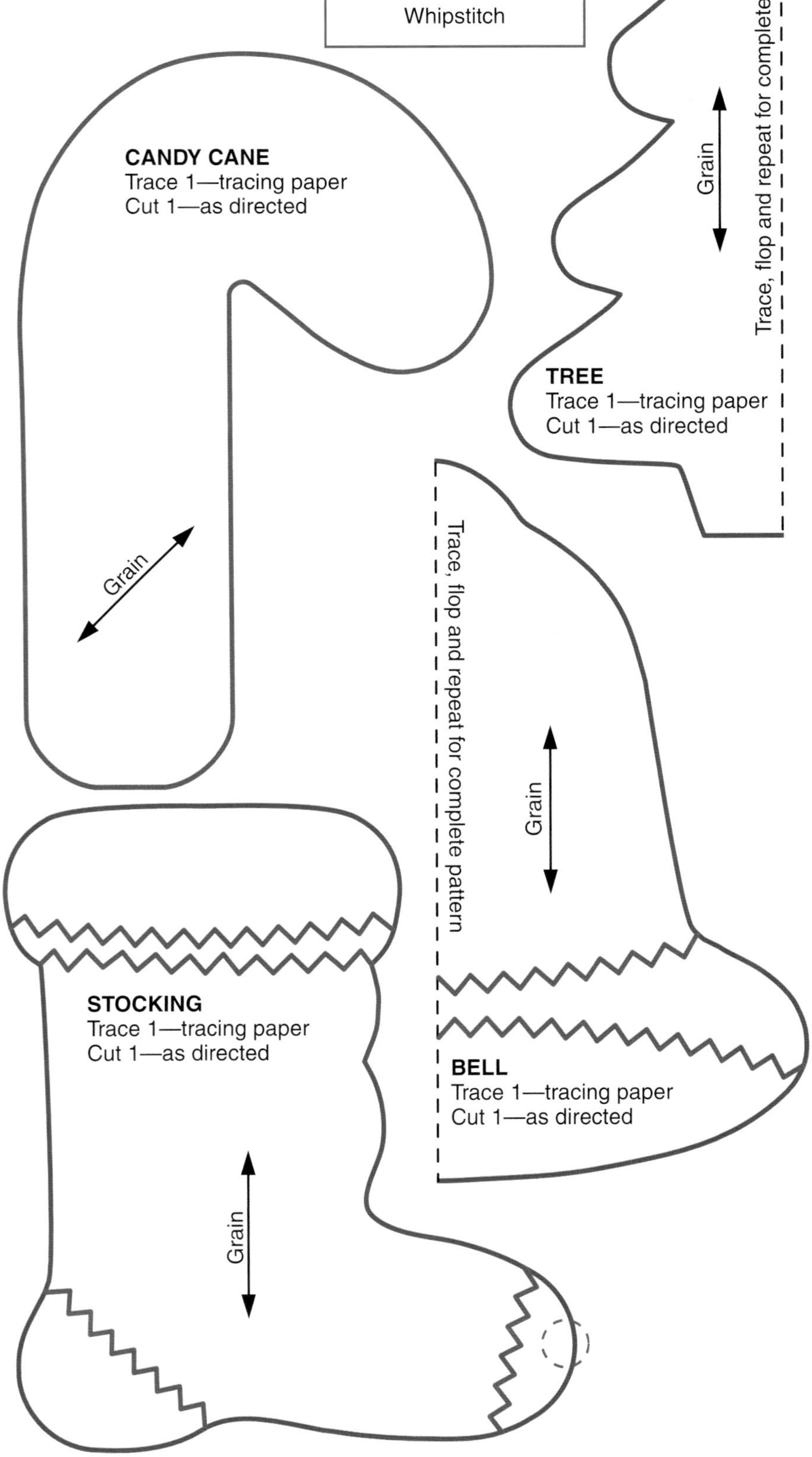

**CANDY CANE**
Trace 1—tracing paper
Cut 1—as directed

Grain

Trace, flop and repeat for complete pattern

Grain

**TREE**
Trace 1—tracing paper
Cut 1—as directed

Trace, flop and repeat for complete pattern

Grain

**STOCKING**
Trace 1—tracing paper
Cut 1—as directed

Grain

**BELL**
Trace 1—tracing paper
Cut 1—as directed

# Recycle Cards For Keepsakes

WHEN people take the time to send you Christmas cards, it's difficult to throw them away...especially if they're pretty as a picture.

So why not recycle them? For starters, you can make the Christmas Card Bowl on page 85. Or try some suggestions here...

"Since I don't like to part with the beautiful greeting cards I receive each year, I use them to create recipe cards. I give them as gifts to friends and family," writes Barbara Steininger of Salisbury, Maryland.

"I carefully cut off the front of the card, turn it over and write out a recipe. Then I cover both sides with clear Con-Tact paper to protect the card from spills. You could also use self-adhesive laminating sheets."

When she hosts a holiday get-together, Barbara asks everyone to bring one of the recipe cards with their name and year on the bottom of the recipe to swap.

"They make wonderful keepsakes," she says.

For fun homespun gift tags, cut out pretty pictures from the front of Christmas cards with pinking shears or decorative-edge scissors. Mount each picture on a piece of construction paper slightly larger than the picture in a coordinating color.

Glue the mounted scene onto a slightly larger folded piece of heavy white paper. You can also trim the edges of the white paper with decorative shears if you wish.

Punch two small holes in the front center or corner of the finished tag, thread a piece of ribbon through the holes and tie a tiny bow. Trim a gift box with the tag.

Some cards are so appealing that they're worthy of framing. Choose cards that coordinate with your holiday decorating theme or colors, and purchase inexpensive, festive frames. Group them on a wall or place on small easels or plate stands.

# Wintry Skirt Circles Tree with Frosty Flair

A BLIZZARD of buttons and bells adorns this snowy tree skirt, designed by Donna Stefanik of Westfield, Massachusetts. Fabric snowmen, stars and evergreens are fused onto a blue-and-white background to provide the perfect setting for a pile of presents.

"The motifs on this skirt can be blanket-stitched as I have done," Donna advises, "or crafters can machine-applique or outline the shapes with dimensional fabric paints."

### Materials Needed:
*Patterns on next page and page 80*
*Tracing paper and pencil*
*44-inch-wide 100% cotton or cotton-blend fabrics—1-1/2 yards of light blue and white print for background and backing; 3/4 yard of white-on-white print for snow and snowmen; and scraps or 1/8 yard each of black print for top hats, green print for trees, orange pin-dot for noses, red pin-dot for all hearts and two hats, two different red prints for two hats and all scarves and yellow print for stars*
*All-purpose thread—white and light blue*
*1 yard of paper-backed fusible web*
*33-inch circle of lightweight quilt batting*
*Seven 3/4-inch gold jingle bells*
*30 white buttons in assorted sizes*
*White crochet cotton*
*Large-eye hand-sewing needle*
*Black six-strand embroidery floss*
*Embroidery needle*
*Black fabric paint pen*
*Standard sewing supplies*

**Finished Size:** The snowman tree skirt measures about 31-1/2 inches across.

### Directions:
Pre-wash all fabrics without fabric softeners, washing colors separately. If the water from any fabric is discolored, wash again until rinse water runs clear. Dry and press all fabrics.

Trace tree skirt patterns for center section and bottom section on page 80 onto folded tracing paper. Cut out and open each for complete pattern.

Cut sections from fabrics as directed on patterns.

With right sides up, lay top of one bottom section over bottom of one top section, matching outside dots. Pin to hold.

Separate six-strand floss and use two strands to blanket stitch along overlapped edge. See Fig. 1 for stitch illustration and refer to photo for position of stitches.

**APPLIQUE:** Trace remaining patterns onto paper side of fusible web as directed on patterns, leaving 1 in. between shapes. Cut shapes apart.

Fuse shapes onto wrong side of fabrics as directed on patterns following manufacturer's directions. Cut out the shapes on traced lines.

Onto four of the sections of the tree skirt, fuse a tree on the left and a snowman on the right. Fuse a star centered above the already fused shapes and a heart to each snowman as shown in the photo. Then fuse a nose, scarf and a black hat to each snowman.

Onto the remaining sections of the tree skirt, fuse a tree on the right and a snowman on the left. Add the star, heart, nose and scarf as before and a red hat to each snowman.

Referring to photo, blanket-stitch with two strands of black floss around all appliques, except the nose.

Use black paint pen to add stick arms and small dots for eyes and mouth to each snowman as shown on pattern.

**ASSEMBLY:** Lay out the sections of the tree skirt, alternating sections as shown in the photo. Sew straight edges of the eight sections together in planned order with a 1/4-in. seam, leaving two edges unstitched for center back opening of tree skirt. Press seams open.

From light blue-and-white print fabric, cut a 33-in. square for the backing of tree skirt.

Lay circle of batting on a flat surface and smooth out wrinkles. Center square of backing fabric right side up over batting. Place pieced tree skirt wrong side up over backing fabric. Smooth out wrinkles and pin as needed to hold all layers together.

Sew around all edges with a 1/4-in. seam, leaving an opening for turning along one straight edge. Trim all layers 1/4 in. from stitching and clip curves. Turn right side out through opening. Hand-sew opening closed. Press lightly if needed.

**FINISHING:** Referring to photo for

placement, hand-sew a jingle bell at end of each seam that joins the sections.

Thread large-eye needle with crochet cotton and sew a button to top center of each section and then add others randomly where desired. To sew buttons on, stitch from front to back through button and all layers of tree skirt. Then stitch from back to front through another hole in the button. Tie threads in a knot on front and trim ends to desired length.

*(Patterns continue on the next page.)*

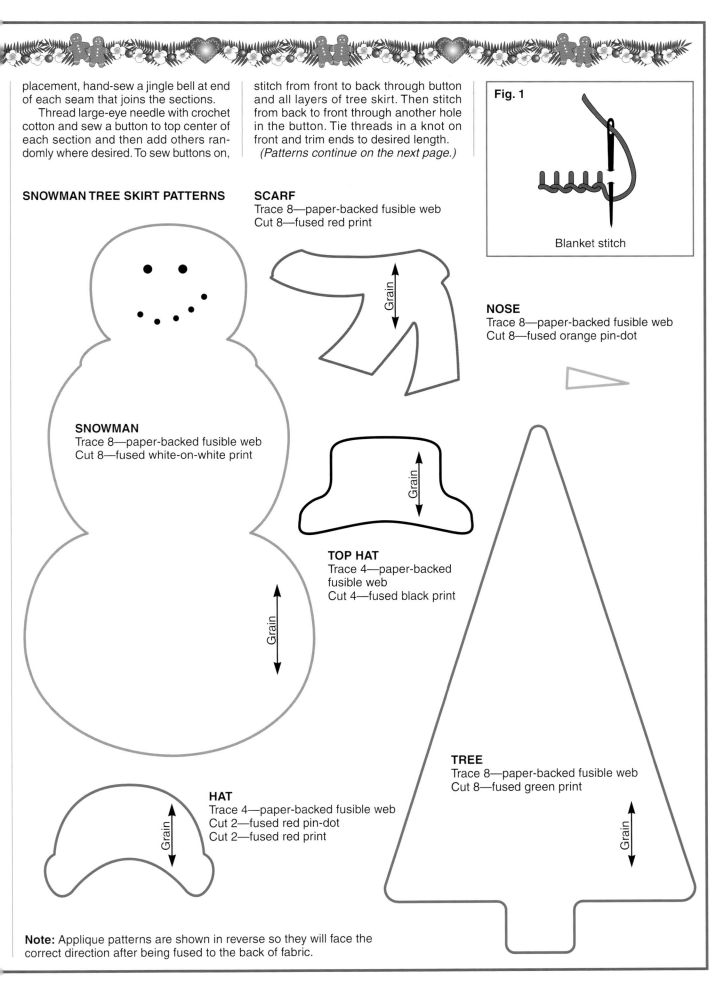

## Fig. 1

Blanket stitch

## SNOWMAN TREE SKIRT PATTERNS

**SCARF**
Trace 8—paper-backed fusible web
Cut 8—fused red print

**NOSE**
Trace 8—paper-backed fusible web
Cut 8—fused orange pin-dot

**SNOWMAN**
Trace 8—paper-backed fusible web
Cut 8—fused white-on-white print

Grain

**TOP HAT**
Trace 4—paper-backed fusible web
Cut 4—fused black print

Grain

**TREE**
Trace 8—paper-backed fusible web
Cut 8—fused green print

Grain

**HAT**
Trace 4—paper-backed fusible web
Cut 2—fused red pin-dot
Cut 2—fused red print

Grain

Grain

**Note:** Applique patterns are shown in reverse so they will face the correct direction after being fused to the back of fabric.

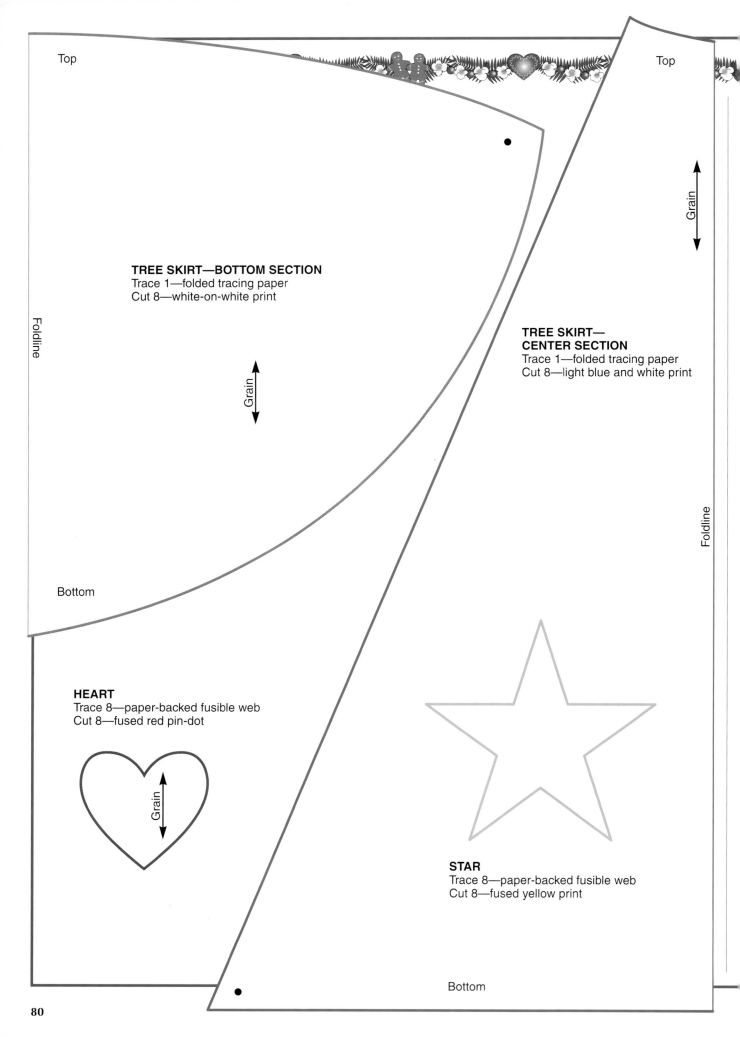

Top

Foldline

**TREE SKIRT—BOTTOM SECTION**
Trace 1—folded tracing paper
Cut 8—white-on-white print

Grain

**TREE SKIRT—
CENTER SECTION**
Trace 1—folded tracing paper
Cut 8—light blue and white print

Top

Grain

Foldline

Bottom

**HEART**
Trace 8—paper-backed fusible web
Cut 8—fused red pin-dot

Grain

**STAR**
Trace 8—paper-backed fusible web
Cut 8—fused yellow print

Bottom

# You'll Feed Birds for a Song

LOOKING FOR a thrifty way to treat your winged friends at Christmas or anytime of the year? This simple-to-construct bird feeder dishes out tasty fare handily from an inverted glass jar no matter what the weather's like.

"It's quickly and easily made at almost no cost," reveals Patricia Schroedl of Jefferson, Wisconsin. "I used wood scraps, jute string, a few wooden beads and nails, some paint and a recycled mayonnaise jar."

## Materials Needed:

*Pattern below*
*Tracing paper and pencil*
*8-inch x 2-inch piece of stencil plastic or freezer paper*
*8-inch square of 1-inch pine for seed tray of feeder*
*34 inches of 2-inch-wide x 1/4-inch-thick basswood for sides of feeder*
*Drill with 3/16-inch bit*
*Scroll saw*
*Sandpaper and tack cloth*
*Paper towels*
*Paper plate or palette*
*Acrylic craft paints—black, light blue, brown, green and red*
*Paintbrushes—liner, stencil brush and 1-inch sponge brush*
*Craft (X-Acto) knife*
*Masking tape*
*Exterior varnish*
*1-inch nails or brads*
*Hammer*
*Quart jar with metal screw-on band or plastic lid*
*Three 1/2-inch wooden beads*
*Three 1-1/4-inch flat-head screws*
*Screwdriver*
*Two 40-inch-long pieces of 3-ply jute string*
*Birdseed*

**Finished Size:** Bird feeder is 8 inches wide x 8-1/2 inches deep x 9 inches high without hanger.

## Directions:

Use scroll saw to cut basswood into two 8-in.-long pieces and two 8-1/2-in.-long pieces for sides of feeder.

Drill holes through seed tray of feeder about 3/4 in. from each corner.

Center metal band or plastic lid on top of seed tray. Drill three equally spaced holes through outside edge of band or lid and into seed tray to make pilot holes for screws.

Remove band or lid. If using plastic lid, drill into top of lid to make starter hole. Then use scroll saw to cut out center of lid, making a 2-in. circle for seed to fall through.

Sand all wooden pieces smooth. Wipe each with tack cloth.

Use sponge brush to paint sides of feeder light blue. Let dry.

Nail 8-in.-long sides to opposite sides of seed tray with bottom edges and ends even. Then nail 8-1/2-in.-long sides centered along remaining opposite sides of seed tray.

Trace stencil pattern onto tracing paper as directed on pattern. Tape pattern onto stencil plastic or freezer paper. Use craft knife to cut out stencil pattern on traced lines. Discard shaded areas.

Center stencil pattern along one side of feeder. Tape pattern to hold securely.

Dip stencil brush into green paint and wipe off excess paint until brush is nearly dry. Holding brush perpendicular to piece, apply paint with up-and-down motion to tree of stencil pattern. In same way, stencil birds red. Remove pattern and let dry. Repeat procedure on remaining sides of feeder.

Reposition pattern along one side of feeder, centering trunk pattern directly under tree shape as shown in photo. Stencil trunk brown. Let dry. Repeat on remaining sides of feeder.

Use liner and black paint to add legs to each bird as shown in photo. Then dip handle of brush into black paint and dab a small eye onto each bird. Let dry.

Apply exterior varnish. Let dry.

Insert screws into drilled holes of band or lid from the inside to outside. Slip a wooden bead over end of each screw for a spacer. Attach band or lid to seed tray, aligning screws with drilled pilot holes.

Working with both lengths of jute string as one, fold string in half. Then tie an overhand knot about 4 in. from fold.

Thread an end of jute string through each hole in corners of seed tray from top to bottom. Tie a knot in each, making sure feeder hangs level. Trim ends even.

Fill quart jar with birdseed. Invert feeder over jar and screw feeder onto jar. Quickly turn feeder right side up, allowing some seed to fall into seed tray.

Hang feeder outdoors during the holidays—and beyond! ♥

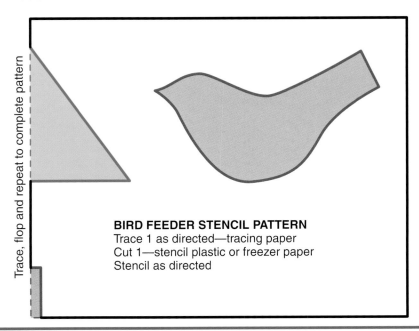

Trace, flop and repeat to complete pattern

**BIRD FEEDER STENCIL PATTERN**
Trace 1 as directed—tracing paper
Cut 1—stencil plastic or freezer paper
Stencil as directed

# Handy Trimmed Totes Help Handle Gift Giving

GET a grip on packaging presents with these sturdy seasonal sacks! Alida Macor of Martinsville, New Jersey shares her easy-to-make plastic canvas bags right here.

Accented with metallic cord and gold bells, the attractive jingling sacks are a gift in themselves. So make an extra one for your home to stash cards, candies or whatever you fancy.

**Materials Needed (for both):**
*Charts on next page*
*Craft scissors*
*Size 18 plastic canvas needle or tapestry needle*

**Materials Needed (for large bag):**
*Two 10-1/2-inch x 13-1/2-inch sheets of clear 7-count plastic canvas*
*4-ply worsted-weight yarn or plastic canvas yarn—33 yards of white, 14 yards of red and 7 yards of green*

*12 yards of gold metallic cord (Alida used Darice Metallic Gold No. 149)*
*Eight 5/8-inch gold jingle bells*
*Two 9-inch x 12-inch pieces of white self-adhesive felt*

**Materials Needed (for small bag):**
*One 11-inch x 14-inch sheet of clear 10-count plastic canvas*
*DMC No. 3 pearl cotton—27 yards of white, 11 yards of red and 6 yards of green*
*10 yards of gold metallic ribbon floss or six-strand gold metallic floss*
*Eight 3/8-inch gold jingle bells*
*One 9-inch x 12-inch piece of white self-adhesive felt*

**Finished Size:** Large bag is 8 inches high x 6 inches wide x 2 inches deep. Small bag is 5-1/2 inches high x 4 inches wide x 1-1/4 inches deep. Measurements do not include handles.

**Directions:**
**CUTTING:** Remembering to count bars and not holes, cut the plastic canvas as directed in instructions that follow.

**STITCHING:** Working with 18-in. to 20-in. lengths of yarn, pearl cotton, cord or floss, follow charts and instructions that follow to stitch pieces.

Do not knot strand on back of work. Instead, leave a 1-in. tail on the back of the plastic canvas and work the next few stitches over it. To end, run strand on back of canvas under completed stitches of the same color and clip close to work.

**LARGE BAG: Cutting:** From 7-count plastic canvas, cut two 40-bar x 54-bar pieces for front and back and two 14-bar x 54-bar pieces for sides. Also cut one 6-bar x 91-bar piece for handle and one 40-bar x 14-bar piece for bottom of bag.

Following charts and referring to Fig. 1 for stitch illustration, fill in front of bag with green, red and white yarn and gold metallic cord, using straight stitches as shown and leaving edges unstitched. Fill in back of bag in same way.

Stitch each side with red and white yarn and gold metallic cord straight stitches as shown

on chart, leaving edges unstitched.

Straight-stitch handle with red yarn as shown on chart, leaving edges unstitched. Then overcast long edges with red yarn.

The bottom of the bag is not stitched.

**Lining:** From self-adhesive felt, cut a piece slightly smaller than the front, back and two sides of the bag.

Remove paper backing from felt. Apply adhesive side of felt to the wrong side of each matching piece, centering each and avoiding the outer unstitched edges.

**Assembly:** Referring to photo, assemble bag as follows: Using white yarn, whipstitch the matching edges of each side to the front and back of the bag, making sure the right sides are facing out. Then whipstitch the unstitched bottom to the bottom edges of the front, back and sides.

Overcast top edge of bag with white yarn, attaching a short end of handle to center of each side of bag.

Using matching yarn, attach a 5/8-in. jingle bell above each gold metallic diamond as shown in photo.

**SMALL BAG: Cutting:** From 10-count plastic canvas, cut two 40-bar x 54-bar pieces for front and back and two 14-bar x 54-bar pieces for sides. Also cut one 6-bar x 91-bar piece for handle and one 40-bar x 14-bar piece for bottom of bag.

Following charts and referring to Fig. 1 for stitch illustration, fill in front of bag with green, red and white pearl cotton and gold metallic ribbon or floss, using straight stitches as shown and leaving edges unstitched. Fill in back of bag in same way.

Stitch each side with red and white pearl cotton and gold metallic ribbon or floss straight stitches, leaving edges unstitched as shown on chart.

Straight-stitch handle with red pearl cotton, leaving edges unstitched. Then overcast the long edges with red pearl cotton.

The bottom of the bag is not stitched.

**Lining:** Follow instructions for lining large bag.

**Assembly:** Referring to photo, assemble bag following assembly instructions for large bag and using white pearl cotton instead of yarn.

Using matching pearl cotton, attach a 3/8-in. jingle bell above each gold metallic diamond as shown in photo.

Fill the decorative holiday bags with festive gifts!

# PLASTIC CANVAS GIFT BAGS CHARTS AND COLOR KEYS

## HANDLE
**LARGE BAG**
6 bars x 91 bars
Cut 1—7-count plastic canvas
**SMALL BAG**
6 bars x 91 bars
Cut 1—10-count plastic canvas

**Fig. 1**

Straight stitch

Overcast/Whipstitch

**COLOR KEY**
**STRAIGHT STITCH**
— Green
— Red
— White
— Gold Metallic
**WHIPSTITCH/OVERCAST**
— Red
— White

## FRONT AND BACK
**LARGE BAG**
40 bars x 54 bars
Cut 2—7-count plastic canvas
**SMALL BAG**
40 bars x 54 bars
Cut 2—10-count plastic canvas

## SIDE
**LARGE BAG**
14 bars x 54 bars
Cut 2—7-count plastic canvas
**SMALL BAG**
14 bars x 54 bars
Cut 2—10-count plastic canvas

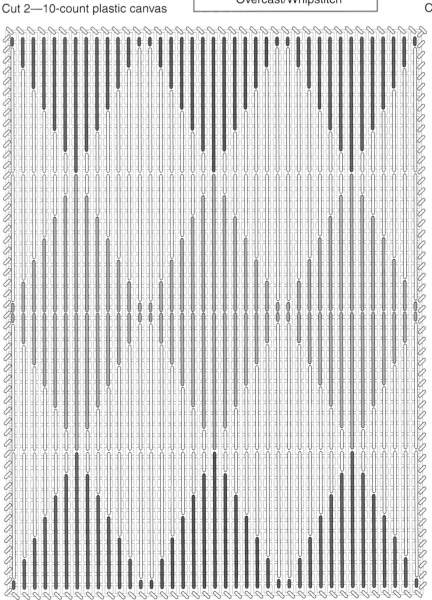

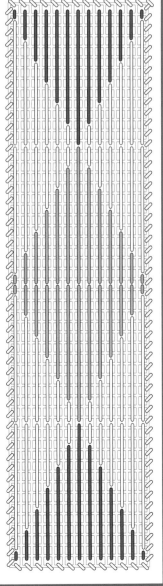

# Fast Festive Bookmarks Figure Extra Fun into Yuletide Reading

THESE craft stick creations make novel stocking stuffers for the little book lovers in your life. They're so much fun, kids might want to read even more in the snowy days ahead.

"Children love my bookmarks because the sparkle glaze and dimensional paint I apply make them eye-catching," confirms Sandra McKenzie of Braham, Minnesota.

**Materials Needed (for all):**
*Acrylic craft paints—flesh, pink, white and gold*
*Sparkle glaze*
*Small flat paintbrush*
*White (tacky) glue*
*Scissors*

**Materials Needed (for each snowman):**
*Patterns on next page*
*Tracing paper and pencil*
*One jumbo craft stick*
*One 1/16-inch-thick x 1-1/4-inch-wide wooden circle (Sandra used a large Woodsies circle)*
*Two 7mm glue-on wiggle eyes*
*Black and red dimensional paint*
*Sequins or holiday confetti—two silver snowflake shapes for snowman with earmuffs*
*Felt—small scrap each of orange and red for nose and bow tie and 2-inch square of black for snowman with top hat*
*Red pom-poms—two 3/8-inch for snowman with earmuffs and three 1/8-inch for snowman with top hat*
*Red pipe cleaner (chenille stem) for snowman with earmuffs*
*1-1/2-inch x 7-inch piece of green and tan check fabric for scarf and hatband*

**Materials Needed (for Santa):**
*One jumbo craft stick*
*One 1/16-inch-thick x 1-1/2-inch-high wooden Santa head (Sandra used a large Christmas Woodsies II Santa face)*
*Two 3mm glue-on wiggle eyes*
*White glitter*
*White bulky textured yarn, doll hair or cotton ball for beard*

**Materials Needed (for angel):**
*One jumbo craft stick*
*Two 1/16-inch-thick x 1-1/2-inch-long wooden lightbulb shapes (Sandra used large Christmas Woodsies II lightbulbs)*
*Toothpick*
*Two 3mm glue-on wiggle eyes*
*3-inch length of gold tinsel pipe cleaner (chenille stem) for halo*
*1-inch length of 1/4-inch-wide gold braid for trim*
*3-inch length of white yarn for hair*

**Finished Size:** Snowman with top hat measures about 1-1/2 inches across x 6-3/4 inches tall. Snowman with earmuffs measures about 1-3/4 inches across x 6-5/8 inches tall. Angel measures about 3 inches across x 6-1/4 inches tall. Santa measures about 1 inch across x 6-3/8 inches tall.

**Directions:**
Use flat brush to paint all sides of craft sticks and wooden shapes as directed. Apply additional coats of paint as needed for complete coverage, allowing drying time between each coat.

**SNOWMAN:** Paint craft stick and wooden circle white. Let dry.

Glue circle onto one end of craft stick for head with edge of circle even with end of craft stick. Let dry.

Apply sparkle glaze to assembled snowman. Let dry.

Referring to photo for position, glue eyes to head. Apply dots of black dimensional paint for mouth and red dots for cheeks. Let dry.

Cut a 5-in.-long strip of fabric. Wrap strip around craft stick below head for scarf and tie the ends in a loose knot.

Trace patterns onto tracing paper and cut out. Cut out each shape from felt as directed on patterns.

Referring to photo for position, glue bow tie to scarf and nose to face.

Glue two sequins to craft stick for buttons for snowman with earmuffs. Add a small dot of red dimensional paint to the center of each. Let dry.

Glue two 1/8-in. pom-poms to snowman with hat for buttons.

For snowman with hat, glue hat to top of head. Cut a 1/4-in. x 1-in. piece of fabric for hatband and glue to hat. Glue a 1/8-in. red pom-pom to hatband for trim.

For snowman with earmuffs, cut a 2-1/2-in. length of red pipe cleaner or chenille stem. Glue ends to sides of head above cheeks. Glue a 3/8-in. red pom-pom to each side of head, covering ends of pipe cleaner or chenille stem.

**SANTA:** Use flat brush to paint all sides of the craft stick red and the entire Santa face white. Let dry.

Paint a small oval on one side of Santa face flesh. On same side, paint a narrow band of red across top for Santa's hat, leaving tip white as shown in photo. Let dry.

Apply sparkle glaze to assembled Santa. Let dry.

Dip toothpick into red and dab a dot onto Santa's face for nose. Let dry.

Glue back of Santa's head onto one end of craft stick so craft stick does not show above top of hat. Apply a bit of glue to tip of hat and to white band above face. Sprinkle with white glitter and shake off excess. Let dry.

Glue eyes to Santa's head above nose. Let dry.

Glue yarn, doll hair or pieces from cotton ball to Santa's face for beard and mustache. Trim as desired. Let dry.

**ANGEL:** Use flat brush to paint all sides of craft stick and lightbulbs gold. Let dry.

Paint 1 in. at one end of craft stick white. When dry, paint a small oval at same end flesh for face. Let dry.

Referring to photo for position, glue lightbulbs to back of craft stick for wings.

Apply sparkle glaze to body and wings of assembled angel. Let dry.

Glue yarn on head for hair. Trim.

Glue eyes to face and braid across craft stick below head. Trim ends even with sides of craft stick.

Dip handle of paintbrush into pink

paint and dab a small dot onto face for mouth. Let dry.

Cut a 4-in.-long piece of tinsel pipe cleaner. Wrap pipe cleaner around finger to make a loop. Twist ends together and remove from finger. Glue ends to back of craft stick and bend circle of tinsel forward for halo as shown in photo. 🤍

**CRAFT STICK BOOKMARK PATTERNS**

**HAT
(for snowman with hat only)**
Trace 1—tracing paper
Cut 1—black felt

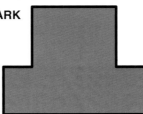

**BOW TIE AND NOSE
(for each snowman)**
Trace 1 each—tracing paper
Cut 1 each—color of felt as shown on patterns

# Christmas Card Container Will Bowl You Over

DON'T know what to do with Christmas cards that are just too pretty to toss? Fashion them into a lively holiday bowl with crochet!

"The thrifty bowls are a great way to recycle cards and scraps of leftover yarn," notes Carolyn Porter Stone of Harrisonburg, Virginia. "They can be made rather quickly as last-minute gifts, and they're perfect projects for scouts or other children's groups."

**Materials Needed:**
*Patterns below*
*Tracing paper and pencil*
*14 used Christmas cards*
*Round hole punch*
*Glue stick or white (tacky) glue*
*Approximately 25 yards of 4-ply worsted-weight yarn in color of choice*
*Size G (6mm) crochet hook*
*Tapestry needle*
*Scissors*

**Finished Size:** Card bowl measures about 10-1/2 inches across and is about 3-1/2 inches tall.

**Directions:**
Use copy machine to enlarge pattern to 200%, or mark tracing paper with a 1-in. grid and draw pattern as shown onto tracing paper.

Trace patterns onto tracing paper. Cut out patterns.

Trace around patterns onto right side of cards as directed on patterns with chosen design

of card centered under pattern. Cut out each just inside traced lines. Repeat, making 12 side pieces and two bottom pieces.

Glue two side pieces with wrong sides together and edges matching. Repeat with remaining side pieces to make six double-sided pieces. Glue the two bottom pieces together in the same way.

Place side pattern over a side piece with edges matching and use hole punch to punch holes at each X on pattern. Repeat with remaining side pieces and with bottom pattern and bottom piece.

**CROCHET:** With slip knot on hook, work 3 scs in any corner hole of a side piece, * [ch, 3, sc in next hole] to next corner, work 3 scs in corner hole; repeat from * around, join with sl st in beginning sc. Fasten off. In same way, crochet around each remaining side piece and bottom piece.

Thread tapestry needle with a long piece of yarn. With wrong sides together, whipstitch bottom edge of each side to one edge of bottom piece, catching one loop of each piece. See Fig. 1 for stitch illustration.

Then lift sides to join edges and in

same way, sew side edges together to form bowl shape. Fasten off.

Use tapestry needle to weave in all loose ends. 🤍

---

**ABBREVIATIONS**

| | |
|---|---|
| ch | chain |
| sc(s) | single crochet(s) |
| sl st | slip stitch |
| * [ ] | Instructions following asterisk or between brackets are repeated as directed. |

---

**Fig. 1**

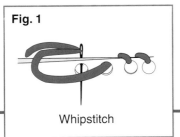

Whipstitch

**CROCHETED CARD BOWL PATTERNS**

Enlarge pattern 200%
Each square = 1 in.

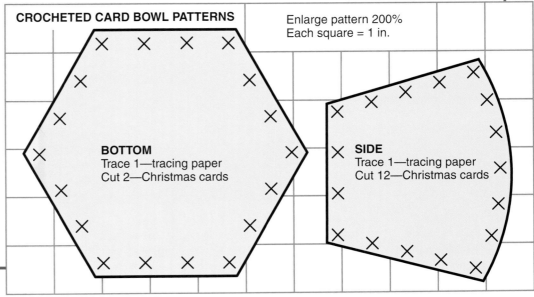

**BOTTOM**
Trace 1—tracing paper
Cut 2—Christmas cards

**SIDE**
Trace 1—tracing paper
Cut 12—Christmas cards

# Holly Wreath Sweatshirt Warms Up Wardrobe

WRAP a round of fabric holly leaves into a wreath and turn a plain white sweatshirt into a nifty Noel pullover. It takes only a few supplies to complete this easy project, assures Cheryl Ricketts of Washington, Illinois. So gather some fabric scraps and red pom-poms, then fuse, sew and go!

## Materials Needed:
*Patterns at right and on next page
White sweatshirt
44-inch-wide 100% cotton or cotton-blend fabrics—1/8 yard each or scraps of three different green plaid or check fabrics for holly leaves and 1/4 yard of red pin-dot for bow
Matching all-purpose thread
1/4 yard of paper-backed fusible web
Pencil
1/3 yard of tear-away stabilizer or typing paper
Red pom-poms—16 each of 1/2-inch and 1/4-inch
Standard sewing supplies*

**Finished Size:** The wreath applique measures about 12 inches across x 13 inches high and is shown on an Adult size Large sweatshirt. The design can be enlarged or reduced on a copy machine to fit other size garments.

## Directions:
Pre-wash all fabrics, washing colors separately. Dry and press fabrics. Wash and dry sweatshirt following manufacturer's instructions.

Trace patterns onto paper side of fusible web, leaving 1/2 in. between shapes. Cut shapes apart. Fuse shapes onto the wrong side of fabrics as directed on the patterns following manufacturer's directions.

Transfer inside design lines on bow by machine-stitching through lines traced on paper backing. Cut shapes out on traced lines.

Remove paper backing from appliques. Arrange holly leaves on right side of front of sweatshirt, forming a wreath as shown in photo. Place bow over holly leaves at the bottom of wreath as shown. Fuse appliques in place.

Pin tear-away stabilizer or typing paper to wrong side of garment behind the appliques.

Using green thread and a medium satin stitch, applique around the holly leaves.

Using a narrow satin stitch and red thread, stitch over inside design lines on bow. Using red thread and a medium satin stitch, applique around outside edges of bow.

Remove tear-away stabilizer or typing paper. Pull loose threads to wrong side. Tie off and clip threads close to knots.

Hand-stitch pom-poms to sweatshirt where shown in photo.

Don your holly-jolly top.

## WREATH SWEATSHIRT PATTERNS

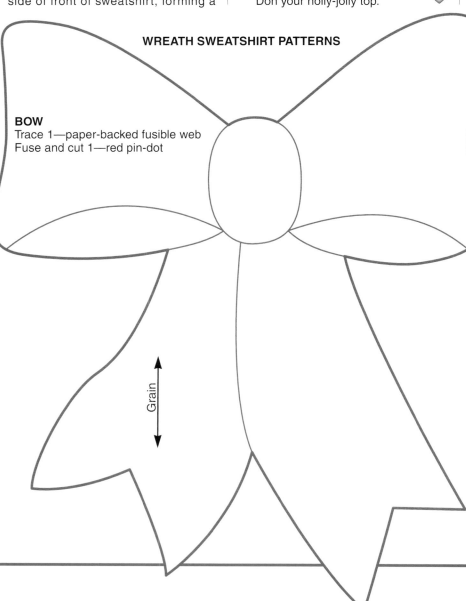

**BOW**
Trace 1—paper-backed fusible web
Fuse and cut 1—red pin-dot

Grain

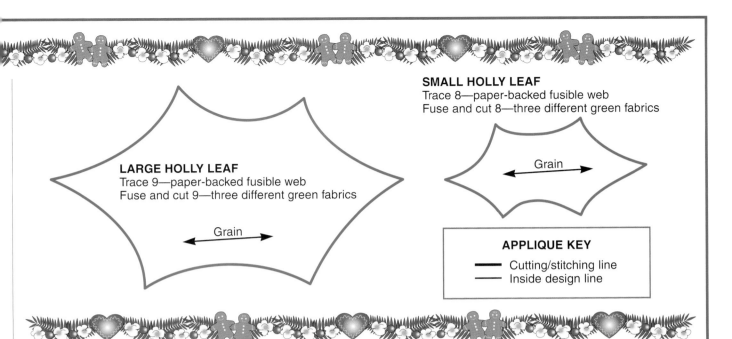

**SMALL HOLLY LEAF**
Trace 8—paper-backed fusible web
Fuse and cut 8—three different green fabrics

Grain

**LARGE HOLLY LEAF**
Trace 9—paper-backed fusible web
Fuse and cut 9—three different green fabrics

Grain

**APPLIQUE KEY**
—— Cutting/stitching line
— Inside design line

# Snowman Pins Fasten Fun On Christmas

THESE cheery winter accents fashioned from wood and bits of fabric will dress up your Yuletide apparel...and still be at home on a jacket or sweater after December 25.

"My snow folk pins are so popular that I made 75 one Christmas for gifts and to sell at local craft fairs," relates Bette Veinot of Bridgewater, Nova Scotia.

**Materials Needed (for one):**
*Wooden domed furniture plugs—one 1-inch diameter for head and one 1/4-inch diameter for nose*
*Paper plate or palette*
*Paper towels*
*Acrylic craft paints—black, pink, white and silver or gold metallic*
*Small flat paintbrush*
*Toothpick*
*Two 1-1/2-inch-long x 7/8-inch-wide pieces of dark blue and silver print, brick red and tan check or green and tan check fabric for scarf*
*2-1/2-inch square of light blue, brick red or dark green T-shirt ribbing for hat*
*All-purpose thread to match ribbing*
*Hand-sewing needle*
*Small amount of polyester stuffing*
*1/2-inch-high x 1/8-inch-thick wooden star or small gray or gold button for trim on hat*
*Textured snow paint*
*1-inch pin back*

*Glue gun and glue sticks*
*Scissors*

**Finished Size:** Each pin measures about 2 inches across x 3-1/2 inches high.

**Directions:**
**HEAD:** Place small amounts of paints on paper plate or palette as needed. Paint all pieces as directed. Apply a second coat as needed for complete coverage, allowing drying time between each coat.

Paint large wooden furniture plug white for head and small wooden furniture plug silver or gold metallic for nose. If using wooden star for hat trim, paint it gold metallic. Let dry.

Referring to photo for position, glue flat side of nose onto domed side of head.

Dip handle of paintbrush into black paint and dab small dots onto head for mouth and eyes where shown in photo. Let dry.

Dip paintbrush into pink paint and wipe brush on paper towel until no brush strokes show. Then add cheeks to each side of nose with a circular motion. Let paint dry.

Dip toothpick into white paint and dab three tiny dots onto each pink cheek. Let dry.

**HAT:** Fold T-shirt ribbing in half with ribs running parallel to fold. Hand-sew long raw edges together with an 1/8-in. seam, making a tube. Turn tube right side out.

To make brim of hat, fold one end of tube 1/4 in. to right side. Then fold again 3/8 in. to right side. Glue or hand-sew brim to seam to hold.

Place hat on head with seam in back. Pull hat down onto head so brim on back is about 1/2 in. from bottom of head. Fold

front of brim as before. Glue front of hat to head so fold of brim is just above eyes. Pull sides of brim down around head and glue to hold. Let dry.

Lightly stuff open end of hat. Wrap thread around open end about 1/2 in. from raw edge and tie to secure.

**SCARF:** Pull threads of each piece of scarf fabric to fringe, making 1/8-in.-long fringe on both long edges and 1/4-in.-long fringe on one short edge of each.

Referring to photo for position, glue unfringed end of one piece to back of head so end hangs straight down. Glue unfringed edge of other scarf piece to back of first piece so end extends to the side.

**FINISHING:** Glue pin back onto back along seam of hat.

Glue button or star to brim of hat.

Use paintbrush to apply a dab of textured snow to the hat where desired. Let dry.

Pin on a favorite outfit!

# Cherub-Trimmed Basket Fills A Bushel Of Yuletide Uses

SHOWING plenty of Christmas spirit, this charming basket makes a heavenly addition to your holiday decor. Even better, it's a delight to do!

"If you're a beginner, allow about an hour for this project," says weaver Jodi Shebester of Concord, North Carolina. "The more you make, the quicker you'll be. I can make five baskets in 55 minutes, so I call this my '11-Minute Special'."

**Materials Needed:**

*Natural reed—3/8-inch flat for stakes and weavers and 1/4-inch flat for locking row*
*Red reed\*—11/16-inch or 3/16-inch flat for weavers*
*Heavy scissors or side cutters*
*Tape measure*
*Pencil*
*Large plastic bucket to soak reed*
*Old towel*
*Spring-type clothespins*
*Needle-nose pliers*

*Trim—2-1/2-inch-high tie-on ceramic angel and 8 inches of 1/8-inch-wide white satin ribbon or same-size wooden angel cutout (painted white or color of choice) and white (tacky) glue*

*\*To dye your own reed, use red Rit dye and follow the instructions included in the package.*

**Shopping Information:** To order a kit for this basket, write to The Basket House, 527 Union St. South, Concord NC 28025-5570 or phone 1-704/782-5993.

**Finished Size:** Basket measures about 7 inches long x 5-1/4 inches across x 4 inches high.

**Directions:**
For stakes, cut eight 24-in.-long pieces of 3/8-in. natural reed.

Soak reed in warm water for about 5 minutes or until pliable. Measure and mark the center on wrong side of stakes.

Place towel on a flat surface. Lay out and weave the eight pieces as shown in Fig. 1. Adjust base so it measures 4-3/4 in. x 2-1/2 in.

**Locking row:** Soak 1/4-in. natural reed until pliable.

Weave with reed rough side up, alternating under and over the stakes and weaving parallel to one long edge of the base.

Bend and crease the reed diagonally at the corner so the reed is parallel to the short edge of the base. Weave along the short edge, alternating over and under the stakes.

Bend and crease reed at next corner. Continue weaving along the remaining edges and corners as before. When beginning stake is reached, continue over and under next couple of stakes, clipping end of weaver in the middle of the last stake.

**Upsetting the stakes:** Working with dampened basket base, gently bend each stake upward from the base by rolling the stakes over your finger. Hold stakes in place with clothespins as needed.

**Sides: Rows 1-2:** Soak 3/8-in. natural reed until pliable. Weave with natural reed, alternating over and under the stakes.

**Rows 3-8:** Soak red reed until pliable. Wipe the reed with the towel to remove excess dye. Weave with red reed, alternating over and under the stakes.

**Rows 9-10:** Weave with 3/8-in. natural reed, alternating over and under the stakes.

**Row 11:** Place a piece of 3/8-in. natural reed around the inside of the basket, overlapping beginning and end of piece. This piece is not woven in. Use clothespins as needed to hold the piece in place.

**Rim:** Bend any stake to the inside of basket. At the same time, insert the end of the stake from the inside to the outside between Rows 10 and 11 and in front of its neighboring stake. Tuck the end in back of the top of the next stake. See Fig. 2. Using the next stake to the right, continue in the same way around top of basket.

**FINISHING:** Find the center of the best side of your basket.

Thread ends of ribbon through reed from inside to outside on best side of basket. Then thread ribbon from back to front through holes in angel. Tie ends in a bow to secure. Or glue wooden angel cutout to side of basket.

Fill with pine boughs, ornaments or whatever you like to make a festive table or mantel decoration! ♥

**Fig. 1** Layout  **Fig. 2** Finishing the rim

2-1/2 in.

4-3/4 in.

# Top Off Decor with Curtain Trim

WHEN it comes to easy elegance, these appealing country accents are tops—and they're a breeze to make from a simple square of fabric. Arranged in a "V" over a valance or curtain, the dapper drapery garnishes create a merry mood inside and out.

"The toppers can be made larger or smaller to suit your window," suggests designer Betty Veinot of Bridgewater, Nova Scotia.

**Materials Needed (for one):**
*13-1/2-inch square of fabric to coordinate with room*
*Two 1-1/4-inch-high plastic cups*
*Gold metallic spray paint*
*3 inches of 1/4-inch gold bead garland or gold string beads for clappers*
*4-1/2 inches of 3mm gold string beads for hangers*
*Tweezers or needle-nose pliers*
*Glue gun and glue sticks*
*36 inches of 1-1/4-inch-wide velvet*

*ribbon in color of choice to coordinate with fabric*
*Matching all-purpose thread and hand-sewing needle (optional)*
*Scissors and pinking shears*

**Finished Size:** Curtain topper measures about 18-1/2 inches across x 12-1/2 inches deep.

**Directions:**
Spray-paint inside and outside of each plastic cup gold. Let dry.

Tie velvet ribbon into a bow measuring about 7 in. across. Trim ends of bow in an inverted "V" to desired length.

Cut a 1-1/2-in. length of larger gold bead garland or string beads. Apply glue to the inside of bottom of plastic cup. Use tweezers or pliers to glue one end of length of beads into cup for clapper. Repeat to add a clapper to the other plastic cup.

Cut a 4-in. length of smaller gold string beads and glue an end to bottom of each gold plastic cup.

Use pinking shears to trim 1/4 in. from all sides of fabric square, making a 13-in. square.

Fold fabric square in half diagonally with wrong sides together.

Glue or hand-tack bow centered along fold as shown in photo.

Glue or hand-tack length of beads joining bells to a bottom point of curtain topper, allowing bells to hang unevenly as shown in photo.

Improve your view with this pretty Yuletide topper! ♥

89

# Cheery Cross-Stitched Cubbies Will Sew Up Beary Merry Yule

THESE cute little critters are so cuddly, you'll wish you could give them all bear hugs! Renee Dent of Conrad, Montana illustrated the teddy bear trio getting ready for Christmas.

"One chubby bruin holds a tree, one has a stocking and one is ready to hang candy canes, which are crossed to form a heart," Renee explains.

Bear in mind, they're so adorable that you might have to stitch sets for friends and family, too!

**Materials Needed (for all):**
*Pattern on next page*
*Tracing paper and pencil*
*Charts on next page*
*Three 6-inch squares of white 14-count Aida cloth*
*Three 6-inch squares of fusible interfacing*
*Three 7-inch squares of coordinating felt for backing*
*DMC six-strand embroidery floss in colors listed on color key*
*Size 24 tapestry needle*
*1/4-inch-wide white satin ribbon—three 6-inch lengths for hangers*
*and three 8-inch lengths for bows*
*Three 15-inch lengths of 1/2-inch-wide pre-gathered white lace*
*White (tacky) glue*
*Scissors*
*Iron and ironing surface*

**Finished Size:** Each ornament is about 4-1/8 inches wide x 6-1/2 inches high without the hangers. Design area of bear with candy cane and bear with stocking is 51 stitches high x 28 stitches wide. Design area of bear with tree is 59 stitches high x 36 stitches wide.

**Directions:**
Zigzag or overcast edges of Aida cloth to prevent fraying. Fold Aida cloth in half lengthwise and then in half crosswise to determine center and mark this point.

To find center of charts, draw lines across charts connecting arrows. Begin stitching each at this point so designs will be centered.

Working with 18-inch lengths of six-strand floss, separate strands and use two strands for cross-stitching and French knots and one strand for back-stitching. See Fig. 1 for stitch illustrations.

Each square on chart equals one stitch worked over a set of fabric threads. Use colors indicated on color key to complete cross-stitching, then backstitching.

Do not knot floss on back of work. Instead, leave a short tail of floss on back of work and hold it in place while working the first few stitches over it. To end a strand, run needle under a few neighboring stitches in back before cutting floss close to work.

**ASSEMBLY:** Fuse interfacing onto wrong side of each completed design.

Use copy machine to enlarge pattern to 200%, or mark tracing paper with a 1-in. grid and draw pattern as shown onto tracing paper.

Trace oval pattern onto tracing paper. Center pattern over each completed design and cut out oval shapes.

Glue felt onto interfacing side of each, making sure edges of ovals are securely glued. Let glue dry. Trim excess felt, cutting along outside of oval.

Glue ends of each 6-in. length of ribbon together. Then glue ends centered onto top of each ornament.

Starting and stopping at the top, glue lace trim around front edge of each design and trim excess.

Tie each 8-in. length of ribbon into a small bow. Glue a bow to front of each ornament, covering ends of lace trim.

Trim your Christmas tree with these cuddly cuties! ♥

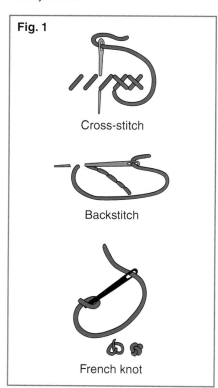

Fig. 1

Cross-stitch

Backstitch

French knot

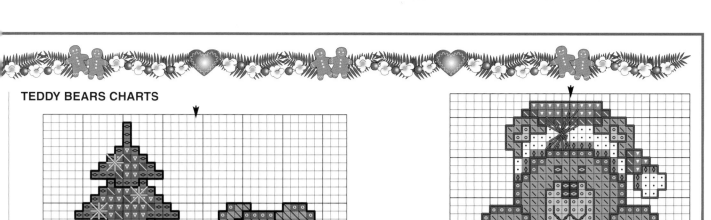

**TEDDY BEARS CHARTS**

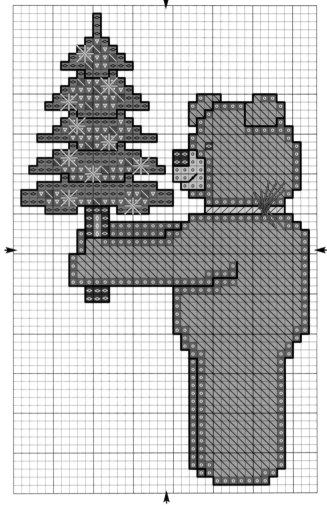

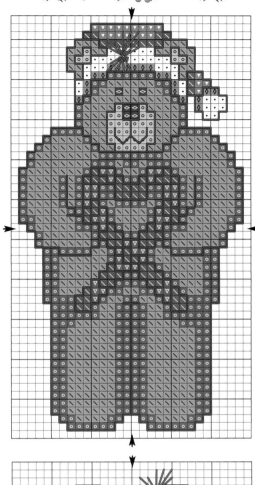

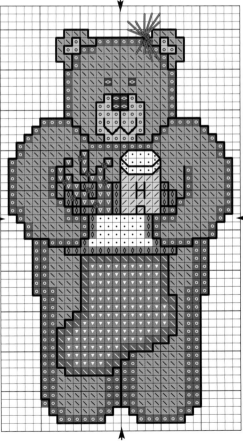

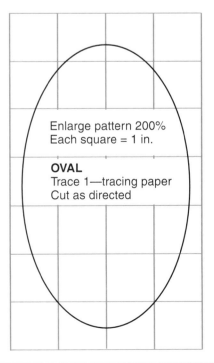

Enlarge pattern 200%
Each square = 1 in.

**OVAL**
Trace 1—tracing paper
Cut as directed

**CROSS-STITCHED TEDDY BEARS**

| COLOR KEY | DMC |
|---|---|
| · White | 000 |
| ▽ Dark Coral | 349 |
| ◈ Pearl Gray | 415 |
| ◎ Light Brown | 434 |
| ◥ Very Light Brown | 435 |
| ● Tan | 436 |
| ▽ Kelly Green | 702 |
| ◣ Very Dark Coral Red | 817 |
| ◊ Medium Beige Brown | 840 |
| ◈ Very Dark Parrot Green | 904 |
| ■ Black Brown | 3371 |
| ◨ Dark Mocha Brown | 3781 |
| ╱ Straw | 3821 |

**BACKSTITCHING**
| — Kelly Green | 702 |
|---|---|
| — Black Brown | 3371 |
| — Straw | 3821 |

**FRENCH KNOT**
| ❀ Very Dark Coral Red | 817 |
|---|---|

# Wooden Nativity Scene Holds Season's Reason

MOLD meaning into your Christmas celebration with this heartwarming manger scene from Loretta Kemna of St. Elizabeth, Missouri.

To make it, you fashion figures with modeling clay, then build the stable and manger from craft sticks and dowels. The divine display will add joy to a table, mantel or any spot you place it during the holidays.

**Materials Needed:**

*Oven-bake polymer clay—beige, blue, brown, translucent, white and yellow (Loretta used Sculpey III clay in Beige 093, Blue 063, Chocolate 053, Translucent 010, White 001 and Yellow 072)*
*Polymer clay glaze and small paintbrush (optional)*
*Waxed paper*
*Rolling pin*
*Compass and pencil*
*Permanent fine-line markers—black, gold and red*
*2-inch length of 3mm gold string beads for halo*
*Purchased 5-inch x 7-inch wooden plaque or same-size piece of 3/4-inch-thick pine*
*16 jumbo craft sticks*
*Scroll or band saw*
*Transparent tape*
*Ruler*
*Two 3-inch lengths of 3/8-inch wooden dowel*
*Spanish moss*
*White (tacky) glue or glue gun and glue sticks*
*Scissors*

**Finished Size:** Wood Nativity is 7 inches long x 5 inches deep x 4 inches high.

**Directions:**
**NATIVITY FIGURES:** Knead clay until soft and smooth, making sure to wash

hands each time you use a new color of clay.

Use rolling pin to roll out clay between sheets of waxed paper. When joining pieces, press them into place firmly or work clay together with a knife to avoid having them come apart during baking.

After shaping, bake the clay pieces according to manufacturer's directions.

**Mary:** To make body, shape a 1-in. ball of white into a 1-1/4-in.-long tapered log. Lay log on a flat surface and press down on wide end while gently lifting narrow end to create a 1-1/4-in.-tall kneeling figure.

Shape two large pea-size pieces of white clay into arms. Press arms onto each side of body.

Roll two pea-size balls of beige clay and attach one to end of each arm for hands.

For Mary's shawl, roll out blue clay to 1/16-in. thickness between sheets of waxed paper. Use compass to draw a 2-in. circle onto waxed paper. Cut out circle, cutting through all layers. Then cut a slit from edge into center of circle.

Remove waxed paper. Drape shawl over figure with slit on top of figure, leaving space for head.

Roll a 3/8-in. ball of beige for head. Press head onto top of body.

Flatten a pea-size ball of brown clay onto top of head for hair.

For head covering, roll out blue clay to 1/16-in. thickness and cut out a 1-1/2-in. circle using same technique as for shawl. Fold one edge of circle back 1/4 in., forming a straight edge. Place the straight edge of head covering over head and drape remainder around figure as shown in photo.

**Joseph:** Make Joseph, following the instructions for Mary and using yellow clay for the body and arms and brown

clay for the shawl.

For head covering, roll brown clay to 1/16-in. thickness and cut a 1-1/4-in. triangle from clay. Drape triangle over Joseph's head as shown in photo.

**Angel:** Make angel following instructions above, using a 1-1/4-in.-high cone of translucent clay for body and shaping arms from translucent clay as before. Omit shawl and head covering.

Roll beige clay to 1/16-in. thickness and cut a 1-1/2-in. x 3/4-in. rectangle for wings. Use scissors to round all corners. Press wings onto back of angel below head.

**Baby:** Roll white clay to 1/16-in. thickness and cut a 1-in. square for blanket. Roll a pea-size ball of beige clay for head. Place head at one corner of blanket. Fold opposite corner up 1/4 in. and then overlap right and left corners.

**Finishing:** Bake all clay pieces following manufacturer's directions. Let cool.

Use paintbrush to apply glaze to figures if desired. Let dry.

Use markers to add black eyes and nose and a red mouth to each figure as shown in photo. Use gold marker to add hair to angel's head and to color angel's wings.

Glue gold beads into a small circle for halo. Glue halo to top of angel's head.

**STABLE:** Stack three craft sticks with edges even and wrap with tape to secure. Use scroll or band saw to cut craft sticks in half crosswise, making six 3-in.-long pieces for back of stable.

Place the six pieces on a flat surface with long edges about 1/4 in. apart and ends even. Glue a craft stick across top (curved ends) with ends even. See Fig. 1. When glue has dried, turn assembled back over and glue a craft stick

**Fig. 1** Making back of stable

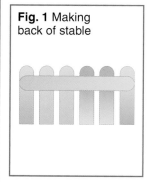

**Fig. 2** Making top of stable

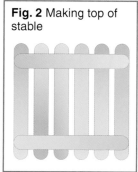

**Fig. 3** Making manger

across top of back with back sandwiched in between and ends even as before. Let dry.

For top of stable, lay six craft sticks on a flat surface with long edges about 1/4 in. apart and ends even. Glue a craft stick across top with one long edge about 1/2 in. from curved ends. Glue another craft stick across bottom in same way. See Fig. 2.

When glue has dried, turn assembled top over and glue a craft stick to top

with top sandwiched in between and ends even. Let dry.

Glue ends of dowels to top of wooden plaque about 1 in. from corners along one long edge. Glue back of stable to edge of opposite long side. Let dry.

Apply glue along top edge of back and to tops of dowels. Glue top of stable to edge of back and to tops of dowels as shown in photo.

**MANGER:** From remaining craft sticks, cut two 1-1/2-in.-long pieces and

two 1-in.-long pieces.

Glue one long edge of each 1-1/2-in.-long piece together to form a V. Then glue a short piece centered across each end. See Fig. 3.

**FINISHING:** Referring to photo for position, glue Mary, Joseph, angel and manger to plaque. Glue Spanish moss to top of plaque and inside manger.

Place baby in manger.

Display the finished scene and spread the holiday spirit. ♥

---

# Wreath Makes a Sharp Name Tag

THIS welcome wreath pin will put everyone on a first-name basis. Fashioned from plastic canvas, the seasonal accessory leaves room for a purchased name tag.

"This pretty pin makes a great stocking stuffer for anyone who wears a name tag, such as a teacher, nurse or store clerk," offers Mary Cosgrove of Rockville, Connecticut. "If you don't want to add a name tag, add a hook and hang it on the tree instead."

**Materials Needed:**
*Chart below*
*4-inch square of 7-count plastic canvas*
*Plastic canvas yarn—3 yards each of green and red and 1 yard of white*
*Plastic canvas needle*
*Purchased name pin*
*Scissors*

**Finished Size:** Wreath is 3 inches high x 3-1/4 inches across.

**Directions:**
**CUTTING:** Remembering to count the bars and not holes, cut out wreath following outside cutting lines on chart. Then cut out and discard the shaded areas as shown.

**STITCHING:** Working with 18- to 20-in. lengths of yarn, follow chart and instructions below to stitch piece. See Fig. 1 for stitch illustrations.

Do not knot the yarn on back of work. Instead, leave a 1-in. tail on the back and catch it in the first few stitches. To end a yarn, run yarn on back of canvas under completed stitches of the same color and clip close to work.

Using green yarn, fill in wreath with Continental stitches.

Add red mosaic stitches and red reverse Continental stitches. Then add white Continental and reverse Continental stitches.

Stitch ends of the bow with red long slanted straight stitches. Then fill in center of bow with red vertical straight stitches, stitching two stitches per hole.

Overcast outside edges with matching yarn as shown on chart.

Place name pin over wreath and attach to clothing. ♥

---

**WREATH COLOR KEY**
**CONTINENTAL STITCH**
╱ Green
╱ Red
⬭ White
**REVERSE CONTINENTAL STITCH**
╱ Red
⬭ White
**MOSAIC STITCH**
╱ Red
**STRAIGHT STITCH**
— Red
**OVERCAST**
— Green
— Red

---

**PLASTIC CANVAS WREATH CHART**
22 bars x 20 bars

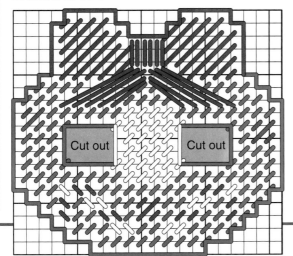

**Fig. 1**

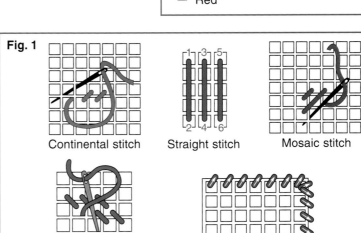

Continental stitch    Straight stitch    Mosaic stitch

Reverse Continental stitch    Overcast

# Tiny Snowman Trim Contains Lots of Charm

Round toothpick for snowman's nose
3/4-inch-high wooden star
Two 3mm black beads for eyes
Drill with 5/64-inch bit
Glue gun and glue sticks
Scissors

* Karen used a 1.25-ounce bottle. If your bottle does not have a round ball cap, use an appropriate size Styrofoam ball in place of the cap for the head.

**Finished Size:** Snowman measures about 3 inches tall x 3-1/2 inches across.

**Directions:**
**CROCHETED HAT:** With black, ch 6, join to first ch with sl st to form a ring. Work in rounds without turning. Move stitch marker with each round.

**Round 1:** Work 12 sc in ring, add stitch marker: 12 scs.

**Round 2:** * Work 2 scs in next sc; repeat from * around: 24 scs.

**Round 3:** Sc in each sc around: 24 scs.

**Round 4:** Working in back loops only, sc in each sc around: 24 scs.

**Rounds 5-11:** Sc in each sc around: 24 scs.

**Round 12:** Working in front loops only, * sc in next sc, work 2 scs in next sc; repeat from * around: 36 scs.

**Round 13:** * Sc in each sc around, join with sl st in first st of round: 36 scs. Fasten off and weave in loose ends.

Form into hat shape as shown in photo.

**SNOWMAN:** Screw plastic cap onto top of bottle or push and glue Styrofoam ball onto top of bottle for head. Lightly sand bottle and plastic cap to roughen surface. Do not sand Styrofoam ball.

Using flat brush, paint entire bottle and head white. Let dry.

Using the old scruffy brush and a dabbing motion, apply textured snow paint to bottle and entire head. Let dry.

Apply another coat of white paint over textured snow paint and let dry.

Dip one end of toothpick into orange paint for nose. Let dry.

Use flat brush to paint entire star yellow. Let dry.

Drill a hole into center of one side of plastic cap for nose. Break off about 1/2 in. from painted end of toothpick for nose. Dip wider end into glue and insert nose into hole in cap, with pointed end extending about 3/8 in. from cap. If using

a Styrofoam ball for the head, glue prepared toothpick nose onto ball.

Referring to photo for placement, glue black beads above nose for eyes.

Drill holes on each side of bottle about 1/2 in. down from cap for placement of arms. Dip ends of twigs into glue and insert glued end of twigs into holes. Position arms as shown in photo.

Tie scarf around bottle just below head and spot-glue ends to front of snowman's body as shown in photo.

Cut an 8-in.-long piece of black crochet cotton. Glue ends to top of snowman's head, leaving loop for hanger. Use crochet hook to thread loop of hanger through center of crocheted hat. Position hat on head and glue to hold. Or omit hanger and glue hat to top of head.

Glue star to one end of remaining twig for wand. Glue wand to bottom edge of bottle and to one twig arm as shown in photo.

Set the flaky fellow out for all to enjoy!

THIS frosty fellow sends out a merry message in a bottle. Karen Wittkop of Duluth, Minnesota fashioned her cool character from a recycled plastic container, then dressed him in a crocheted top hat and fabric scarf. Whether you hang him on the tree or set him on a shelf, he's sure to melt your heart!

**Materials Needed:**
Empty, clean and dry 2-3/4-inch-high rounded plastic bottle with round ball cap*
Approximately 12 yards of size 10 black crochet cotton
Size 6 steel crochet hook
Stitch marker
Acrylic craft paint—orange, white and yellow
Textured snow paint
Paintbrushes—small flat and old scruffy brush
Twigs—two 3-inch-long for arms and one 4-inch-long for star wand
3/4-inch x 7-inch strip of Christmas print fabric for scarf

---

| ABBREVIATIONS | |
|---|---|
| ch(s) | chain(s) |
| sc(s) | single crochet(s) |
| sl st | slip stitch |
| st(s) | stitch(es) |
| * | Instructions following asterisk are repeated as instructed. |

# Wrap It Up!

IF YOU wait until the last minute to wrap Christmas gifts, you want the process to be as streamlined as possible. Being organized helps. Here are some tips from craft editor Jane Craig that will tie things up in no time.

• Keep all folded wrapping paper, gift bags, tape, scissors and ribbon in a portable container so you can pick up everything at once and take it to your work area.

• Stand rolls of wrapping paper in a tall wastebasket to keep them contained in one area.

• Use a piece of ribbon to measure the distance around large packages, allowing for an overlap. Then use it to measure your wrapping paper before cutting.

• For tangle-free ribbon, store rolls and spools of ribbon on a dowel with a spring-type clothespin at each end to hold them in place. ♥

# Adorable Country Angels Add Joyful Note to Christmas Tree

YOUR spirits will soar when this host of heavenly figures takes wing. Doll up the curly-haired cherubs in Noel print dresses, bits of lace and ribbon, then let them fly around the tree and spread good cheer.

"They're perfect gifts for teachers or baby-sitters," notes Susie Germundson of Fargo, North Dakota. "You can make them just for Christmas or give them a summertime look with flower prints and a straw hat. Each angel seems to take on its own personality when it's finished."

## Materials Needed (for one):
*Patterns below*
*Tracing paper and pencil*
*Two 7-inch squares of 100% cotton or cotton-blend Christmas print fabric (Susie used a fabric with a printed seasonal greeting)*
*4-inch x 6-inch piece of paper-backed no-sew fusible web*
*3/4-inch wooden bead for head*
*Curly doll hair in color of choice*
*Assorted trims (Susie used scraps of lace, pearl trim, gold mini-star garland and 1/16-inch-wide red, green and white ribbon bows to trim her angels)*
*6 inches of metallic gold elastic for hanger (optional)*
*Craft pick or three toothpicks*

*Acrylic craft paints—brown, red and white*
*Liner brush*
*Glue gun and glue sticks*
*Scissors*

**Finished Size:** Each angel measures about 2-1/2 inches across x 4 inches high without hanger.

**Directions:**
Center fusible web on wrong side of one piece of Christmas print fabric. Fuse in place following manufacturer's directions. Remove paper backing and fuse to wrong side of remaining fabric piece with edges matching.

Trace patterns onto folded tracing paper. Cut out each and open for complete patterns.

Place patterns on fused fabric with grain lines matching. Cut out each on traced lines as directed on patterns.

Break off about a 2-1/2-in.-long piece of craft pick. Glue craft pick into hole on one side of bead for head. If using toothpicks, glue all three toothpicks into hole.

Use liner and brown to add eyes, eyebrows, eyelashes, nose and tiny dots to head as shown in photo. Let dry.

Dip handle of brush into red paint and dab on a small dot for mouth. Let dry.

Wrap pieces for arms and dress into cone shapes, overlapping the edges a bit. Glue the overlapped edges together to hold cone shape.

Slip craft pick or toothpicks through opening in top of dress and glue bottom of head to top of dress.

Glue an arm to each side of dress, referring to photo for placement.

Glue wings centered onto back of dress below head.

Add ribbon or lace trim to front of angel as shown in photo.

If desired, glue ends of metallic cord to top of head, leaving a loop for hanger.

Glue doll hair onto head as shown in photo.

Glue garland, pearl trim or bow to top of head. Cut seasonal greeting from fabric and glue to hands if desired.

Perch on boughs, windows or anywhere you like! ♥

## ANGEL PATTERNS

### WINGS
Trace 1—folded tracing paper
Cut 1—fused Christmas print fabric

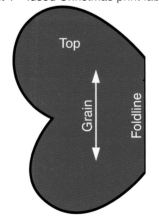

Top

Grain

Foldline

### DRESS
Trace 1 each—folded tracing paper
Cut 1—fused Christmas print fabric

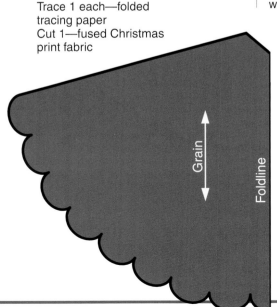

Grain

Foldline

### ARM
Trace 1—folded tracing paper
Cut 2—fused Christmas print fabric

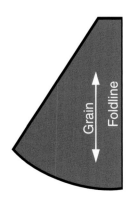

Grain

Foldline

# Her Sampler Stocking Keeps You in Stitches

**REVERSE SINGLE CROCHET: reverse sc:** Holding crochet hk as usual and working from left to right, insert hk in next st to right, yo and draw yarn through hk. Continue working in this way from left to right around or across row as instructed.

**Directions:**
Begin at top of stocking.

**Row 1:** With white yarn, ch 31, sc in second ch from hk and in each ch across, turn: 30 scs.

**Rows 2-11:** Ch 1, working in back lp only, sc in each sc across, turn: 30 scs.

**Row 12:** Ch 2, working in back lp only, hdc in each sc across: 30 hdcs. Fasten off.

**Row 13:** Attach red yarn in first hdc on wrong side, ch 3 (counts as dc), [sk 1 hdc, dc in next hdc, dc in sk hdc] 14 times, dc in top of beginning ch-3, turn: 30 dcs.

**Row 14:** Ch 3 (counts as dc), dc in each dc across, turn: 30 dcs.

**Row 15:** Ch 3 (counts as dc), [sk 1 dc, dc in next dc, dc in sk dc] 14 times, dc in last dc, turn: 30 dcs.

**Row 16:** Repeat Row 14, inc 1 dc in first dc: 31 dcs. Fasten off, turn.

**Row 17:** Attach white yarn in last dc, ch 3 (counts as dc), ch 1, * sk 1 dc, dc in next dc, ch 1; repeat from * across, dc in last dc. Fasten off, turn.

**Row 18:** Attach green yarn in last dc, ch 1, * dc in next sk dc in Row 16, sc in previous dc of Row 17; repeat from * across, sc in third ch of beginning ch-3: 31 sts.

**Row 19:** Attach green yarn in last dc, ch 3 (counts as dc), ch 1, * sk one dc, dc in next sc, ch 1; repeat from * across to last sc, dc in last st: 31 sts. Fasten off, turn.

**Row 20:** Attach red yarn in same st, ch 1, * [dc in next sk st of Row 18, sc in next dc of Row 19; repeat from * across, ending with last sc in third ch of beginning ch-3, turn: 31 sts.

**Row 21:** Ch 3 (counts as dc), dc in each st across, turn: 31 dcs.

**Row 22:** Ch 2, work 2 dcs in same st, * sk 2 dcs, sc in next dc, ch 2, work 2 dcs in same place as sc (shell made); repeat from * across to last 3 sts, sk 2 dcs, sc in third ch of beginning ch-3: 10 shells. Fas-

ten off, turn.

**Row 23:** Attach white yarn in last sc, ch 3 (counts as dc), dc in same st, [work 3 dcs in ch-sp of shell] 9 times, work 2 dcs in ch-sp of last shell, turn: 31 dcs.

**Rows 24-25:** Ch 3 (counts as dc), dc in same st, [work 3 dcs in center dc of next 3-dc group] 9 times, work 2 dcs in last dc, turn: 31 sts. Fasten off at end of Row 25, turn.

**Row 26:** Attach green yarn in last dc, ch 3 (counts as dc), dc in each dc across: 31 dcs, turn.

**Row 27:** Ch 3 (counts as dc), dc in same st, * ch 1, sk 2 dcs, work 4 dc Cl in next dc, ch 1, sk 2 dcs, work 2 dcs in next dc; repeat from * across, turn: 5 dc Cls and 6 2-dc groups.

**Row 28:** Ch 3, * dc in each of next two dcs, dc in next ch-sp, work 2 dcs in next dc Cl; repeat from * across: 31 dcs. Fasten off, turn.

**Row 29:** Attach white yarn in last dc, ch 1, sc in each dc to last 3 sts, work 2 scs in each of last 3 dcs, turn: 34 scs.

**Row 30:** Ch 3, work (dc, ch 2, 2 dcs) in same st, * sk 2 scs, work (2 dcs, ch 2, 2 dcs) in next sc; repeat from * across to last 3 sts, sk 2 scs, work 2 dcs in last sc.

**Row 31:** Ch 3 (counts as dc), turn, dc in next dc, work (2 dcs, ch 2, 2 dcs) in

GET in step with the season by crocheting this fun striped stocking. Sue Childress of Longview, Texas designed the pleasing project that has a variety of stitches. "More experienced crocheters will enjoy this one," she advises.

**Materials Needed:**
*4-ply worsted-weight cotton or cotton-blend yarn in 50-gram balls with 107 yards per ball—one ball each of green and red and two balls of white*
*Size F/5 (3.75mm) crochet hook or size needed to obtain correct gauge*
*Scissors*

**Gauge:** Working in sc, 5 sts and 3 rows = 1 inch.

**Finished Size:** Stocking measures about 14 inches long.

**Special Stitches:**
**DOUBLE CROCHET CLUSTER: dc Cl:** Holding back last lp, work 2 dcs in stitch indicated, yo, draw through all lps on hk.

## ABBREVIATIONS

| | |
|---|---|
| ch(s) | chain(s) |
| dc(s) | double crochet(s) |
| hdc(s) | half double crochet(s) |
| hk | hook |
| inc | increase |
| lp | loop |
| sc(s) | single crochet(s) |
| sk | skip |
| sl st | slip stitch |
| sp(s) | space(s) |
| st(s) | stitch(es) |
| tog | together |
| yo | yarn over |
| ( ) | Stitches within parentheses are all worked in the same stitch or space as directed. |
| * or [ ] | Instructions following asterisk or within brackets are repeated as instructed. |

each of next 10 ch-2 sps, work (2 dcs, ch 2, 2 dcs, ch 2, 2 dcs) in last ch-2 sp. Fasten off, turn.

**Row 32:** Attach red yarn in last dc, ch 3 (counts as dc), [work 5 dcs in next ch-2 sp] twice, [work 3 dcs in next ch-2 sp] 10 times, dc in each of last two dcs, turn: 43 dcs.

**Rows 33-35:** Ch 3 (counts as dc), dc in each dc across, turn: 43 dcs. At end of Row 35, fasten off red, turn: 43 dcs.

**Row 36:** Attach white yarn in last dc, ch 3, [dc next 2 dcs tog] twice, dc in

each dc across, turn: 41 dcs.

**Row 37:** Ch 3 (counts as dc), dc in each dc across to last four sts, [dc next 2 dcs tog] twice, turn: 39 dcs.

**Row 38:** Ch 3 (counts as dc), [dc 2 tog] twice, dc in each dc across to last 4 sts, [dc 2 tog] twice: 35 dcs. Fasten off.

Repeat instructions above to make another stocking.

**FINISHING:** Weave in all loose ends.

Hold both stockings together with raw edges matching. Attach green yarn at top corner of first piece along heel edge, join to second piece with a sl st, ch 20 for

hanger, sc in same place as first st to attach hanger; (* ch 1, sc) through both pieces to join stockings together; repeat from * around spacing sts evenly down stocking to heel, across bottom, around toe and up opposite side to top and adding additional scs as needed to round heel and toe; join with a sl st to beginning st. Fasten off.

Attach green to top edge of a single layer of stocking, reverse sc evenly around top edge of each stocking; join with a sl st to beginning st. Fasten off and weave in loose ends. ♥

# Pretty Paper Trimmer Tolls Glad Tidings

RING in the season with this delicate bell ornament designed by Linda Whitener of Glen Allen, Missouri. It'll make your tree noteworthy!

The appealing three-dimensional paper trim is a snap to fold and snip, reveals Linda. You can cut out a white bell just like she did, or choose colored or patterned paper instead.

**Materials Needed:**
*Patterns at right*
*Tracing paper and pencil*
*Two 5-inch squares each of green and off-white construction paper or card stock*
*70 red seed beads*
*12 inches of green all-purpose thread*
*Stapler*
*Hand-sewing needle*
*White (tacky) glue*
*Small scissors*

**Finished Size:** Paper bell trim measures about 5 inches across without hanger.

**Directions:**
Trace patterns onto tracing paper as directed on patterns.

Fold each square of paper in half to make a rectangle.

Stack two off-white rectangles and bell pattern with all foldlines and outside edges matching. Staple all layers together, taking care not to staple on or inside pattern lines.

Cut out bell along outside lines of pattern. To cut shaded areas, pierce paper with a needle or pin to make an opening large enough for blade of scissors. Then use scissors to cut along lines on pattern and discard shaded areas.

In same way, stack two green rectangles and wreath pattern. Staple layers together as before and cut out wreath. Discard shaded area.

Open each wreath and glue seed beads randomly to one side of each. Let dry.

Apply a thin bead of glue down the outside edge of the fold of one bell. With top and bottom edges matching, glue folds of both bells together so just the folds are touching. Let dry.

Apply a thin bead of glue to outside folds of one wreath. Carefully glue fold at top of wreath to glued fold of bow at top of bell. Repeat with other wreath. Then

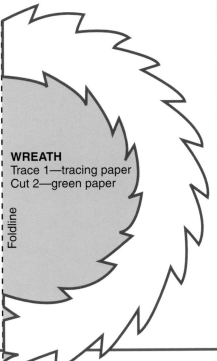

glue bottom of wreaths together along outside edges of folds. Let dry.

Thread hand-sewing needle with green thread. Stitch thread through folds of bow at top of bell. Tie ends of thread in a knot for hanger. Trim excess thread.

Gently open wreath and bell as shown in photo.

Add to your happy holiday decor! ♥

**PAPER BELL PATTERNS**

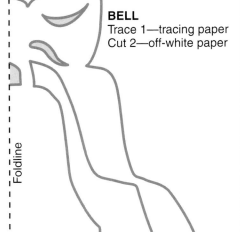

**BELL**
Trace 1—tracing paper
Cut 2—off-white paper

Foldline

**WREATH**
Trace 1—tracing paper
Cut 2—green paper

Foldline

# Her Well-Heeled Garland's in Step with the Holiday Season

NEED a little festive help to dress up your house for the holidays? Jane Rosenau of Carrington, Louisiana's well-heeled design will do the trick! She stitched up a stocking-filled homespun garland and shares the easy instructions here so you can do the same.

### Materials Needed:
*Patterns at right and on next page*
*Tracing paper and pencil*
*5-inch x 7-inch piece of lightweight cardboard*
*Transparent tape*
*44-inch-wide 100% cotton or cotton-blend fabrics—1/8 yard each or scraps of three different prints for stockings (Jane used green and tan check, brick red and white print, and navy and cream print); and scraps of coordinating plaid and check fabrics for toe and heel sections of stockings and prints for heart, star and tree appliques*
*Quilter's marking pen or pencil*
*Two 15-inch squares of cotton quilt batting*
*6 yards of 3-ply jute string*
*1/8 yard of paper-backed fusible web*
*1/2-inch buttons—three each of dark*
*blue, dark green and tan*
*Six-strand embroidery floss—brick red, dark blue and gold*
*Black all-purpose thread*
*Black permanent fine-line marker*
*Pinking shears*
*Glue gun and glue sticks*
*Standard sewing supplies*

**Finished Size:** Stocking garland measures about 9 feet long x 5 inches high. Each stocking measures about 4 inches across x 5 inches high.

### Directions:
Trace stocking and cuff patterns onto tracing paper as directed on patterns. Tape the patterns onto cardboard and cut out shapes for stocking and cuff templates.

Fold one piece of quilt batting in half with wrong sides together and edges matching. Trace around the cuff template nine times onto batting. Use pinking shears to cut out the cuffs, cutting out two at a time.

Cut nine 4-1/2-in. squares from remaining batting and six 4-1/2-in. squares each of green and tan check, brick red and white print and navy and cream print fabrics.

Place cardboard stocking template on right side of one green and tan check square with grain lines matching. Trace around template with quilter's marking pen or pencil. Trace around stocking onto two more green and tan check squares.

In same way, trace around template onto right side of three brick red and white print and navy and cream print squares. The remaining fabric squares will be used for backing of stockings.

Trace heart, star and tree patterns onto paper side of fusible web as directed on patterns, leaving a 1/2-in. margin between shapes. In same way, trace toe and heel patterns onto paper side of fusible web.

Fuse shapes onto wrong sides of fabrics as directed on patterns.

Remove paper backing from shapes. Referring to photo for placement, fuse a heart onto right side of each navy and cream print stocking shape.

In same way, fuse stars onto brick red and white print stockings, and tree trunks and trees onto green and tan check stockings. Then fuse a toe and heel onto each stocking shape.

Use marker to add "stitching" around fused shapes and to each toe and heel where shown on patterns.

For each button, thread a hand-sewing needle with floss. Stitch through button, leaving long threads of floss on front. Tie floss in a knot on front of button and trim ends as desired. Use brick red floss with dark blue buttons, dark blue floss with dark green buttons and gold floss with tan buttons.

Glue buttons to heart, tree and star appliques where shown in photo.

Place a green and tan check backing piece wrong side up on a flat surface. Center a piece of batting on top. Place a piece of matching fabric with a traced stocking right side up on top of batting with edges matching.

Assemble remaining backing, batting and traced stocking pieces in the same way.

Sew around each stocking with black thread, stitching 1/4 in. inside the traced outlines.

Use pinking shears to cut out each stocking, cutting a scant 1/4 in. outside stitching.

Cut length of jute string in half. Fold one length in half and mark center. Then measure and mark every 11 in. from each side of center, making nine evenly spaced marks along the jute string.

Referring to photo for placement, center and glue a set of cuffs over first mark on jute string with jute string sandwiched between cuffs. Then glue the top of a stocking sandwiched between bottom of cuff pieces. Repeat, alternating stockings.

**CUFF**
Trace 1—tracing paper
Cut 1—lightweight cardboard
Cut 18—cotton batting

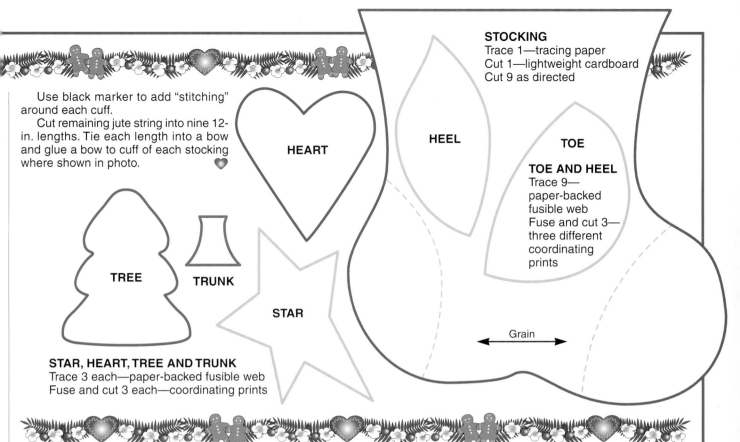

Use black marker to add "stitching" around each cuff.

Cut remaining jute string into nine 12-in. lengths. Tie each length into a bow and glue a bow to cuff of each stocking where shown in photo. 💙

**HEART**

**TREE**

**TRUNK**

**STAR**

**STAR, HEART, TREE AND TRUNK**
Trace 3 each—paper-backed fusible web
Fuse and cut 3 each—coordinating prints

**STOCKING**
Trace 1—tracing paper
Cut 1—lightweight cardboard
Cut 9 as directed

**HEEL**

**TOE**

**TOE AND HEEL**
Trace 9—paper-backed fusible web
Fuse and cut 3—three different coordinating prints

Grain

# Yuletide Card Is Nice and Spicy

THIS gleeful gingerbread man will send heartfelt hellos to all those on your Christmas card list in no time! The felt fellow is easy to roll out, reveals Kathy Meyer from Mapleton, Minnesota.

You can pen her message to the outside or add one of your own. Either way, it'll sweeten anyone's day!

**Materials Needed:**
*Patterns at right*
*Tracing paper and pencil*
*8-1/2-inch x 5-1/2-inch piece of natural card stock or a purchased 4-1/4-inch x 5-1/2-inch blank card*
*Felt—3-1/2-inch x 2-1/2-inch piece of tan for gingerbread man, 1-1/2-inch*
*square of red for heart and 1-inch x 2-inch piece of green for holly*
*4 inches of 3/8-inch-wide lace trim*
*One 1/4-inch red pom-pom and three 1/8-inch white pom-poms*
*Markers—black fine-line and brown medium point*
*Cosmetic powdered blush*
*Cotton swab*
*Gold metallic thread*
*Red pearl cotton or embroidery floss*
*1-inch-long spring clothespin*
*White (tacky) glue*
*Scissors*

**Finished Size:** Folded card measures 4-1/4 inches across x 5-1/2 inches high.

**Directions:**
Trace patterns onto tracing paper.

Cut gingerbread man from tan felt, heart from red felt and holly from green felt.

If using card stock, fold it in half to make a 4-1/4-in. x 5-1/2-in. card.

Place card on a flat surface with fold on the left. Glue gingerbread man onto

front of card.

Referring to photo for placement, glue lace trim to arms, legs and head of gingerbread man. Trim excess.

Use black marker to add the eyes and mouth.

Glue left edge of heart to right arm of gingerbread man.

Glue holly to lower left corner.

Tie two small bows about 6 in. apart along an 18-in.-long piece of gold metallic thread. Do not cut bows apart or trim ends. Glue bows to upper corners on front of card.

Clip clothespin over center section of metallic thread and then onto right edge of heart as shown in photo. Then glue clothespin to card.

Tie a piece of red pearl cotton or embroidery floss into a small bow. Glue bow to gingerbread man and trim ends as desired.

Glue white pom-poms to gingerbread man for buttons and red pom-pom to lower left corner of card for holly berry.

Use cotton swab to apply blush to cheek area. Dab blush onto buttons.

Use brown marker to write "Rejoicing with You" in lower right corner. 💙

**GINGERBREAD MAN**

**GINGERBREAD CARD PATTERNS**
Trace 1 each—tracing paper
Cut 1 each as directed

**HOLLY**

**HEART**

# Noel Wreath Opens Door to Fun

YOU'LL have a ball transforming an artificial wreath into this sparkling showpiece. Joanna Rott of Fort Washington, Pennsylvania embellished the boughs with shining stars, gold beads and glittering ornaments. She rounded out her design with a felt "Noel" banner that's sure to make guests feel welcome.

## Materials Needed:
*Patterns below*
*Tracing paper and pencil*
*Purchased 20-inch artificial wreath*
*1-1/2 yards of 3-inch-wide red metallic net ribbon*
*10 yards of 4mm gold string beads*
*1 yard of 8mm gold string beads*
*4 yards of gold mini-star garland*
*Faceted ball ornaments —six large gold, seven small gold and seven small red*
*Stiffened felt—scraps or one 12-inch x 18-inch sheet each of green and red (Joanna used Easy Felt— regular felt may be substituted)*
*9-inch x 4-inch piece of lightweight cardboard*
*Toothpick*
*Wire cutters*
*White (tacky) glue*
*Transparent tape*
*Scissors*

**Finished Size:** Wreath measures about 20 inches across.

## Directions:
Cut length of 8mm gold string beads in half. Loosely wrap one half around wreath, starting and stopping at the top of the wreath.

In same way, wrap remaining length around wreath, wrapping in the opposite direction and crisscrossing the strands of beads on the front of the wreath. Spot-glue beads as needed to hold.

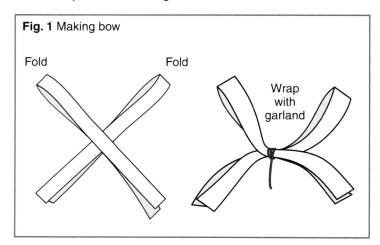

**Fig. 1** Making bow

Fold          Fold

Wrap with garland

**WREATH PATTERNS**
Trace 1 each—tracing paper
Cut 2 each as directed

Use wire cutters to cut star garland into six 18-in. lengths. Thread garland through hangers on six large gold ball ornaments. Twist star garland around branches of wreath and attach ornaments to wreath where desired.

Slip branches of wreath through hanging loops of remaining ball ornaments, attaching them where desired.

Cut length of red metallic ribbon in half. Fold each length in half and fashion into a bow as shown in Fig. 1. Wrap center of bow with remaining star garland.

Twist garland around center of bow to hold. Then bring ends to front and wrap ends around pencil to coil.

Trace patterns onto tracing paper. Tape patterns to lightweight cardboard and cut out each on traced lines.

Place cardboard letters on green felt with right side of each letter facing the felt. Trace around each letter. Cut out letters, cutting 1/8 in. outside traced lines.

In same way, place patterns on red felt and trace around each. Cut out letters, cutting 1/8 in. inside traced lines.

With toothpick, apply glue to back of each red letter. Center and glue red letters to right side of corresponding green letters. Let dry.

Glue assembled letters centered onto a 4-in. x 18-in. piece of green felt.

Cut a length of 4mm gold string beads to fit each letter. Use toothpick to apply glue to beads. Glue beads to letters where shown in photo. Let dry.

Glue the "Noel" banner centered across back of wreath.

Hang on the door for all to enjoy! ♥

# Angelic Frame Shows Off Your Little Stars

PICTURE your precious darling in this star-studded frame, designed especially for holiday viewing.

Crafter Janna Britton of Firebaugh, California dressed up a plain acrylic photo frame with wooden stars and angels, glittering braid and glimmering metallic paints. It's a snap to make, so you'll want to craft one for each little cherub in your life.

## Materials Needed:
*5-inch x 7-inch all-clear acrylic picture frame*
*Construction paper or acid-free paper—5-inch x 7-inch piece of royal blue and 3-inch x 4-3/4-inch piece of white*
*1/16-inch-thick purchased wooden cutouts—one 1-1/2-inch-high angel, one 1-1/8-inch-high angel and one 5/8-inch-high angel; three 1-1/2-inch stars, three 1-1/4-inch stars and five 3/4-inch stars (Janna used Woodsies)*
*Acrylic craft paints—flesh, gold metallic, silver metallic and white metallic*
*Paintbrushes—small flat and small round*
*Extra-fine gold paint pen*
*12 inches of 22-gauge copper craft wire*
*25 inches of 3/8-inch-wide gold and silver metallic braid*
*Three small white feathers*
*3-inch square of adhesive-backed white felt*
*White (tacky) glue or acid-free photo glue for gluing paper and photo*
*Pencil*
*4-inch length of clear monofilament fishing line*
*Glue gun and glue sticks*
*Scissors*

**Finished Size:** Angel picture frame measures about 6-1/2 inches wide x 10 inches tall.

## Directions:
With flat brush, paint all sides of angels, one large star, one medium star and two small stars white metallic. Let dry.

With flat brush, paint all sides of one large, one medium and two small stars gold metallic. Let dry.

With flat brush, paint all sides of remaining stars silver metallic. Let dry.

Referring to Fig. 1, paint angels as follows: Use round brush and flesh to add a face and hands to one side of each. When dry, paint gold metallic hair on each angel. Then use gold paint pen to add eyes, mouth and remaining details to each angel.

Glue a white feather onto the back of each angel. Trim feathers if needed.

Glue one end of monofilament fishing line to back of smallest angel. Then glue opposite end to back of largest angel.

Wrap copper wire around pencil to coil. Remove pencil and glue ends to upper corners of picture frame. Stretch wire to form an arc above frame as shown.

**Fig. 1** Painting angels

Glue angels to front of coiled wire where shown in photo.

Cut a piece of adhesive-backed felt slightly smaller than each angel. Adhere a felt piece centered onto back of each angel with wire and feather sandwiched in between.

Glue braid around outside edge of front of frame, starting and stopping at one upper corner. Trim excess. Let dry.

Referring to photo for placement, glue stars to upper corners of frame.

Glue white paper centered over royal blue paper and a picture of your favorite "angel" to center of white paper.

Referring to photo for placement, write "Angels All Around..." with gold paint pen.

Insert mounted picture into frame and use to brighten your home for the holidays! ♥

# Fabric Bells Ring with Merry Magnetism

YOUR seasonal celebration will be a re-sounding success when you snap these holiday print bells into place. Winnie Malone of Westerville, Ohio produced the pretty ringers, then trimmed them with ribbon, lace and metallic rickrack.

Magnetic strips on the back allow you to place them on metal surfaces. "Or you can add a ribbon loop to hang them from a hook," Winnie suggests.

**Materials Needed:**
*Patterns below*
*Tracing paper and pencil*
*44-inch-wide 100% cotton or cotton-blend fabrics—1/2 yard each of red print and green print and 1/4 yard each of red solid and green solid*
*2-5/8 yards of 1-inch-wide pre-gathered lace trim*
*2-5/8 yards of gold metallic rickrack*
*1 yard of 5/8-inch-wide white*
*satin ribbon*
*1 yard of 3/8-inch-wide gold stripe metallic ribbon*
*Two 1-inch gold buttons*
*4 inches of gold metallic cord*
*Matching all-purpose thread*
*Polyester stuffing*
*12 inches of 1/2-inch-wide adhesive-backed magnetic strip*
*Standard sewing supplies*

**Finished Size:** Bell wall hanging measures about 19 inches across x 15 inches high.

**Directions:**
Use copy machine to enlarge patterns to 200%, or mark tracing paper with a 1-in. grid and draw patterns as shown onto tracing paper.

Cut two each of entire bell pattern from red print and green print.

Cut bell insert pattern away from bell pattern, cutting along dotted line. Cut one each of bell insert from green solid and red solid fabrics.

Pin green solid bell insert right side up on top of right side of green print bell, with bottom and side edges matching.

Sew along top edge of bell insert with a narrow zigzag stitch and matching thread. Repeat, using red solid insert and red print bell.

Pin front and back of green print bell together with right sides facing and edges matching. Sew around outside edges of bell with 1/4-in. seam, leaving an opening for turning where indicated on pattern. Clip curves and turn right

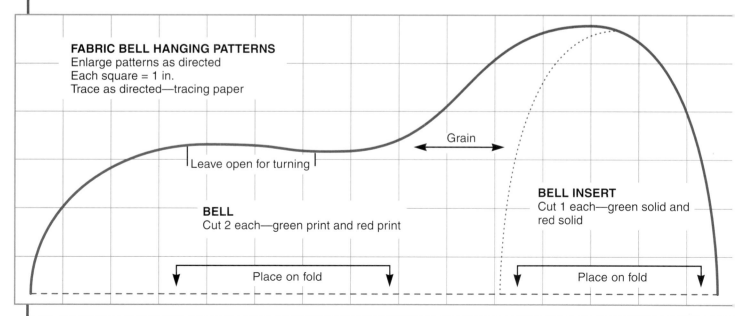

**FABRIC BELL HANGING PATTERNS**
Enlarge patterns as directed
Each square = 1 in.
Trace as directed—tracing paper

Grain

Leave open for turning

**BELL**
Cut 2 each—green print and red print

**BELL INSERT**
Cut 1 each—green solid and red solid

Place on fold

Place on fold

side out. Repeat, using front and back of red print bell.

Stuff each bell lightly. Turn raw edges of openings in and hand-sew openings closed.

Referring to photo for position, place red print bell over green print bell and pin. Hand-tack along overlapped edges on front and back of bells.

Cut gold cord in half. Hand-sew each half to center of bell inserts. Then sew a button to bottom end of each, stitching through all layers.

Pin rickrack to right side of gathered edge of lace trim. Sew along center of rickrack to attach it to lace trim.

Hand-sew rickrack and lace trim over stitching that joins bell and bell insert on green bell as shown in photo, making sure zigzag stitching is completely covered. Trim excess. In same way, add trim to red bell insert.

Hand-sew combined rickrack and lace trim to right edge of front of green bell. Trim excess. Then hand-sew trim around entire red bell, starting and stopping at top of bell. Trim excess.

Form white and gold metallic ribbons into two same-size double-loop bows. Stack gold metallic bow centered on top of white bow. Hand-sew stacked bows to top of bells, referring to photo for position.

Cut magnetic strip into two 6-in. lengths. Adhere across back of bells.

Hang your noteworthy decoration!

# Teachers Will Eat Up Jolly Apple Claus

GET to the core of Christmas fun with this delicious decoration. Renee Dent of Conrad, Montana plucked a ripe red apple for Santa's pudgy figure and buckled it with a strand of black ribbon.

The roly-poly Nick is so easy to make that youngsters will want to create one for their favorite teacher. And when used as a yummy table favor, it's sure to bring bushels of grins from good girls and boys.

## Materials Needed:
*Patterns below*
*Tracing paper and pencil*
*3-1/2-inch square of medium-weight white paper or white card stock*
*Acrylic craft paints—black, flesh, gold, pink, red and white*
*Paintbrushes—small flat and small round*
*Black Sharpie ultra-fine permanent marker*
*Decoupage finish*

*Length of 1/4-inch-wide black satin ribbon to fit around apple*
*Toothpick or craft pick*
*White (tacky) glue*
*Transparent tape*
*Scissors*
*Apple*

**Finished Size:** Santa measures about 3 inches across x 2-3/8 inches high. Finished size will vary depending on size of apple used.

**Directions:**
Trace patterns onto tracing paper. Tape patterns to white paper or card stock and cut out on traced lines.

Use flat brush to paint entire Santa white and buckle gold. Let dry.

Cut slits on dashed lines of buckle where shown on pattern.

Turn Santa pattern over and rub flat side of pencil lead over traced lines to darken. Place tracing paper pattern right side up over Santa cutout with edges matching. Trace over inside design lines to transfer pattern onto paper. Remove pattern.

Use flat brush and flesh to paint Santa's face. Let dry.

Use round brush and pink to paint his nose, mouth and cheeks. Use flat brush and red to paint hat. Let dry.

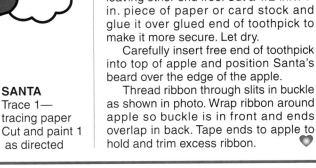

Dip the handle of the brush into black paint and dab on two small dots for eyes. Let dry.

With marker, outline Santa and buckle and add inside design lines as shown on patterns.

Use flat brush to apply decoupage finish to Santa and buckle. Let dry.

Glue about 1/2 in. of one end of toothpick onto back of Santa's face, leaving other end free. Cut a 1/2-in. x 1-in. piece of paper or card stock and glue it over glued end of toothpick to make it more secure. Let dry.

Carefully insert free end of toothpick into top of apple and position Santa's beard over the edge of the apple.

Thread ribbon through slits in buckle as shown in photo. Wrap ribbon around apple so buckle is in front and ends overlap in back. Tape ends to apple to hold and trim excess ribbon. ♥

## APPLE SANTA PATTERNS

**BUCKLE**
Trace 1—tracing paper
Cut and paint 1 as directed

**SANTA**
Trace 1—tracing paper
Cut and paint 1 as directed

# Cozy Pennsylvania Teahouse Is Steeped in Holiday Flavor

HOLIDAYS suit Janet Young to a "tea." So do birthdays, graduations and bridal showers.

But Christmastime is when this Camp Hill, Pennsylvania woman really gets things brewing in her quaint teahouse. At Over the Teacup, she creates a festive atmosphere steeped in old-fashioned charm and pot after pot of hot soothing tea.

"November and December are especially busy," Janet says. "In addition to the three holiday teas I host, local folks book a lot of parties. I also offer a post-Thanksgiving tea as a respite for weary shoppers.

"I serve afternoon tea year-round, but I specialize in themed occasions, from Valentine's Day and Halloween teas to a Japanese tea ceremony and a 'Down on the Farm Tea'. I host meetings and private parties and teach tea etiquette, too," she adds.

Each Yuletide, the pink cottage with its stenciled walls and lacy curtains is trimmed inside and out with garland, wreaths, white lights and a beautifully bedecked tree. Tables are set with fine linens, napkin rings, lovely silverware and new and antique teacups.

The mouth-watering holiday menu offers an assortment of goodies, from tea sandwiches and quiches to fancy cookies, cakes, plum pudding, mulled cider and, of course, brewed tea.

Janet even infuses entertainment into the mix, whether it's a decorating demonstration or a costumed hostess straight out of a Charles Dickens novel.

"The tranquil 2-hour-long teas give people the chance to spend quality time with family or friends while rediscovering what I call the 'art of conversation'," Janet says.

Her clients aren't all adults, either. A certified tea consultant and expert in proper behavior, Janet helps out youthful Brownies hoping to earn their manners badges.

Janet's family also enjoys an occasional sipping session. She stirs up festive teas for her husband, Bob, and their two grown children as well as birthday teas for other relatives.

"Whether I'm pouring tea for family, friends or first-time visitors, it's exciting to know that I have played a role in creating happy times for others," Janet shares.

**Editor's Note:** *Afternoon tea is served from 11 a.m. to 1 p.m. and 2-4 p.m. Wednesday through Friday at Over the Teacup, 3814 Old Gettysburg Rd., Camp Hill PA 17011. Reservations are required, except for the post-Thanksgiving tea. For more information, call 1-717/737-5099 or visit Janet's Web site at www.overtheteacup.com.* ♥

**TIMELY TEA** leaves Over the Teacup guests craving another cup. Owner Janet Young, top left, and costumed hostess pour and serve while visitors savor some traditional treats of the season.

## A Perfect Pot of Tea

WANT to polish up your brewing skills? Janet offers these tips.

● First bring the water to a boil. While you are waiting, put hot tap water into the teapot to warm it, then empty the pot.

● If you are using tea leaves, place 1 teaspoon per cup in a perforated holder called an infuser. For teabags, use 1 for every 2 cups of tea.

● Place the tea in the pot and take the pot to the stove. As soon as the water comes to a boil, fill the teapot. Steep for 3-5 minutes. Then remove the infuser or teabags, so the tea does not become bitter, and serve.

# For Porcelain Tree Trims, Timing Is Everything

AS summer breezes begin to blow, Gina Conway is already getting fired up about Christmas.

The rural Ridgefield, Washington crafter starts working on her hand-painted porcelain ornaments a good six months before the holiday season starts. That's because producing 1,200 large ornaments and 300 miniatures is a painstaking process.

The time-consuming technique has eye-catching results, however. Gina turns out a seasonal smorgasbord of Santas, snowmen, angels, doves, reindeer and bears as well as teardrop-shaped floral ornaments and other fancy shapes.

"To make them, I prepare a watery clay mixture called slip, pour it into purchased molds and let the mixture dry," describes Gina, who works with 60 different designs.

"The next step is removing the pieces from the molds and checking them for defects. They are air-dried for 24 hours, cleaned and then fired for 14-1/2 hours in one of my three kilns.

"Because the process takes so long, I fire about 60 to 70 pieces per load," she says. "The ornaments are cooled, smoothed and polished by my chief polishers—my husband, Tom, and our son, Kevin."

Gina decorates her fragile ornaments freehand, even the delicate floral designs, with china paints. "I paint a kiln-load at a time," she says. "I layer the paints and fire between layers to embed the colors in the porcelain.

"Most ornaments have three paintings and firings. Between firings, each piece cools for 7 to 8 hours."

Friends and family—including her

in-laws, Jackie and Richard Conway—pitch in to help Gina prepare for a handful of craft shows. They add ribbon hangers, sprinkle on glitter and price and box the little treasures.

"During the busy season, my studio looks like Santa's workshop," she says. "When my friends comment on this, I always invite them to come on over and be one of my elves!"

Gina has been pouring out ornaments for over 17 years. When she's not brushing up for the holidays, she paints tea sets, baby shoes, plates and vases and does commission work.

"Folks come back regularly to buy gifts or add to their collections. They use the trims on wreaths, garlands and mantels, in shadow boxes and even as cabinet knobs," Gina shares.

And the porcelains are certainly going places—from Japan and Brazil to Iceland and New Zealand.

"I'm amazed at where the ornaments have found homes," she says. "My customers truly make all the hard work worthwhile."

**Editor's Note:** *For more information, send a self-addressed stamped envelope to Gina Conway, 2508 N.E. 199th St., Ridgefield WA 98642.* ♥

**POURING IT ON.** Producing 1,500 porcelain trims, from fancy florals to smiling snowmen, takes hundreds of hours, so Gina Conway, top, slips into holiday "mold" during summertime.

Deidre Pearce Weiland

# Christmas Fiction

# The Wise Men's Gifts

*By Betty Fulgham of Frankfort, Kentucky*

MAGGIE FOSTER shivered as she watched her husband, Jake, drive off in the snowstorm. Another lonely weekend lay ahead for her and baby Charlie…another weekend of wondering how they would manage now that there were three of them.

After the factory closed, Jake had to find work wherever he could—and Maggie had to find them places to stay. At least this job—on a horse farm—came with a ramshackle house, a benefit they both appreciated now that they had a newborn infant to care for.

Little Charlie was snug and content in his cradle. So Maggie went back to stuffing old newspapers around the doors and windows to keep out the cold.

A sudden knock on the door made her jump. Maggie peeked out and saw Mr. Shaw, the farm's foreman.

### Warm Welcome

"Hi, Mrs. Foster," he said as Maggie opened the door. "My wife sent me to bring you and the baby to the church. We're decorating for the play, and later we're having a potluck dinner."

"Oh, thank you, but I couldn't," she answered, worried that her meager food supply wouldn't stretch through the weekend if she brought a dish to share.

"You know I can't take no for an answer," Mr. Shaw said. "Just get your coat, and I'll take the little one."

He scooped up Charlie and wrapped the baby in a warm blanket.

The quaint church glowed through the falling snow as they drove up the lane. Inside, the warmth felt good. Everybody wanted to hold Charlie, and they encouraged Maggie to help decorate the sanctuary with candles, red bows and greenery.

She enjoyed talking with the ladies, who were nervous about the annual Christmas play just 4 days away.

"You'd think it was the first time they ever did that play," Mr. Shaw chuckled. "Why, my wife, Eleanor, once played Baby Jesus!"

The delicious dinner would have rivaled any good restaurant's menu. Everyone joked that they had eaten too much to rehearse, but soon they were reciting the familiar verses of the Nativity story.

"You'll come back for the play on Tuesday, won't you?" asked Mr. Shaw. "I'd be glad to pick up you, Jake and Charlie on my way."

The evening had her in such a good mood that she quickly agreed.

On Tuesday night, the deep snow drifted up around the radiant church. Still, the sanctuary was nearly full when Maggie, Jake and the baby arrived with Mr. Shaw. Immediately, one of the ladies rushed up to Maggie.

"Mrs. Foster," she said breathlessly. "Our Baby Jesus' family is snowed in. Could you and your husband and Charlie stand in for them at the manger scene? We've worked so hard and…"

"We'd be happy to," Maggie said, already feeling a kinship with the parishioners. "Just tell us what to do."

Charlie made a perfect Baby Jesus, and even Jake relaxed and enjoyed his role. But the wise men's gifts weighed more than Maggie expected. Thinking they were empty boxes, she almost dropped one of them before lowering it to the floor.

*What do they have in these boxes?* she thought as one after another nearly fell out of her hands. Luckily, no one seemed to notice.

### Birthday Presents

Later, as she put on her coat, Maggie felt a tiny hand take hers. One of the angels from the play gently pulled her to the front of the church, where the wise men's gifts were stacked.

"Will you open them now so I can see?" asked the little girl.

"Oh, no, sweetie, they're not mine," Maggie told her. "They were for the play. There's nothing in them."

*Except maybe rocks,* she thought.

"Becky's right, Mrs. Foster. They *are* yours," said Mr. Shaw, who was standing behind her. The rest of the congregation had gathered around, too, all with knowing smiles on their faces.

"Every year we collect gifts for the newest baby in the church, in honor of Jesus' birth," he explained. "But this year, no one had a baby.

"I knew that you had just had Charlie, so we'd like him to be our Baby Jesus this year…if that's okay with you."

While Jake held Charlie, Maggie and the girl tore into the boxes, which suddenly numbered more than the wise men had brought. Inside were blankets, toys, clothes, food and diapers for Charlie, a work jacket and gloves for Jake and a sweater for her.

Jake shook hands all around while Maggie smiled through her tears. No words could express her gratitude.

She had been wondering where they would raise Charlie. This neighborly little town might be a perfect place to start.

# Angelic Fascination Fuels Crafter's Heavenly Hobby

A HOST of celestial beings has materialized in Michele Beckenthal's house. They alight on windowsills, shelves and the corner hutch, hover atop the Christmas tree and take shape on the dining room table.

Among the throng are Renaissance angels adorned with metallic ribbon, country angels wrapped in shawls, garden angels bearing birdhouses and guardian angels watching over precious infants.

Michele has been creating the charming cherubs for over 9 years in her Alburtis, Pennsylvania dining room, lifting spirits not only at Yuletide, but all year-round.

"People request my angels for Christmas, birthdays, Mother's Day, weddings and other special occasions," she says.

"Sometimes they request specific material, trims or colors. I've even worked with vintage fabrics, such as an heirloom tablecloth."

Michele styles most of her heavenly figures on a sturdy cardboard cone so they can double as tree toppers. She attaches commercial porcelain heads and hands and molds papier-mache wings that are hand-painted with acrylics. Her smaller angel ornaments have porcelain legs, too.

To fashion flowing gowns, Michele stitches print or hand-dyed fabric cut from an original pattern. After the final fitting, embellishments are added.

"I use dried flowers, raffia, pearls, pinecones and lace. For the halos, I rely on fabric, twine, ribbon and beads."

During the holiday season and other busy times, Michele's daughters—Ashley, 18, Lauren, 15, and Victoria, 13—lend a hand. And they've certainly earned their wings!

"They've made angels from start to finish," Michele says proudly. "Best of all, they really enjoy doing it."

The appealing angels have flown across the United States and as far away as Australia. Although Michele works, her fascination with angels and the moving requests she receives keep enthusiasm for her hobby at its height.

"From time to time, people who have lost loved ones request angels as reminders of those family members or friends," Michele details.

"And my neighbor asked me for an angel to hang over her granddaughter's hospital crib. She felt that having the angel there would help."

Michele, too, believes in the power of angels.

"Angels *are* among us," she affirms wholeheartedly. "I do not believe in coincidence. Anything coincidental is really angels at work."

**Editor's Note:** *For more information about Michele's angels, contact her at Brookdale Collection, P.O. Box 353, Alburtis PA 18011, 1-610/966-0648. Or check her Web site at www.brookdale collection.com.* ♥

**HEAVEN-SENT.** Michele Beckenthal (above and at top) fashions her delicate angels using a mix of materials, including papier-mache, porcelain, fabric and a bevy of embellishments.

# Holidays Bloom Brilliantly For This Poinsettia Grower

COME Christmastime, Rhonda Jones starts seeing red...and pink and white and mauve.

Rhonda and her husband, Mike, color the season with pretty poinsettias, which populate 15 of the 46 greenhouses on their plant farm outside New Summerfield, Texas.

"Poinsettias require special care, from planting, spraying, cutting and watering to packing and shipping," Rhonda explains. "But you get such satisfaction when people tell you how beautiful the flowers are."

The growing season begins in August when the couple sows 20,000 starter plants from a local grower in 6-1/2-inch pots. Rhonda waters the plants daily and fertilizes them. After a month, she prunes the tops of the poinsettias to promote fuller growth.

"I like to have six to eight blooms per plant," she explains.

They start showing their colors by mid-October, and by mid-November the poinsettias are bloomin' beauties.

"The greenhouses take on such pretty hues," Rhonda says. "We grow red, pink and white versions—and other variations, too.

"We also cultivate mauve and white and pink marbled poinsettias, plus a variety called 'jingle bell' that sports red with splashes of white. Another kind, called 'peppermint', features white leaves with splashes of light pink."

Sales begin Thanksgiving weekend, and the annual crop disappears fast in December.

"Some of our customers drive from Arkansas, Oklahoma and Louisiana to buy the poinsettias," shares Rhonda. "In addition to what we offer ourselves, we supply a lot of school fund-raisers as well as florists and churches."

Mike handles shipping and deliveries. Other help comes from relatives and the couple's three children, Courtney, 21, Miranda, 20, and Cory, 8.

Once the greenhouses are emptied, Rhonda and clan dig right into their next project. "By the time we finish with the poinsettias, we have already started planting for spring," she informs.

Rhonda's green thumb stems from childhood. After her family moved to the country in 1972, her father started his own plant business. Rhonda and her three siblings helped plant, prune, pick and sort the tomatoes from his first greenhouse.

After she and Mike married, Rhonda worked at a local plant farm before going to work for her dad. "That's when I learned about growing poinsettias," she recalls.

"In 1995, my dad offered to sell his business to us, and we jumped at the opportunity," she relates. "That's how we got into the poinsettia trade—I had to keep the tradition going."

**Editor's Note:** *For more information, call toll-free 1-888/466-9413 or send an E-mail to Rhonda at jonesplant farm@risecom.net.* ♥

**SEA OF RED.** Poinsettias populate about a third of Rhonda and Mike Jones' 46 greenhouses. She learned all about growing the holiday favorites from her father (shown with Rhonda at top). Now, the Texas couple sells about 20,000 of the pretty plants each season.

Photos: Glynda Ross Photography

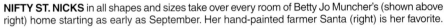

NIFTY ST. NICKS in all shapes and sizes take over every room of Betty Jo Muncher's (shown above right) home starting as early as September. Her hand-painted farmer Santa (right) is her favorite.

# Collector Finds Christmas A 'Claus' for Celebration

YOUNGSTERS better be on their best behavior at Betty Jo Muncher's house during the holidays, because Santa will be watching…from every nook and cranny.

The Clanton, Alabama farm wife has gathered more than 1,400 Santas that, come Christmas, fill her 100-year-old Victorian home from top to bottom.

Her Kris Kringles come in all manner of materials, from spools and shells to golf balls and baseballs, embroidery and cross-stitch, wood and ceramic. Betty Jo painted a good portion of her collection, which started to shape up after she took a ceramics class.

"I think I've been bringing home Santas for about 20 years now," says the mother of two grown daughters and grandmother of four. "In addition to the ceramic Santas I've painted, I took a brush to several wood pieces my husband, Richard, cut for me.

"People also give them to me for birthdays, Christmas and Mother's Day. Some I buy myself. Richard and I are retired and love to prowl around flea markets and antique shops."

Her prize possessions pop up on shelves, tables and walls as early as September. "It takes several months to get them all unwrapped and cleaned," Betty Jo explains.

"By Halloween, we have a Christmas tree in the den trimmed with almost 300 Santa ornaments, including a thimble, yo-yo and corncob. It really confuses the little trick-or-treaters!"

Once the decorating is done, the house is a wall-to-wall Claus encounter featuring elegant Father Christmas figures and a variety of roly-poly St. Nicks on mugs, candy dishes, gourds, rocks, lightbulbs, towels, pillows, baskets, cookie jars and lamps.

They congregate in the living room, kitchen, bedrooms and den. "But the most talked-about room is the powder room, which spotlights my Coca-Cola collection," Betty Jo notes. "There are about 50 Santas and two collectible Yuletide Coke signs in there."

She likes to share her holiday collection with others, so Betty Jo opens her doors to nursing home residents, clubs and groups who travel from around the state to "ooh" and "aah" over her batches of bearded fellows.

"The first thing people ask is 'Where in the world do you store all of these Santas?'" she says, surveying her assortment of jolly gents. "Each one is wrapped in tissue paper and then newspaper, packed up in large boxes and stacked in a room-size closet with wide shelves.

"We do have a lot of Santas," admits Betty Jo. "But we enjoy sharing our Christmas tradition with others. I've become known as the 'Santa Lady' around these parts!" ♥

109

# Wreaths and More Round Out Crafter's Christmas

THERE'S always a holiday just around the corner for New Jersey crafter Patricia Carty, but her busiest time of year is, naturally, Christmas. That's when demand soars for her adorable "sandbag angels" and decorated wreaths.

"I style at least one wreath design for most holidays, but I have 15 offerings for the Yuletide season," says Patricia, who lives in Spring Lake Heights. "The angels represent holidays as well as various hobbies and professions."

For her colorful wall and door decor, she spruces up artificial evergreen

wreaths with florals, ribbons, bells, bows, fruit, pinecones and other festive embellishments.

Her snow-tipped "Country Christmas" wreath features pinecones, holly, fruit, nuts and a flannel ribbon. Red and gold accents adorn her "Christmas Magic" creation. A Hanukkah wreath is decked out with dreidels, lace and a big blue bow.

Patricia, who offers her items at craft fairs and on the Internet, got into business in a roundabout way.

"I fashioned a Valentine's wreath for the entrance doors on the restaurant we owned," she explains, "and customers loved my design so much they asked if there were others for sale."

The queries prompted her to cook up a business, Corner Crafters. Husband Mark, a chef by trade, whipped up a Web site, and Patricia made room for an in-home studio.

Wreaths make up most of her business, but every year the product line has grown, often in response to requests.

"One was for an angel to cheer up a sick friend in the hospital," Patricia detailed. "That resulted in my first sandbag angel. I have sold over 2,000 of the cheery cherubs."

Each angel's round body is made of a sand-filled sock, with a wooden ball for a head. She adorns the doll with curly hair, lace wings, a golden halo and a handmade fabric dress.

"Customers can choose the hair color and, on some angels, we can write personalized messages," says Patricia, who also fashions angel magnets and angelic tree trims.

"We work full-time most of the year, but from September until Christmas—when we sell hundreds of wreaths and angels—the work is nonstop," she says.

Then she enlists extra help, including eldest sons Derek, 14, and Kyle, 11, who pitch in at the craft shows. Tommy, age 6, offers enthusiastic support, and Mark manages Internet activity and handles orders, shipping and customer service.

"Certain orders hold a special place in my heart," Patricia says. "For example, a woman named Angel Louise or-

**AROUND THE HOLIDAYS**, Patricia Carty (shown above and below) crafts decorative wreaths and angels galore. Her wreaths sport seasonal themes, while the spirited dolls also represent professions and hobbies.

dered our angel magnets to give to over 100 children who have cancer.

"It's people like her who make me feel that I, too, can touch the lives of others through my crafts."

**Editor's Note:** *For more details on Patricia's accents, contact her at Corner Crafters, P.O. Box 5, Spring Lake, NJ 07762 or call 1-732/449-9427. You can visit her Web site at www.cornercrafters.com.* ♥

## Christmas Candles

Christmas candles in a row,
Burnished by the firelight's glow,

Give the room a festive air,
Ocher peaks that weave and flair.

Short or tall, slender or wide,
All bespeak of Christmastide.

Flickering flames that rise and fall,
Making shadows on the wall.

Christmas candles burning bright,
Welcoming the Holy Night.

—*Peggy Stevens*
*Bartlesville, Oklahoma*

## I'll Never Forget...

# Visiting Grandparents' Farm Was a Happy Holiday Ritual

*By Sonja Walters Asendorf of Georgetown, Texas*

MEMORIES of childhood Christmases flit in and out of my thoughts throughout much of the year, but especially during December. I only have to look in the starry eyes of my grandchildren and see their excitement to remember my own.

As a child in the 1940s, holiday happiness for me was packing the family car with people, gifts and food, and driving from Houston to my grandparents' place in Ace, Texas. That 30-acre farm in the backwoods of eastern Texas was so inviting at Christmas.

My two sisters and I would be so excited about our country holiday that we'd ask our parents to make the 2-hour drive at night instead of waiting until the next morning.

The tin-roofed farm buildings gleamed and the landscape shimmered in the moonlight as we drove up my grandparents' lane. Soon their quiet farmhouse was alive with the sounds of barking dogs and squawking children jarred from a deep sleep.

Inside, the fireplace would still be aglow with enough warmth to take the chill off before heading to bed. Once we were warm, my sisters and I would crawl between the cold sheets topped with layers of quilts, and our Christmas dreams would take over.

### An Early Start

We would never sleep late. Each day began with prayers at 6 a.m. and breakfast at 6:30. To my grandparents, one was as necessary as the other.

I can still feel the wood floor under my knees and my grandmother's hand on my shoulder as she calmed my impatient wriggling. I can still hear my grandfather's resonant voice as he conversed with God.

But uppermost in my mind during those reverent moments were the delicious smells from the kitchen. They'd finally get to Grandpa, too, and he'd end his prayers so breakfast could begin.

Then we'd eagerly dig into Grandma's hot biscuits with freshly churned butter and homemade preserves, fried eggs, hash browns, fresh milk and Grandpa's smoked sausage. With a meal like that under our belts, we had plenty of energy for our morning activities.

We children had the most important duty of the day—bringing home the best Christmas tree we could find.

The farm was perfectly suited for our explorations, with its open fields and small pastures. Sloping away from the cleared land were wooded areas with fern-fringed creeks and evergreen groves. We'd return by noon, exhausted but satisfied with the small pine or cedar we managed to haul home.

It took enthusiasm and ingenuity, too, to decorate for Christmas in those days when money was too precious to be spent on baubles.

Popcorn, which my grandfather raised, was our most plentiful resource, and we spent many joyful hours stringing fluffy white kernels into decorative ropes. We also made sweet, sticky popcorn balls—some to eat and some to dangle from the ceiling as pretend snowballs.

Colorful paper rings, joined in a chain, also embellished the tree, and holly branches, heavy with red berries, vied with mistletoe for places of honor throughout the living room.

### Precious Gifts

Christmas Eve would come at last. Evening prayers would be accompanied by Scripture readings retelling the story of the birth of Jesus, and bedtime would be enhanced by whispered hints of Santa's imminent visit.

Before the fires were lit on Christmas morning, we would find our stockings...stuffed with navel oranges, red Delicious apples, giant peppermint sticks and Texas pecans. And before the call to morning prayers, we'd be on our knees shaking presents, wondering what treasures awaited us.

It took very little to fulfill our Christmas wishes back then. A toy, a book, new clothes or paper dolls were precious to us.

Every year, my grandparents would tuck a card with five silver dollars for each grandchild somewhere in the branches of the Christmas tree. We always delighted in finding that note!

One year my uncle with the college degree gave me a gold-plated pencil with retractable lead. I thought this was the ultimate gift. My Christmas spirits soared the year my parents surprised me with a purple velveteen jacket I had coveted in a store window.

Over the years, my golden pencil rusted and the purple jacket faded...but my memories of Christmas have survived untarnished. Those memories surface every holiday, reminding me of a childhood too lovely to forget. ♥

*May the joy and beauty of the holiday season remain with you and yours the whole year through.*

# INDEX

## Food

## Crafts

---

 **Share Your Holiday Joy!**

DO *YOU* celebrate Christmas in a special way? If so, we'd like to know! We're already gathering material for our next *Country Woman Christmas* book. And we need your help!

Do you have a nostalgic holiday-related story to share? Perhaps you have penned a Christmas poem…or a heartwarming fiction story?

Does your family carry on a favorite holiday tradition? Or do you deck your halls in some festive way? Maybe you know of a Christmas-loving country woman others might like to meet?

We're looking for *original* Christmas quilt patterns and craft projects, too, plus homemade Nativities, gingerbread houses, etc. Don't forget to include your best recipes for holiday-favorite main-dish meats, home-baked cookies, candies, breads, etc.!

Send your ideas and photos to "*CW* Christmas Book", 5925 Country Lane, Greendale WI 53129. (Enclose a self-addressed stamped envelope if you'd like materials returned.) ♥